Alabama
Bible Records

Collected by
Jeannette Holland Austin

HERITAGE BOOKS
2008

HERITAGE BOOKS

AN IMPRINT OF HERITAGE BOOKS, INC.

Books, CDs, and more—Worldwide

For our listing of thousands of titles see our website
at
www.HeritageBooks.com

Published 2008 by
HERITAGE BOOKS, INC.
Publishing Division
100 Railroad Ave. #104
Westminster, Maryland 21157

International Standard Book Numbers
Paperbound: 978-1-58549-611-2
Clothbound: 978-0-7884-7564-1

NOTE TO THE READER

This collection of 249 Alabama Bible Records and 7,344 names in the index, contains an itemized list of the births, marriages, and deaths found in approximately 256 family Bibles. Many of the records were sent to me over the past twenty years by the actual owners, while others I copied from Bibles located in the Georgia State Archives, local libraries, or other genealogical publications. The collection spans a period stretching from the early 1700s to the 1900s and because of this range and diversity should be of assistance to the researcher of Alabama families.

Jeannette Holland Austin

TABLE OF CONTENTS

JOHN WILLIAM KILGORE BIBLE
Owner: Miss Essie Kilgore

John William Kilgore b. Cleburn Co., Ala. 1/26/1878 m. 12/20/1898, d. 4/21/1947
Ida Bell Kilgore b. Cleburn Co., Ala. 8/12/1880 m. 12/20/1898 Hattie Bell Kilgore b. Cleburn Co., 5/23/1900 m. 12/24/1919 Chester Lee Kilgore b. Cleburn Co., Ala. 10/19/1901
Effie Mae Kilgore b. Cleburn Co. Ala. 8/26/1904, unmd. Lessie Mat Kilgore b. Cullman Co., Ala.; 2/17/1905 d. 10/5/1906
Tollie Tellro Kilgore b. Cullman Co., Ala. 1/7/1907 d. 4/6/1949 Lillian Gladys Kileore b. Cullman Co., Ala. 3/23/1910 Viola Beatrice Kilgore b. Cullman Co., Ala. 2/28/1912
Odus Lee Kilgore b. Cullman Co., Ala. 2/14/1914
Dcwie Wilson Kilgore b. Cullman Co., Ala. 4/28/1916
John Floyd Kilgore b. Cullman Co., Ala. 6/16/1918 m. 9/7/1937 Irene Kilgore b. Cullman Co., Ala. 12/5/1920 d. 12/5/1920
Thelma Oneda Kilgore b. Cullman Co., Ala. 9/8/1921

WILLIE ALBERT CRANBERRY AND WIFE, MARY MALISSA EVELINE LANEY BIBLE
Owner: Lula Cranberry Newton, Riverview, Alabama

William Albert Cranberry of Ala. m. Mary E. Laney of Ala. 11/30/1882 at David Laneys by Preacher Motley.

Births

Willie Albert Cranberry 6/26/1860
Mary Malissa Eveline Laney Cranberry 8/12/1867

Their children:
E. J. (Emery Jesse) Granberry 10/3/1983
C. S. (Charlie Sanford) Cranberry 6/24/1885 James Willie Cranberry 9/3/1886
Lela A. (Leila Arminta) Cranberry 10/19/1888

1

(William Albert Cranberry Bible continued...)

Bertha E. (Bertha Elizabeth) Cranberry 10/18/1891
Ola Cranberry 9/23/1893
Lula H. (Lula Hettie) Cranberry 8/15/1895
Amos D. Cranberry 8/5/1901
Dazy M. (Dazy May) Cranberry 12/7/1903

WILLIAM DALE HUGHES BIBLE
Owner: Mrs. Hazel Yates Love
1309 E. South St., Kosciusko, MS 39090

William Dale Hughes m. Martha Kelley 10/15/1835 in Talladega, Ala.

Births
William D. Hughes 8/31/1813
Martha K. Hughes 8/2/1818

Their children:
Margaret Elizabeth Hughes 11/17/1836
Lydia C. Hughes 12/18/1838
Moses Gilliland Hughes 3/7/1840
Mary A. Hughes 11/8/1842
William A. Hughes 6/11/1845
A Third Son 3/17/1848
Marinda A. Hughes 2/22/1850
Louisa C. F. Hughes 2/23/1853
Martha L. Hughes 5/18/1855
Edward W. Hughes 7/5/1857
Isadora M. Hughes 2/7/1860

2

(William Dale Hughes Bible, contd....)

Marriages

Margaret Elizabeth Hughes to Archibald Blue 3/10/1856
Marinda Ann Hughes to Joel Harvey Yates 2/7/1973, by the Rev. W. C. Lloyd
Isadora Hughes to William W. Wood 1/25/1887
Edward W. Hughes to Johnnie Fortune Neel 12/3/1894
William A. Hughes to Sarah Richardson
Louisa L. Hughes to Jasper Owen
Mary Hughes to Oliver Parker
Martha L. Hughes to Curtis F. Temple

Deaths

Lydia C. Hughes 1/1/1839
Martha Hughes Temple 2/7/1923
Third son 6/1/1848
Louisa C. Hughes Owen 1925
Moses G. Hughes 9/19/1864
William A. Hughes 2/28/1927
William Dale Hughes 9/18/1875
Edward W. Hughes 5/5/1949
Mary Hughes Parker 1876
Isadora Hughes Wood 2/21/1952
Margaret E. Hughes Blue 2/11/1896
Martha Kelley Hughes 6/6/1882
Marinda A. Hughes Yates 6/25/1903

REV. JOHN COOK HENDON BIBLE, Baptist Minister

John Cook Hendon m. Mary Ann Reynolds 1/11/1848 in Pickens Co., Ala.

Births

John Cook Hendon, (son of Rev. Benjamin Morris Mendon, Baptist Minister and his wife, Aly Clements), 4/1/1829
Mary Ann Reynolds 10/24/1828 in Pickens Co., Ala., (dau. of George Reynolds and his wife, Martha Stewart)

Their children: (all b. Pickens Co., Ala.)

James S. Hendon 10/10/1848
William R. A. Hendon 3/5/1861
Margaret K. Hendon 6/6/1850
Emley Nehdon 11/12/1862
Martha F. Hendon 7/21/1851
Dicey Caroline Hendon 3/9/1864
Joseph D. Hendon 11/25/1852
George Abraham Hendon 12/31/1865
Nancy Lucinda Hendon 1/17/1855
Ulysia Booker Hendon 8/13/1868
Sarah Lovie Ann Hendon 12/29/1856
Julia Rebecka Hendon
8/13/1868 Mary H. Hendon 11/30/1858
John S. P. Hendon 3/30/1871

Deaths

Rev. John Cook Hendon 7/22/--, Comanchie Co., Tx.
Mary Ann Reynolds Hendon 12/2/1887 Marion Co., Ala.

(Rev. John Cook Bible continued…)

Emley Hendon 5/28/1863 Pickens Co., Ala.
Mary H. Hendon 11/2/1865 Pickens Co., Ala.
John S. P. Hendon 8/23/1871 Pickens Co., Ala.
Dicey Caroline Hendon Evans 7/10/1857 Marion Co., Ala.
Ulysia Booker Hendon 11/4/1887 Marion Co., Ala.
William R. A. Hendon 12/1/1890 Guin, Marion Co., Ala.
Margaret R. Hendon Mulenix, 1909, Brilliant, Marion Co., Ala.
Nancy Lucinda Hendon Harris 12/13/1911 Clay Co., MS.
Joseph D. Hendon, 1912, Monroe Co., MS.
James S. Hendon 5/4/1924, Chickasaw Co., MS.
Rev. George Abraham Hendon 10/18/1931 Dublin, Erath Co., Tx. Sarah Lovie Ann Hendon
Burleson 1/15/1934 Pittsburg Co., Okla. Martha F. Hendon Graham, 1936, Tenn.
Julia Rebecka Hendon Crow 8/23/1953 Marion Co., Ala.
Mary Ann Hendon, her dau., Dicey Caroline and son, Booker, all d. during typhoid epidemic in
Marion Co., Ala. and are buried in Old Mars Hill Cemetery in Marion Co.
William K. A. Hendon was a policeman in Guin, Ala. and was shot and killed by a drunk.

Marriages James S. Hendon and Mary Jane Margaret Hendon and Mr. Mulenix

Martha F. Hendon and John Graham Joseph D. Hendon and Betty Harris
Nancy Lucinda Hendon and Robert Mitchell Harris 11/27/1873
Sarah Lovie Ann Hendon and Peter Simon Burleson, 1879
William R. A. Hendon and Georgia Ann
Dicey Caroline Hendon and William Morris Evans, 1883
Rev. George Abraham Hendon and Sarah Drucilla Barton 10/18/1885, Marion Co., Ala.
Julia Rebecka Hendon and William Abraham Crow 6/22/1885

Rev. John Cook Hendon m. second Dicy Cox 2/2/1888 in Marion Co., Ala. by Elder J. S. Stanley
Dicey b. 10/18/1843 Ga. and d. 1/7/1920 Lamesa, Dawson Co., Tx. She was the dau. of John Cox
and his wife, Mary.

5

WILLIAM ROBERTS' BIBLE
Owner: Mrs. Preston Payne
1011 Dripping Springs Rd, N. W., Cullman, Ala. 35055

William Roberts b. at Penprise? 1863 12/4, d. at 48 yrs of age, buried 5/22.
Wife, Mary Ann Roberts b. 1863

Births of Their children

Eliz Ann Roberts 10/13/1884
Catherine Roberts 1/25/1892
Mary Eliz Roberts ---
Mary Ellen Roberts 11/8/1895
Ann Roberts ---
William Thomas Roberts 9/11/1903
Margaret Roberts 3/17/1889

A. H. BOBO BIBLE
Owner: Mrs. Lynda Eller
P. O. Box 249, Lanett, Ala. 36863

Births

Hety Jane Bennett 10/18/1882
Tathaneise Bennett 9/17/1861
R. C. Bennett 9/29/1865
W. P. Bennett 10/2/1888
G. W. Bennett 12/6/1864
L. R. Bobo 9/13/1886
A. H. Bobo 5/5/1984

(A. H. Bobo Bible continued...)

Deaths

William Bennett b. 3/25/1792 d. 1/3/1877
Martha E. Bennett 7/17/1890

Marriages

W. P. Bennett to Bertha Chatham 12/24/1908
George W. Bennett to Mary A. Yarbrough
8/21/1881 William Bennett to Martha E. Bobo 10/12/1859
M. E. Arrington to H. J. Bennett 8/12/1902

MARCUS LAFAYETTE HICKS' BIBLE
Owner: Mrs. Christine L. Armacost
Spruce Hill Farm, Hampsted, Md. 21074

Marriages

Marcus L. Hicks to Lizzie E. Morris 5/12/1870
Walter T. Hicks to Christine F. Beavers 4/28/1897
William S. Lunger, Jr. to Inez I. Hicks 8/12/1920
Marcus P. Hicks to Lola Britt ---

Births

Marcus Lafayette Hicks 12/25/1846
Inez Imogene Hicks 2/14/1899
Lizzie E. Hicks 7/14/1848
Marcus Parks Hicks 7/26/1904

Walter T. Hicks 5/30/1871
Marcus P. Hicks, Jr. 12/10/1924
Christine F. Hicks 2/25/1872
Muriel Christine Lunger 9/30/1922

7

(Marcus Lafayette Hicks' Bible, contd....)

Deaths

Marcus Lafayette Hicks 4/10/1917, buried Oxford, Ala.
Lizzie E. Hicks 4/28/1926, buried Oxford, Ala.
Walter T. Hicks 12/2/1934, buried Oxford, Ala.
Christine Beaver Hicks 8/14/1947, buried Oxford, Ala.

WILLIAM CRAIG ORR BIBLE
Owner: Judge R. C. Orr, Athens, Ga.

Marriages

William Craig Orr 7/7/1814-7/1/18/1859 m. 9/8/1840
Cynthia Ann Montgomery 7/27/1818-8/1/1888
Mary Cornelia Orr b. 10/3/1845 m. 7/2/1868 Cyrus R. Smith
Robert Craig Orr b. 6/28/1859 m. 7/15/1830 Florida Agnes Carr
William Orr b. 8/22/1771 Mecklenburg, N. C. d. 7/2/1861 Talladega, Ala.

THOMAS FRANKLIN BIBLE
Owner: John M. Sparks
4300 Westbourne Drive, Indianapolis, Ind.

Births

Thomas Franklin 3/17/1792
Martha Franklin 10/27/1792
Thomas D. Franklin 12/31/1810
Mary Franklin 6/25/1812
Jacob N. Franklin 1/1/1814
Winney Franklin 9/9/1815

8

Nancy Franklin 11/5/1816
William Franklin 1/19/1818
James Franklin 3/19/1819
John M. Franklin 3/28/1824
Taletha Jane Franklin 12/11/1825
Perlinia Cumy Franklin 4/23/1827
Martha Elizabeth Franklin 11/16/1825
Isaiah Wilshire Franklin W. 5/31/1831
Esikiah Electus Franklin 3/1/1833

Marriages

Thomas Franklin to Martha Harrel 3/13/1810
Thomas D. Franklin to Mary Smith 3/17/1831

Deaths

Mary Franklin 12/7/1824
Thomas Franklin 11/12/1873
Martha Pranklin 3/25/1869

Births

Sarah Tabitha Franklin 4/6/1835
Rebecca Franklin 3/19/1837

WILLIAM AND AMY MALONE HESTER BIBLE

Owner: Mrs. Mary E. Ahlstrom
Rt. 3, Box 28, Florence, Ala. 35630

Marriages

William and Amy Hester 10/18/1805
John and Nancy Richardson 1/3/1826
Roling and Lucindy Hester 12/11/1823
Ebernizer and Polly Bourland 2/25/1830
Simeon and Judy Wates 1/2/1831
Linsey and Saley Moor 12/25/1832
John and Sercy Hester 2/24/1831
William and Malissa Hester 9/20/1840
Levi Rikard and Amy P. Hester 2/18/1841
Chesley B. Hester and Sally Rikard 7/25/1844
John P. Malone and Fartheny E. Hester 11/7/1844
J. Cariole Rikard and Huldah Hester 3/6/1845

Births

William Hester Sr. 1/27/1780
Amy Pertheny Hester 1/12/1824
Amy Hester 3/10/1789
Semirah Mis Hester 12/8/1825
Roling Hester 1/23/1807
Pertheny Elizabeth Hester 7/25/1827
Nancy Hester 10/11/1808
John Nester 7/16/1810
Huldah Rillah Hester 3/31/1829
Poley Hester 7/24/1812
Elizah Jackson Hester 2/22/1831

10

(William Hester Bible continued...)

Judy Hester 5/3/1814
Hudson G. Hester 9/5/1833
Saley Hester 3/26/1816
Lucas N. Hester 7/30/1835
William H. Hester, Jr. 3/25/1818
Robert Whiley Richardson 7/23/1827
Robert B. Hester, Jr. 12/20/1819
Chesley B. Hester 5/24/1822
William Carrol Hester 10/14/1829
John M. Richardson 7/4/1830
John E. Hester 1/5/1839
Gabriel L. Bourland 12/17/1830
Harvey C. Hester 9/24/1840
John Hester 5/28/1832
Fanny Attemier Hester 1/16/1842
Mary Ann Hester 10/11/1831
Robert M. Hester 1/16/1842
Amy Caroline Hester 1/3/1832
Alleney A. Hester 9/6/1845
Luiza M. Bourland 3/20/1833
Perthena C. Bourland 6/18/1837
Cynena R. Wates 4/24/1833
Dubart W. Bourland 12/9/1841
Roling S. Hester 3/20/1833
Therissa Bourland 8/7/1844
Hester Ann Hester 11/19/1834
Semirah Elizabeth Hester 6/15/1845
Mariah T. Moor 9/1832
James G. Hester 9/26/1833
John H. Rikard 3/15/1846

11

(William Hester Bible continued...)

Amos T. Richardson 11/22/1833
William G. Rikard 4/4/1845
Susan W. Bourland 5/14/1835
Julis V. Malone 10/9/1846
William U. Hester 2/7/1836
James S. Hester 10/14/1846
Martha Ann Moor 10/13/1836
Montgomery R. Bourland 1/9/1847
Nancy Cathrin Wates 2/21/1836
Sarah Elizabeth Moore 1/6/1843
Sinthey Ann Hester 2/24/1836
Marget Elizabeth Moor 2/7/1845
Mary D. Hester 8/10/1837
Judy Culpurney Moor 7/5/1846
Amy Anthem Waits 9/24/1837
Lervira Ebers Moor 8/12/1845
Daniel G. Richardson 10/23/1837
Roling B. Hester 5/20/1840
Mary Ellender Hester 8/22/1838
Serling B. Hester 8/9/1842
Parthenia Catherine Bourland
Wiley R. Hester 7/25/1844 6/18/1838
Nancy L. Hester 9/26/1846
James P. Bourland 9/1837
 Robert M. Hester 8/26/1848
---Hester 6/4/1839
J. C. Richardson 2/22/1848
Robert Franklin Rikard 2/10/1842
Amy Hester 1/23/1840

(William Hester Bible continued...)

William Lewis Rikard 12/19/1843
William Hester 10/5/1847

Juda Waits 7/24/1899
Sinthey Ann Hester 1/26/1937
Roling Denton Hester 10/11/1900
John E. Hester 6/23/1842
James Goodloe Hester 12/20/1905
Harvey C. Hester 6/23/1842
John Chesley Hester 2/23/1907
Sidney D. Wates 7/7/1842
Nancy Loucenda King 5/14/1907
Fancy Attemier Hester 11/12/1843
Roland Benton Hester 10/11/1900
William Carrol Hester 11/21/1908
Miles V. Malone 12/17/1846
Wiley R. Hester 8/28/1928
Theressa Bourland 10/1846
Robert M. Hester 8/21/1928
E. P. Hester 11/9/1852
Nancy Richardson 1/26/1853
William Hester 5/2/1853
Albert Hester 10/8/1853

G. W. PELT BIBLE
Owner: Mrs. Jessie Williams
2411 Deaumont Drive, Pensacola, Fla.

G. W. Pelt of Jackson Co., Fla. and M. E. Howard of Henry Co., Ala. were m. 2/12/1853 at Leroy Aleys? by Rev. John Stuard. Witnesses: Jesy Coley, I. W. Pelt, Henry Dykes and wife.

Births

G. W. Pelt 11/2/1862
Margaret Morris 9/29/1903
S. A. Pelt 1/3/1851
Jesse Lee Morris 7/5/1905
Elijah Morris 10/28/1873
Eva Clyde Morris 10/1/1907
Catherine Morris 1/6/1876
James A. Morris 6/11/1898
Ethel Morris 7/4/1896

Brothers of G. W. Pelt:

Robert F. Pelt 4/7/1865
Lenard Martin 1/19/1879
W. J. Pelt 8/15/1867
Caresell Martin 6/19/1896
Henry N. Pelt 8/24/1870
J. M. Martin 10/8/1915
G. H. Pelt 10/11/1889
George W. Martin 4/11/1917
Dessie Lee Pelt 5/31/1892
Cecil Martin 1/27/1921

(G. W. Pelt Bible continued...)

Marriages

G. W. Pelt to M. E. Howard 2/12/1888
G. W. Pelt to Sarah A. Sadler 5/3/1896
E. W. Martin to Miss Caribell Hancock 11/9/1914
Elijah Morris to Catherine Martin 7/4/1895
Ethel Morris to W. B. Haddock 6/13/1913
Margaret Morris to I. L. Blanton 12/30/1917
Jesse Lee Morris to Lula Feagle 3/10/1928
Eva Clyde Morris to E. B. Feagle 4/22/1922

Deaths

G. W. Pelt 10/24/1892
M. E. Pelt 3/2/1896
Bessie Lee Pelt 4/3/1911
G. W. Pelt 4/8/1913
Sarah Pelt 2/17/1924
Ellie Morris was Elijah Morris' Father
Margaret Morris his mother Ellie Morris d. 1911, wife Margaret, 1906
Elijah Morris 2/1954
Catherine Morris 1956
Catherine Martin Morris
James Martin, father, Delilah Sadler, mother.
Lenard Martin 9/28/1966

STEPHEN BOYER BIBLE
Owner: Jim Henry Boyer, Prattville, Ala.

Births

Stephen Boyer 4/10/1827
Adam Boyer 11/5/1831
Harriet Boyer 11/17/1833
Jenny Boyer 5/13/1838
Anetta Boyer 1/11/1845
James Henry Boyer 2/2/1857
Thomas Jefferson Boyer 8/14/1861
W. E. Boyer 7/23/1887

Bisahler Hiler 12/8/1877

Thomas W. Dobbs 9/29/1818
Samuel A. Dobbs 1/14/1884
Lucinda Ann Dobbs 9/2/1886
Mary Caroline Dobbs 8/1/1876
Oliver Dobbs 6/14/1881

Marriages

Henry Boyer to Elizabeth Smith 6/22/1826 (parents of Stephen, Henry, Adam, Harriet and Jenny Boyer)
Stephen Boyer to Lucinda Henderson 2/17/1856
Thomas Boyer to Martha Tatum 9/7/1884 (2nd marriage)
Henry Boyer to -----A. Scott 4/1/1858
Thomas Boyer to Lutisha Compton 8/26/1881
Jim Henry Boyer to Eloise Thomas 2/7/1942
Annetta Boyer to Elemined Dobbs 10/20/1875

16

(Stephen Boyer Bible continued...)

Deaths

Henry Boyer 4/18/1856
J. R. Boyer 6/23/1924
Elizabeth Boyer 5/9/1868
Henry Boyer 4/3/1911
Lutisha Boyer 6/6/1882
Elen Boyer 2/12/1905
J. V. Henderson 4/17/1884
W. T. Boyer 3/29/1943
Stephen Boyer 5/10/1909
Mrs. Alice Boyer 6/25/1947
George Cothran 7/5/1918
Mrs. Fanny Lake 10/16/1947

JAMES BRADFIELD BIBLE
Owner: Mrs. E. L. Arrington, Lanett, Ala. 36863

Marriages

James Bradfield to Susan E. Traylor 10/22/1844
Jere Reese to Mary Tabitha Bradfield 9/22/1868
William Robert Bradfield to William Florence Pitman 1/6/1876
Oscar Hightower to Sarah Denton Bradfield 3/27/1879
William R. Bradfield to Fannie Wisdom ---
Mary S. Bradfield to Thomas J. Patterson 8/17/1904
Katie Florence Bradfield to John S. Brown 6/28/1904
William R. Bradfield to Susan Frances Davison 3/17/1893
William R. Bradfield, Jr. to Lizzie Lou Emery 4/22/1903
James D. Bradfield to Bonnie Claire Lambert 5/15/1918
James D. Bradfield to Ruth Darden 3/5/1927

17

(James Bradfield Bible continued...)

Edward Lee Arrington to Lynda Claire Bradfield 11/10/1940
W. Elmo Bradfield to Carolyn Moncrief 10/3/1941
James David Bradfield, Jr. to Frances Smith 5/22/1943
Mary Frances Bradfield to Dr. Edward E. Brown 12/23/1949

Births

James Bradfield 12/16/1808
Susan E. Bradfield 7/3/1821
Their first child was b. 5/16/1845
Mary Tabitha Bradfield 11/3/1849
John Lewis Bradfield 7/16/1849
William Robert Bradfield 6/28/1851
James Bradfield 11/9/1853
Sallie Denton Bradfield 11/6/1855
Thomas J. Patterson 1/21/1880
John S. Brown 2/21/1879
James Pitman Bradfield 1/3/1877
Mary Susan Bradfield 7/16/1878
Kate Florence Bradfield 7/30/1880
Robert Bradfield 9/6/1882
Carrie Davidson Bradfield 9/25/1894
James David Bradfield 10/13/1896
James Bradfield, Jr. 8/14/1919
William Elmo Bradfield 2/16/1921
Lynda Claire Bradfield 3/6/1923
Mary Frances Bradfield 1/28/1930
James Rivers Reese 9/3/1869
This second child was b. 6/22/1872
This third child was b. 8/21/1874

(James Bradfield Bible continued...)

This fourth child was b. 9/24/1879
Jere Reese 2/14/1879
Robert Sidney Bradfield 8/28/1932
Joe Lewis Bradfield 3/21/1934

Lynda Susan Arrington 1/8/1947, dau. of Lynda Claire Bradfield
Robert Lewis Bradfield 11/9/1949, son of William Elmo Bradfield
Katie Fisher Hightower 12/6/1979

Deaths

Lewis Bradfield, Jr. 9/26/1847
James Bradfield, Jr. 9/1854
Mary Catharine Bradfield 5/1855
John Lewis Bradfield 9/24/1855
Lewis Bradfield, Sr. 1870
James Bradfield, Sr. 5/3/1873
Sarah D. Hightower 1/11/1880
Fannie Wisdom Bradfield 6/10/1839
James Pitman Bradfield 6/28/1093
Carrie Davidson Bradfield 1/13/1895
James David Bradfield, Sr. 11/16/1953
William R. Bradfield, Sr. 2/24/1903
Annie Claire Bradfield 2/25/1926
Susan Frances Bradfield 10/2/1936
Mrs. S. E. Bradfield 4/15/1900
Willie Florence Bradfield 10/26/1884
Tabitha Traylor 7/18/18--
Rev. J. C. Traylor 7/27/1850

19

LUCY ANN SIMMONS SMITH BIBLE
Owner: Mrs. P. A. Glenn
104 Glendale Ave., Greenville, Ala. 36037

Marriages

John H. Smith to Mary J. Wilkinson 4/1/1830
John   H. Smith to Elizabeth H. Smith ----, 1850
Lucy S. Smith to James R. Smith 10/30/1850
John Smith to Malinda Johnson 11/1857
Mary J. Smith, dau. of John H. Smith and Mary Smith, his wife, d. 4/7/1858

Births

John H. Smith, son of Charles W. Smith and Sarah Smith, his wife, was b. 10/14/1805
Mary J. Wilkinson, dau. of James Wilkinson and Lucy Wilkinson, his wife, was b. 9/18/1809
Elizabeth H. Smith, dau. of John L. Smith and Hetty Smith, his wife, b. 8/17/1827
Charles Alexandria Smith, son of John H. Smith and Mary J. Smith, his wife, b. 2/27/1832
Lucy Ann Simmons Smith, dau. of John H. Smith and Mary J. Smith, his wife, b. 2/14/1835
John Henry Smith, son o: John H. Smith and Mary J. Smith, his wife, b. 4/5/1836
James Moreland Smith, son of John H. Smith and Mary J. Smith, his wife, b. 9/1/1833
Emma Adaline Smith, dau. of John H. Smith and Elizabeth H. Smith, his wife, b. 9/4/1851
Thomas Levi Smith, son of John H. Smith and Elizabeth H. Smith, his wife, b. 3/20/1853
Sarah Susannah Smith, dau. of John H. Smith and Elizabeth H. Smith, his wife, b. 2/11/1855
Caroline Tucker Smith and Mary Jones Smith, twin daus. of John H. Smith and Mary J. Smith, his wife, b. 8/9/1845
H. Smith and Mary J. Smith, his wife, b. 8/9/1845
Laura E. Smith, dau. of John H. Smith and Elizabeth H. Smith, his wife, b. 12/1857

20

(Lucy Ann Simmons Smith Bible continued...)

Deaths

Mary J. Smith, wife of John H. Smith d. 7/28/1849, aged 39 yrs, 10 mos, 10 days.
Elizabeth H. Smith, wife of John H. Smith d. 2/15/1857, aged 29 yrs, 5 mos. and 29 days.
Laura Elizabeth Smith, dau. of John H. Smith and Elizabeth Smith, his wife, d. 9/5/1857,
aged 8 mos, 28 days.
Robert Jackson Smith, son of John H. Smith and Mary J. Smith, his wife, b. 6/29/1838
John A. Smith, Jr. son of John H. Smith, Sr., d. 5/15/1862
James Moreland Smith d. 7/19/1834
Robert J. Smith d. 3/3/1862
Thomas Levi Smith d. 6/19/1854
Sarah Susannah Smith d. 8/16/1855

FRED HOMER BENSON BIBLE
Owner: Mrs. H. C. Miachels, Albertville, Ala.

Births

Fred Homer Benson 6/18/1889
Martha Glenda Benson 2/7/1947
Ola Belie Brown 6/29/1897
Gina Rae Benson 6/2/1962
Durward Glenn Benson 7/27/1916
Kimberly Kelly Elliott 5/11/1959
Ray Benson 2/18/1919

James Bernard Benson 8/14/1937
Melissa Lynn Bryant 3/5/1963
Barbara Ann Benson 8/25/1939
Jeffery Edwin Bryant 7/20/1964
John Fred Benson 4/8/1941
John Michael Benson 11/3/1967
Sandra Nell Bensen 9/22/1946

(Fred Homer Benson Bible continued...)

Kathryn Denise Benson 3/7/1970
Sandra Michelle Elliott 12/7/1972

Horace Coleman Michaels 8/29/1884

Marriages

Fred Homer Bensen to Ola Belle Brown 8/17/1913
Durward Glenn Benson to Nell Dereath Cooper 3/3/1935
Charles Ray Benson to V. G. Roden 12/25/1937
Robert C. Eliiott to Barbara Ann Benson 9/7/1957
Horace Coleman Michaels to Ola Belle Brown Bensen 6/1958
Max Biddle Bryant to Sandra Nell Bensen 1/22/1862
John Fred Benson to L. G. Walker 6/12/1965
James Bernard Benson to Linda Lou McDerment 6/30/1973
J. F. Odom, Sr. to Martha Glenda Benson 1/21/1977
Terrance Lee Reese to Kimberly Kelly Elliott 8/4/1977
George Richard Monger to Martha Glenda Benson Odem 2/6/1981

Deaths

Fred Homer Bensen 6/14/1940
Horace Coleman Michaels 11/6/1972
John Fred Benson 1/31/1975
Durward Glenn Benson 10/25/1976
Charles Ray Benson 6/20/1977
Ola Belle Brown Benson Michaels 5/21/1981

22

JAMES EARP BIBLE
Owner: Mrs. Ben West, Bianco, Tx

Marriages

James Earp to Mary Sanders 6/20/1818 in Lawrence Co., Ala.
Thomas Harmon to Leah Emeline Earp 2/5/1855
Thomas Harmon to Nannie E. (Earp) Taylor 7/4/1869
Gertrude Harmon to Frank Hoffman 6/1/18/--at Briar, Tx.
Marjorie Hoffman to Ben West 3/2/1933 at Pudacah, Tx., now living Bianco, Tx.

Births

Orlenia Earp 6/17/1819
Robert Earp 11/20/1820
Louisa Earp 3/2/1823
Sarah Earp 10/15/1826
Philip Earp 11/15/1833
Pleasant Earp 10/14/1834
James Earp 5/7/1835
Emaline Earp 1/2/1837
Nannie E. Earp 4/20/1841
Ruel Earp 8/7/1828
Francis Earp 5/10/1831

Thomas Harmon 3/1/1835
Ira L. Doak Harmon 3/6/1872
Mary Abigail Harmon 12/1/1855
James K. Polk Harmon 3/6/1872
Sabrina Gertrude Harmon 10/7/1869
Flora Fidelia Harmon 12/8/1876
Thomas Augustus Harmon 9/7/1873

23

(James Earp Bible continued...)

Francis Eliz. Hoffman b. 11/14/1894 at Los Angeles, Calif. (d. 8/17/1895) 3/2/1933 Paducah, Tx.

Daus. of Frank and Gertrude Hoffman (written beside above entry)
Marjorie Hoff

Deaths

Leah Emaline Earp 4/7/1857
James Earp 8/7/1861
Mary Earp 1/17/1863
Philipp Thomas Harmon b. 2/12/1857, d. 10/19/1857
James K. Polk Harmon 3/10/1873
Thomas Harmon 3/11/1890
Nanie Elizabeth Harmon 11/20/1906
Thomas Augustus Harmon 6/27/1904
Ira L. Doak Harmon 12/27/1932
Mary Abigail Harmon Pope 8/1916
Sabina Gertrude Harmon Hoffman 2/20/1957, buried Bianco, Tx. Flora
Fidelia Harmon Shankle 4/30/1969 in Decatur, Tx., buried in Abilene, Tx.

REV. ROBERT ALLEN FOSTER BIBLE
Owner: Henry Chandler Foster, Sr., Brantley, Ala.

Family Record - Miscellaneous
(Rev. Foster recorded birth alld death dates of his parents,
himself, and his siblings)

John Lewis Foster 3/22/1835-3/15/1883
Martha Ann Foster 3/6/1842-8/3/1933
Robert A. Foster b. 4/8/1859
Sheppard Walter Foster b. 6/11/1861

(Rev. Robert Allen Foster Bible continued...)

Judson Hansford Foster b. 3/28/1866
Lula Foster b- 2/6/1870
Mattie Foster b. 3/28/1872
Minnie Foster b. 7/23/1874
Marvin Fletcher Foster b. 7/9/1878
Robert Allen Foster was b. 4/8/1859 near "Malones' Chapel" five miles from Eufaula, Barbour Co., Ala.
Esther McKerness was b. in Luton Bedfordshire, England, 2/28/1856. She moved with her father and brothers and sisters to Ala.
Robert Allen Foster and G. McKerness m. 4/4/1885 at Montgomery, Ala.

Births

Esther Rosalie Foster 12/19/1885 at Elbert, Elbert Co., Cole.
Ethel Elizabeth Foster 9/26/1857 at
Elizabeth, Elbert, Cole.
Beulah Foster 9/14/1889 at Beulah, Pueblo Co., Cole.
Martha Foster 4/12/1891 at Salem, Lee Co., Ala.
Robert McKerness Foster 12/10/1992 at Salem, Lee Co., Ala.

Walter Washington Foster 2/22/1895 at Phoenix City, Lee Co., Ala.
Lucile Foster 8/6/1903, baptised by W. S. Wade 1903, at Perote
Susie Peach Foster 10/2/1905 (at Parsonage) in Havana, Hale Co., Bullock Co., Ala.
John Lewis Foster 5/11/1907 at Havana (Parsonage), Hale Co. Ala.
Just 78 years after the birth of his grandfather, John Hiram Peach. He was baptised in the parsonage at Pine Apple, Ala., Wilcox Co., by Rev. T. Y. Abernathy, Presiding Elder, on 3/15/1908 - just 25 years after the death of his grandfather, John Lewis Foster.

(Rev. Robert Allen Foster Bible continued...)

Marriages

Henry Candler Foster was b. in parsonabe at Pine Apple, Ala. on Thanksgiving morning 11/25/1909. He was baptised by Rev. O. S. Welch 1910.

Abigail Foster was b. in parsonage at Jernigan, Ala. 10/4/1912, baptised by L. B. Lathram in parsonage at Graceville, Fla.

Deaths

Esther Foster 9/15/1901, Aberfoil, Bullock Co., Ala.
John Lewis Foster 12/20/1908, at parsonage, Pine Apple, Ala., aged 19 mos, 9 days, sick only 42 hrs, membranous croup.

Judson H. Foster 2/4/1940
Sister Lula 8/29/1939

Robert Allen Foster d. at his home Brantley, Ala. 9/12/1942
Abigail Peach Foster, wife of Robert
Allen Poster, d. at Henry Candler Foster's home Brantley, Ala. 11/22/1959. She was buried 11/24 beside her husband at Little Oak, 7 miles from Troy, Ala.

Miscellaneous

Robert A. Foster and Abigail Peach were m. at Perote, Bullock Co., Ala. 10/29/1902. Rev. W. H. Wild and Rev. C. C. Rush, members of the Ala. (Methodist) Conference officiating.

26

RODGER McKINSTRY BIBLE
Owner: W. D. McKinstry
939 Saulter Rd., Birmingham, Ala. 35209

Marriages

Alexander McKinstry to Elizabeth Thompson in Augusta, Ga. 1820
Alexander McKinstry, son of the last, to.Virginia T. Dade, Mobile, 3/20/1845 by Joshua Heard
Alexander McKinstry, son of Alexander and Virginia T. Dade McKinstry, to Annie D. Poss
In Eureka, Calif. 5/19/1878
William D. McKinstry, son of Alexander and Virginia T. Dade McKinstry, to Evelyn V.
Sheldon, youngest dau. of Thomas F. and Fannie Sheldon, Mobile, Ala. 1/12/1881 by Mr. J. O.
Andrew
Keith S. Moffatt, son of R. D. Moffatt and Elizabeth Moffatt to Louisa Dade McKinstry, dau of
Alexander McKinstry and Virginia T. Dade McKinstry by Rev. Mr. Johnston, Mobile Ala.,
3/20/1882
Thomas S. McKinstry, son of W. D. and Eva S. McKinstry, to Maude

Leland Bancroft, dau. of Catherine Bancroft, by Rev. Rush, Mobile, Ala. 11/16/1909
Ida Louise McKinstry, dau. of W. D. and Eva S. McKinstry, to William Harrison Bruner, son of I.
O. and C. C. Bruner, by H. H. McNeill, Mobile, Ala. 12/6/1910

Births

Rodger McKinstry - Scotland
John McKinstry, son of Rodger, Scotland, 1680 Alexander McKinstry, son of John
Ezekiel McKinstry, son of Alexander, Ellington, Conn. Alexander McKinstry, son of Ezekiel,
Ellington, Conn. Alexander McKinstry, son of Alexander, Augusta, Ga.

Children of Alexander McKinstry and Virginia T. Dade are as follows:

(Rodger McKinstry Bible continued...)

Robert Dade McKinstry, Mobile, Ala. 11/24/1845
Mary Middleton McKinstry, Mobile, Ala.
1/14/1847 Mordecai McKinstry, Mobile, Ala. 9/21/1848
Elizabeth McKinstry, Mobile, Ala.
9/29/1850 William Dade McKinstry, Mobile, Ala. 2/27/1856
Alexander McKinstry 7/8/1852
Louise Dade McKinstry 7/16/1858
Agnes Tankersley McKinstry 3/1/1860
Virginia McKinstry (twin) 6/6/1862
Ben Fontaine McKinstry (twin) 6/6/1862
Mary Ingersoll McKinstry 7/12/1867
Alexander McKinstry, son of William D. and E. V. McKinstry, 2/24/1882, Mobile, Ala.
Tom Ingecsoll Moffatt, son of Keith S. Moffatt and Louise D. Moffatt 2/23/1883, Mobile, Ala.
Thomas Sheldon McKinstry, son of William D. and E. V. McKinstry, 11/3/1984, Mobile, Bla.
William Dade McKinstry, son of William D. and Eva V. McKinstry, 10/17/1856, Mobile, Ala.
Ida Louise, dan. of William D. and Eva V. McKinstry, 1/7/1885, Mobile, Ala.
Fannie Bragg, dau. of William D. and E. V. McKinstry, 6/29/1890
George Sheldon, son of William D. and E. V. McKinstry, 12/18/1893, Mobile, Ala.
    Children of T. S. McKinstry and Elma S. McKinstry Thomas S. McKinstry, Jr. 1/12/1909
Jerome Dade McKinstry 4/6/1911
William Dade McKinstry 10/18/1912
Alexander McKinstry 4/17/1916

Evelyn Margaret Michael, dau. of R. B. and F. McK. Michael, 9/13/1912, Mobile, Ala.
Caroline Clark Bruner, dau. of W. H. and I. McK. Bruner, 10/24/1912, Mobile, Ala.
Evelyn Lee KcKinstry, dau. of W. D. and M. B. McKinstry - no date Evelyn Sheldon Bruner,
dau. of W. H. and I. M. Bruner 3/20/1914, Mobile, Ala.
Margaret Mac McKinstry, dau. of W. D. and M. B. McKinstry - no date.
Catherine McKinstry, dau. of W. D. and Maude B. McKinstry - no date.

Children of Jerome Dade and Caesarina Edey McKinstry
28

(Rodger McKinstry Bible continued...)

Thomas Ingersoll 4/12/1931, Washington Sanitarium, Takoma Pk., Md., birth registered at Baltimore, Md.
Jerome Dade McKinstry, Jr. 5/10/1937, Washington Sanitarium, birth registered at Baltimore, Md.
Richard Edey McKinstry - no date

William Dade McKinstry, Jr., son of William Dade and Mary Griffin McKinstry 6/21/1942 Jefferson Hospital, Birmingham, Ala.
Eloise McKinstry, dau. of William Dade and Mary Griffin McKinstry, 5/26/1946, Jefferson Hospital, Birmingham, Ala.
Mary Elizabeth McKinstry, dan. of William Dade and Mary Griffin McKinstry, b. 6/5/1948

Deaths Children of Alex and Virginia McKinstry:

Robert Dade McKinstry 12/11/1845, Mobile, Ala. Elizabeth McKinstry 6/11/1852, Mobile, Ala.
Alexander McKinstry 8/1853, Mobile, Ala.
Agncs Tankersley McKinstry 9/1/1861, Mobile, Ala.
Benjamin Fontaine McKinstry 6/27/1862, Macon, Miss.
Mary Middleton McKinstry 1/20/1866, Mobile, Ala.
Louise D. Moffatt 4/4/1883, Mobile, Ala.
Virginia T. McKinstry, wife of Alexander, 2/5/1895, Mobile, Ala.
Alexander McKinstry 10/9/1879, Mobile, Ala.
W. D. McKinstry 4/22/1900
Eva S., wife of W. D. McKinstry, 5/9/1900
Thomas Sheldon McKinstry, Jr., 1912
Alexander McKinstry 12/15/1915
Fannie Bragg Me. Michael 2/13/1923
Virginia Dade McKinstry 6/12/1929
Catherine McKinstry, dau. of W. D. and M. B. McKinstry - no date Elma Stapleton McKinstry 5/20/1931, Mobile, Ala.
Alexander McKinstry 5/20/1931, Mobile, Ala.

(Rodger McKinstry Bible continued...)

William Dade McKinstry II 4/19/1832, Mobile, Ala.
Mary Ingersoll McKinstry (Lovie) 12/16/1934 Thomas Sheldon McKinstry 3/19/1953
Virginia McKinstry 11/28/1951, Birmingham, Ala.

BENJAMIN BAGLEY PRESTRIDGE BIBLE
Owner: Nancy Ann Prestridge Black (wife of E. A. Black)

Marriages

Benjamin B. Prestridge and Mary Ann Ezzell 9/3/1836, Perry Co., Ala.
Benjamin Bagley Prestridee and Georgie Ann C. Compton 4/8/1847, Sumter Co., Ala.
Benjamin Bagley Prestridge and Sarah Adline Barbour, wid. of Thomas Barbour and dau. of Henry and Nancy Williams, 4/5/1855, Sumter Co., Ala.

Births

Benjamin Bagley Prestridge 2/8/1816, Bibb Co., Ala.
Mary Ann Ezzell 11/20/1821, Perry Co., Ala.
Sarah Adline Williams 3/10/1823, Green Co., Ala.
Georgie Ann C. Compton 2/12/1827, Escambia Co., Fla.
James Burton Prestridge, son of B. B. and M. A. Prestridge, 6/18/1838, Sumter Co., Ala.
William Asmund Prestridge, son of B. B. and M. A. Prestridge, 11/5/1839, Sumter Co., Ala.

Children of B. B. and G. A. C. Prestridge:

Ellen Jane Prestridge 7/8/1848, Sumter Co., Ala.
Georgia Harris Prestridge 12/8/1855, Sumter Co., Ala.
Benjamin Bagley Prestridge 3/4/1858, Sumter Co., Ala.
Charles Henry Prestridge 5/20/1860, Sumter Co., Ala.

(Benjamin Bagley Prestridge Bible continued...)

Sarah Elizabeth Prestridge, 3/3/1862, Sumter Co., Ala.
Joseph Gideon Prestridge, 4/10/1864, Sumter Co., Ala.

Deaths

Mary Ann Prestridge, dau. of John and Elizabeth Ezzell 10/19/1846 Georgie Ann C. Prestridge, dau. of Richard and Orpah Compton 3/30/1849
James Burton Prestridge, son of B. B. and M. A. Prestridge, 7/6/1856
Joseph Gideon Prestridge, son of B. B. and M. A. Prestridge, 2/12/1865
    too dim to read---
Mary E. Prestridge, wife of George H. Prestridge 10/9/1879, Johnson Co., Tx.

Nancy Ann Prestridge, dau. of B. B. and S. A. Prestridge, b. Sumter Co., Ala. 2/26/1866 McLeskey b. 8/27/1827
Mary C. Prestridge, Santa Barbara, San Paulo Province, Brazil 10/10/1868 dau. of W. A. and Arie Prestridge and granddau. of B. B. and M. A. Prestridge.
William A. Prestridge and Victoria C. Mills m. Choctaw Co., Ala. 10/5/186-
B. D. Prestridge and Cuscba? J. Maxwell, wid. of Nicholas Maxwell m. Johnson Co., Tx. 7/15/1875
George H. Prestridge and Mary E. Roberts m. Johnson Co., Tx. 1/8/1878
William A. Vernon and Sarah E. Prestridge, dau. of D. B. and S. A. Prestridge m. Johnson Co., Tx. 12/12/1878
Benjamin D. Prestridge, Jr., son of B. B. and Sarah C. Prestridge and M. C. King, dau. of William and ----King m. 1/9/1881
Charles Henry Prestridge, son of D. B. and Sarah A. Prestridge and Lula Cloudus m. 5/1/1883
George Harris Prestridge, son of B. B. and Sarah A. Prestridge and S. C. Waller, wid. of Drue Waller and dau. of Samuel and Adda Elizar Snodgrass m. 10/23/1883
Elijah H. Black and Nancy Ann Prestridge, dau. of B. R. and S. A. Prestridge, m. 12/10/1884, Johnson Co., Tx.
D. B. Prestridge, Sr. d. 6/9/1888

D. B. Prestridge, Jr. d. 1910
George Prestridge d. 5/31/1914

JOSEPH DAVENPORT BIBLE
Owner: Clyde D. Fischer, Jr., DeKalb Co., Ala.

Joseph Davenport (Colonel) b. 6/2/1789 d. 1/22/1876 m. Ist 4/16/1812 Mary Thomas b. 3/31/1789 d. 8/7/1849. Buried in family cemetery, DeKalb Co., Ala. (They moved from Va. to Tenn. between 1812-1816, were in Jackson Co., Tenn. in 1820 and DeKalb Co., Ala. by 1842. All children were b. in Tenn.:)

Emeline Davenport b. 1/28/1813 d. 11/10/1896 m. 2/10/1831 William Howard Holleman (1812 1852), 3 children
Orville J. Davenport b. 6/28/1815 d. 5/1/1875 m. Ist 11/26/1839 Mary Grant (1822-1857), 12 children; m. 2nd Mary Caroline Allman (1830-1900), 4 children
Adron Davenport b. 7/27/1817 d. 1/4/1847, never married.
Carrol Davenport b. 1/23/1820 d. 3/22/1820
Montraville Davenport b. 5/4/1821 d. 11/17/1890 m. 12/2/1843 Amelia Easter McSpadden, 8 children
Rudolphus R. Davenport b. 8/8/1823 d. 9/18/1870 m. Ist 5/20/1840 Margaret Ann Spring (1826-1906), 10 children
Delcour L. Davenport b. 2/26/1827 d. 2/1/1864 m. 8/31/1847 Elizabeth Moore (1827-1911)
Eveline C. Davenport b. 4/6/1830 m. 8/4/1847 Samuel N. Moore
Adaline Ledbetter b. 2/18/1834 d. 8/18/1912 m. 2/14/1849 David Heniger Spring (1829-1912), no children

Colonel Joseph Davenport m. 2nd 10/1/1860, age of 71, to Barbara Stallings who d. 4/23/1876.

PHILLIPS-PARMELE BIBLE
Owner: Mrs. J. C. Richards
5211 Chicapeek, Houston, Tx. 77056

Original owner of Bible: Martha Mumford Cobbs, Raleieh, N. C. who m. William Henry Phillips Of Hillsborough, N. C. (They had 3 daus. and lived in N. C., Ala. and Miss. before removing to Texas. Children: Elizabeth Ann m. William Carter Oliver of Ala.; Julia Feliciana m. Joseph Farmer, lived Middleton Miss., Maria Louise m. James Parmele had children-Bettie who d. age 14 and Julia who m. Taylor and had no descendants)

Deaths

William Henry, infant son of William C. and Elizabeth A. Oliver, aged 3 mos, 2 days, Middleton, Miss.

William Henry Phillips (b. 4/22/1793), aged 54 yrs, 7 mos, 8 days, 11/28/1854, Jackson, La.
James Parmele 6/20/1862, 36 yrs, 4 mos, 1 day (b. 2/19/1826), near Middleton, Miss.
Bettie Parmele, aged 14 yrs, 6 mos, 23 days (b. 1856), at Scooba, Kemper Co., Miss.

Mrs. Julia F. Farmer, dan. of William H. and Martha M. Phillips, 1874, aged 43 yrs, 26 days.
Lilkin? Hinton, Kemper Co., Miss. 6/10/1875, aged 6 yrs, wanting 9 days.

Mrs. Julia F. Taylor 6/26/1902, Granger, Tx.
Mrs. Maria Louise Parmele 9/11/1914, Austin, Tx.

Births

Rebekah James 10/16/1792
Sarah James 5/26/1794
Leroy Harrison James 1/1796
Edgar Rees James 4/26/1798

Martha Hicks James 12/27/1802

William T. James 12/7/1803
Margaret Elizabeth James 7/8/1806
Mary Josephine James 8/9/1809
Robert Madison James 7/9/1812
Orlanda Rees James ---

Talafero James m. Martha Hicks 9/1/1759
Talarfero James m. Frances Hicks -/19/1801
Charles Polk m. Martha H. James 10/14/1824
W. W. Wilson and Mary James m. 6/1/1837

Births

Angus Ray Fairley 6/1/1827
David Fairley 1/20/1861
Laura M. James 1/1/1840
Laura Emily Fairley 4/16/1864
Edgar Riece Fairley 3/12/1857
Daniel Fairley 11/14/1865
John Gale Fairley 10/12/1858

Isabella Fairley -/20/1868
Archibald Fairley 9/21/1870
Angus R. Fairley, Jr. 2/3/1876
M. J. Fairley 4/1874
Neil Fairley 7/1579

Deaths

Laura Emily Fairley 10/24/1864 Isabella Fairley 1/24/1873

Marriages

A. R. Fairley m. Laura M. James 3/27/1856

Note: These Pages found in papers of Archibald Fairley and wife, Mollie Rawls after their deaths. Archibald was one of eight sons of Angus Ray Fairley and Laura M. James. From obituary of Laura, her birthplace was Clarke Co., Ala. 1/1/1840 and she m. in Ocean Springs, Miss. 3/27/1856 and d. 11/4/1909, the dau. of Edgar James and Mariah Gale and niece of Gov. Gale of Ala.

CAROLINE ARMINTA HAYNES CRANBERRY SMYRL BIBLE
Owner: Mrs. Eleanor Smyrl Stephens, Wadley, Ala.

Births

James A. Granbery 10/31/1832
Caroline A. Granbery 5/12/1830

(Caroline Smyrl Bible, contd....)

Their children:

Alice Granbery 6/30/1857
Docia Granbery 3/4/1859

Albert W. Granbery 6/26/1860
Thomas Smyrl 1/23/1886
Sallie Smyrl 11/7/1870
Eveline Hand Smyrl 1/23/1886
Annie Smyrl 1/28/1872
Eleanor Smyrl 10/9/1909
Fannie Smyrl 6/20/1875
Annie Lorine Smyrl 12/10/1912
Lula Smyrl 1/24/1879
Thomas Clifford Smyrl 9/2/1916
Johnie W. Smyrl 12/17/1882
James T. Smyrl 4/14/1834
Elizabeth Smyrl 5/6/1860
Delila Smyrl 7/8/1866
Nannie Smyrl 7/2/1861
Mammie C. Smyrl 4/6/1869
Carrie Lane 5/23/1882

Marriages

Elizabeth Smyrl to R. E. Sullivan 517/1878, Ashville, Ala.
Nannie Smyrl to J. W. Harrison 6/1/1884, Macon, Ga.
Mammie C. Smyrl to J. M. Laney 9/24/1888, Stroud, Ala.
Annie Smyrl to R. D. Evans 7/1889, Stroud, Ala.

(Caroline Smyrl Bible, contd....)

Fannie Smyrl to D. M. Laney 9/28/1890, Davistown, Ala.
Johnie Smyrl to Evelin Hand 12/20/1908, Wadley, Ala.

Deaths

Delila Smyrl 4/18/1870
Docia Kewley 3/22/1939
Sallie Smyrl 1871
Willie Cranberry 12/30/1940
Alice Lane 9/9/1896
Tommie Evans 8/20/1941
Thomas Smyrl 3/7/1903
Fannie Laney 11/15/1855
Lula Smyrl 4/10/1913
Mammie Laney 7/1/1965
J. Thomas Smyrl 6/15/1922
Johnie W. Smyrl 4/24/1968
Caroline A. Smyrl 2/15/1931

Annie Evans 8/18/1968

Lizzie Morgan 6/30/1933

Fannie Smyrl Laney 8/1/1969

C. B. Kewicy 7/6/1933

Reuben Evans 6/18/1939

37

YOUNG D. HARRINGTON BIBLE
Owner: Young Drew Harrington
16 Davis Drive, Montgomery, Ala. 36105

Marriages

Young D. Harrington to Talitha G. Emfinger 11/8/1839
James Howard to Martha A. S. Harrington 2/10/1861
Young J. Harrington to Mary M. Oliver 11/9/1865
William F. Harrington to Nancy A. Oliver 11/19/1868
James L. Oliver to Matilda C. Harrington 11/3/1870
H. J. Harrington to Sarah C. Turner 12/1/1872
G. M. Harrington to Amelia Lancaster 11/1/1872

Births

Y. D. Harrington 6/4/1818
Talitha G. Emfinger 5/3/1816
Martha An Sophroney Harrington 10/12/1840
James Harvey Harrington 1/10/1842
Drewry Hamilton Harrington 1/10/1844
Jeptha Harrington 11/27/1845
William Franklin Harrington 11/3/1947
Henry Jasper Harrington 2/3/1850
Matilday Caroline Harrington 6/24/1853
George Miles Harrington 10/12/185-
John R. Harrington 10/3/1856
Mary Frances E. Harrington 1/3/1860
G. M. (George Miles) Harrington 1855
Mary Jane Howard 12/27/1861
Drury Anna Howard 7/21/1865

(Young D. Harrington Bible continued...)

Martha Penelope Howard 6/3/1867
Talitha Caroline Howard 2/3/1869

Deaths

James H. Harrington 9/10/1865
Y. D. Harrington 7/9/1868
Talitha G. Harrington 3/10/1889
Mourning Emfinger 11/17/1866

Births
Henry G. Harrington 2/3/1860
Samma James Harrington 12/1/1877
Sarah C. Turner 1/24/1856
Henry Hamilton Harrington 2/3/1880
Young Preston Harrington 11/9/1874
Mary Jane Harrington 5/7/1881
Charley Dartis Harrington 5/1/1876
Willey Lenard Harrington 3/30/1858

Marriages

William G. Johnson to Mary F. E. Harrington 12/19/1878
John R. Harrington to Sophronia Osburn 2/20/1879
Madie Catherine Lyles Harrington, wife of Charlie Dartis Harrington, d. 6/17/1970

Deaths

Nina P. Johnson 8/14/1881
Charlie D. Harrington 8/7/1943

(Young D. Harrington Bible continued…)

Samma J. Harrington 10/16/1901
Henry H. Harrington 12/24/1951
W. J. Harrington 12/29/1911
Mary Jane Harrington 5/27/1951
Young Preston Harrington 7/4/1928
Sarah C. Harrington 8/3/1920

Births

Cora Lee Harrington 5/8/1869
Lula May Johnson 9/30/1881
William Harvey Oliver 9/18/1971
Thelma Harrington 1/7/1897
Nina Pirkins Johnson 11/1/1879
Thelma Dunn Harrington 1/18/1932

W. G. LOWRY BIBLE
Owner: Mrs. Joe C. Waters
409 S. 4th St., Gadsden, Ala. 35301

William W. J. Lowry b. 20/27/1809
Rhoda Ann Green b. 5/25/1820
William W. J. Lowry and Rhoda Ann Y. Green m.

Births of Their Children

William Green Lowry 2/9/1841
Joseph Elisha Lowry 12/6/1842
Sarah Jane Elizabeth Lowry 6/4/1845
Louisa Frances Lowry 10/20/1848
Rhoda Ann Wilkie Lowry 3/21/1851

40

Mattie Ellen Lowry 6/10/1856
Margrit Jane Olena Lowry 7/27/1863

Marriages

W. G. Lowry to Margaret R. Boyd 10/6/1860
Joe E. Lowry to Georgia (or Gloria) A. Nix 11/14/1867

Deaths

Sarah Jane Elizabeth Lowry 12/6/1848, aged 3 yrs, 6 mos, 2 days
William Wilkie Jobes Lowry 10/31/1881
Margrit Jane Olena Presson 12/28/1889, aged 26 yrs, 5 mos, 1 day
William Green Lowry 9/26/1891, aged 50 yrs, 7 mos, 17 days
Rhoda Ann Lowry 12/20/1833, aged 73 yrs, 6 mos, 24 days

"Sister, I received Pops Family Bible Sunday and I have drawn off one for you and one for me. Those 2 pages tells of the ages of Father and Mother Sisters and Brothers. Written by your loving Sister, Rhoda Ann Wilkie King.

TRISTRAM THOMAS BIBLE
Owner: Arthur Caraway
2765 Oak Ridge Lane, East Point, Ga. 30044

Tristram Thomas m. Mary (2nd) 12/27/1780
Joseph Thomas m. Susannah 1/16/1793
T. H. Thomas m. Mary 12/17/1837
Joseph Thomas, son of Phil Thomas b. 8/25/1770 d. 8/3/1841

(Tristram Thomas Bible continued...)

Births of Children of Joseph and Susannah Thomas

Tristram Thomas 8/7/1798 d. 9/1671816
James Thomas 1/7/1798 d. 7/1836
Elizabeth Thomas 2/14/1800 d. 8/11/1821
Sarah Thomas 2/26/1802
Mary Thomas 7/5/1805 d. 2/23/1826
William Thomas 8/28/1807 d. 9/30/1844
John Clothier Thomas 2/12/1810 d. 8/12/1821
Josiah Thomas 4/2/1814 d. 6/1844
Tristram Thomas 9/3/1816 d. 7/20/1857, aged 41 yrs.
Tristram Thomas, son of Stephen Thomas 7/28/1752-9/3/1817
Mary Hollingsworth, now wife of Tristrnm Thomas, 1/6/17511/15/1917, aged 66 y-rs, 9 days,
38 yrs. member of Baptist Church of Christ
Tristram and Mary Thomas' children Elizabeth Thomas b. 12/25/1781
John Thomas b. 3/18/1784
Sarah Thomas 9/26/1786-10/26th
Tristram H. Thomas b. 5/8/1789
James Clothier Thomas b. 7/10/1792

Tristram and Ann Thomas' children

Robert Thomas b. 6110/1775
Philip Thomas b. 10/15/1779
Susannah Thomas 9/10/1777-4/3/1841

David Harry, son of David Harry and Mary, his wife, b. 7/1770 a

Ages of T. H. Thomas' children

42

Births

George Augustus Thomas 9/22/1839-IJ16/1903
Narcissa Elizabeth Thomas 5/8/1942-6/18/1850
Martha Ann Thomas 7/27/1845-7/2/1928
Joseph D. Thomas 5/30/1843-9/22/1863
Narcissa Elizabeth Thomas 4/25/1852-4/9/1922
Cornelia Jane Thomas 3/9/1855-9/12/1932

Notes: Tristran Thomas served as Capt., Major and Colonel during Americaoltion, later appointed Brig. General of Marlborough District, S. C. He was b. in Maryland 7/28/1752. Stephen Thomas b. 5/25/1704 Talbot Co., Maryland d. 4/1774 Anson Co., N. C. Tristram Thomas b. 1666 Sundridge, Kent Co., England, d. 2/1745/6 in Queen Anne's Co., Maryland m. Judith Clayland (1764 Maryland ca 1738 Maryland) Tristram Hollingsworth Thomas was buried in Barbour Co., Ala.

JOHN McDOWELL BIBLE
From: Rev. War Pension #R6694
Morgan Co., Ala.

Births of Children of John McDowell and his wife, Sarah Elizabe th McDowell 1/7/1791

Clarissa McDowell 6/23/1802
William Thomas McDowell 4/26/1792
Harriet McDowell 11/25/1806
Nancy McDowell 1/13/1794
Charlotte McDowell 5/1/1810
John Washington
McDowell 2/12/1808
Tristam McDowell 2/1/1796
James Pressley McDowell 5/12/1812
Mary McDowell 3/12/1738

(John McDowell Bible continued...)

Miles McKinnis McDowell 6/26/1804
Alexander Thomas McDowell 2/12/1800

Note: John McDowell's application Morgan Co., Ala. stated that he was b. 8/10//1755 and that he m. Sarah Thomas b. 6/15/1772 on 3/27/1790, dau. of PhLlemon Thomas in Marlborough District, S. C. 3/1855
Sarah McDowell, widow, aged 83, of Lawrence Co., Ala., applied for pension. John McDowell d 1/1/1841

WILLIAM TABOR BIBLE
From: Rev. War Pension #W6246

John Tabor b. 4/18/1783 eldest son
Karenhappy Tabor, dau. of William and Susannah, b. 4:23/1795
Nathan Tabor b. 8/3/1797
Malinda Tabor b. 1/8/1800
Elijah Tabor b. 10/26/1805
William J. Merrow, son of James and Elizabeth Morrow, b. 4/29/1822
Samuel Merrow b. 2/10/182-
Mary Jane Merrow b. 1/14/1826
William Tabor, son of John and Elizabeth Tabor b. 1/4/1761
Susannah Tubbs, dau. of George and Mary Tubbs, 1/31/1852

Note: William Tabor's application dtd 10/16/1832 Bibb Co., Ala., aged 71 last Jan., entered service from Burke Co., N. C. where his father lived; that he was b. 1/4/1762 in Orange Co., N. C. The application of Susannah Tabor, widow, dtd 2/1/1847, Winston Co., Miss., aged 85, states she m. 7/5/1781 William Tabor in Rutherford Co., N. C., by Joseph Kamp; that her husband d. 6/4/1844, aged 53, in Winston Co., Miss. Susannah Tabor d. 1/31/1852 Winston Co., Miss. Nathan Tabor (identical twin), heir of William and Susannah, both deed, apptd Samuel Knight, Washington, D. C. to prosecute his claim 12/13/1852. Surviving children 1/31/1852 were: John, William, Nathan, Elijah, Mary, Cairen and Malinda.

GEORGE THOMAS McCLUSKY BIBLE
Owner: John McClusky, Jr., Monroe, La.

George T. McClusky of Calhoun Co., Ala. b. 9/16/1854

Emly C. Pickett of Calhoun Co., Ala. b. 11/16/1860 m. 4/20/1879, Clovers Station, Ala.
Witnesses: George McClusky, W. H. White. Minister: Rev. John H. Reeves.

Children:

William Covington McClusky 4/4/1880-11/16/1913 Monroe, La.
Mary Gertrude McClusky b. 2/22/1884
John McClusky b. 8/30/1857
Joisy Irene McClusky b. 4/5/1890
Sam Jones McClusky b. 10/5/1892

Deaths

George Thomas McClusky 9/9/1894, Forksville, La.

PRESLY T. HUMPHRIES' BIBLE

Births

Presly T. Humphries 4/3/1807
Jane Aplin Humphries 12/17/1810-7/31/1875

Walter Green Humphries 11/2/1830
Sarah Elizabeth Humphries 10/4/1832
Amandrew Melvina Humphries 11/30/1834
William Thornton Humphries 8/30/1837

(Presly T. Humphries' Bible continued...)

Martha Jane Humphries 6/13/1840

Mary Adline Humphries 5/25/1843
Presly Aplin Humphries 3/27/1846
Frances Florida Humphries 7/12/1848
David Mitchel Humphries 11/15/1850
Mary Ales Dison 2/14/1855
David Mitchel Humphries 11/15/1850
Ella Humphries 1856
Oscar Wily Humphries 1874
Carry Bell Humphries 12/23/1875-6/26/1929
Robert Lee Humphries 3/1/1878-3/8/1962
Colonel Humphries 4/4/1881-3/20/1926
Nancy Jane Humphries 3/29/1884-7/21/1920
J. J. Lee, husband of Mary Ann Lee, d. 2/12/1929
O. M. Humphries d. 7/5/1957
Onias Mitchel Humphries b. 7/21/1889
Alan Urban Humphries b. 6/14/1879
Emit Embry Humphries 10/26/1885-2/7/1858
Eva Victoria Humphries b. 4/19/1901
David Mitchel Humphries d. 8/16/1907, age 56 yrs., 9 mos.
Ella Humphries d. 1/31/1911, aged 56 yrs., maiden name, Lee

Willis Francis Lee b. 4/1846
Benjamin Franklin Lee b. 1/22/1848
Mary Ann Lee 2/9/1851-10/1925
Hester Ann Lee 10/9/1852-6/17/1854
Ella Lee b. 1/21/1856
Nancy Harris b. 12/30/--

Colonel Ivers Lee b. 11/5/1858
Susan Lee b. 1/9/1861
Milton O. Lee m. Nancy Harris 6/13/1844
M. O. Lee 3/30/1826-3/22/1901

SAMUEL MARION DUFFELL BIBLE

Josephine Rebecca Corbitt, dau. of Jesse W. and Mary Elizabeth McKinnon Corbitt, m. James David Zorn 11/3/1859 by Rev. A. J. Sampler. He was killed at battle of Peachtree Creek, near Atlanta, Ga. 7/20/1864. She was left with three children and later married Samuel Marion Duffell 12/27/1867.

James D. Zorn 11/22/1836-7/20/1864
Josephine R. Corbitt 6/29/1839-5/24/1903
Mary Caroline Zorn b. C/12/1S60 m. Albert F. Powell 12/26/1883
Larkin James Zorn b. 9/25/1862 m. Maggie Lewis 2/3/1892

James David Zorn, Jr. 3/15/1864-10/25/188(Marion Walter Duffell 2/15/1869-10/16/1873
Margaret Josephine Duffell b. 3/23/1874 m. W. H. Benton 1/12/1890
Ella Fances Duffell b. 10/19/1872 m. William Bundy 11/28/1907 at River Palls, Ala. by Rev. Daniels. She d. 7/15/1970
Mary Ludie Duffell b. 1/9/1875 m. J. L. Movey 12/29/1897. She d. /5/1901
Jesse Alexander Duffell b. 3/6/1878
Alberta Viola Duffell b. 12/30/1880

Joseph Johnson b. 7/5/1883
Samuel Marion Duffell 4/29/1843-5/6/1911
Frances Eloise Bundy, dau. of Ella F. D. Bundy b. 3/25/1910 m. Randall Carlton Holley 4/16/1941
Marion Willette Bundy b. 9/22/1915, dau. of Ella F. D. Bundy, m. D. A. O'Gwynn 3/19/1937. He was b. 5/3/1914 d. 3/14/1971
Marion Ranella Holey b. 11/25/1943, dau. of Eloise D. Holley
W. E. Benton b. 4/7/1892
M. E. Benton 10/18/1893-12/1893
S. G. Benton b. 8/8/1896
V. J. Hovey 12/27/1898-2/13/1899
Traci Ludie Hovey 8/17/1901-9/6/1901
Priscilla O'Gwynn b. 5/6/1941 m. Edward Michael Young b. 8/9/1940

LARKIN STRICKLAND BIBLE

Owner: Mrs. Harrison Latimer, Anderson, Ga.

Larkin Strickland m. Margarett Stewart, dau. of Rev. War Soldier,
James Stewart and his wife, Margery McGee in Jackson Co., Ga. in 1821. Lived in Troup Co.,
Ga. 1830 and Randolph Co., Ala. 1843.

Births

Larkin Strickland 5/1/1799
George Washington Strickland 6/1/1838
Margarett Strickland 7/3/1799
James 0. Strickland 2/8/1822
Margery Margarett Strickland 5/26/1840
Julius A. Strickland 5/14/1823
Mary Strickland 12/29/1824
Jefferson Strickland 5/8/1842
Sarah Ann Strickland 8/31/1826
Matison Strickland 5/8/1842
Elizabeth Strickland 4/3/1828
Henry Ansel Strickland 3/17/1844
John Carliss Strickland 1/1/1830
Nancy Strickland 8/3/1831
James Larkin Strickland 12/30/1842
David Loyd Strickland 3/20/1833
William F. Strickland 10/29/1834
Mary Elizabeth Strickland 6/14/1845
Larkin M. Strickland 1/1/1837
Leroy Strickland 8/7/1833
Sara C. Strickland 11/3/1855
W. C. Strickland 4/4/1857
Sarah Marget Bishop 4/8/1853

(Larkin Strickland Bible continued...)

J. L. Strickland 1/7/1853
John E. Bishop 7/23/1855
M. J. Strickland 6/30/1868
Florence Virgia Strickland 11/30/1850
C. D. Strickland 1/19/1871
Stephen Bishop 6/23/1825
Margery E. Bishop 8/19/1858
Enoch D. Bishop 10/27/1848
David L. Bishop 5/2/1861
William L. Bishop 10/21/1849
Stephen M. Bishop 8/29/1862
Mary Jane Bishop 8/30/1851
Lanora Strickland 7/4/1869
Derah Strickland 7/4/1869
Ollie Strickland 3/7/1873

Marriages

Larkin Strickland m. Margarett 3/13/1821
James P. Strickland to Margarett C. Lawrence 3/27/1842
Sarah Ann Strickland to William Belcher 5/9/1844
Stephen Bishop to Elizabeth Strickland 12/16/1847
Charley J. T. Cambell to Nancy Strickland 8/22/1850
J. C. Strickland to A. S. Hudson 12/21/1854

Deaths

Leroy Strickland 9/10/1839
Larkin Strickland 5/11/1848
Julius A. Strickland 2/6/1851, Camden Co., Ga.

(Larkin Strickland Bible continued...)

George Washington Strickland 7/7/1860
Jefferson Strickland 1/2/1862
Madison Strickland 1/19/1862
Margrett Strickland 5/21/1869 near Hickory Flat, buried at Standing Rock Church, Chambers Co., Fla.
David L. Strickland 4/30/1853, buried Bethel Church, Chambers Co., Ala.
Elizabeth Bishop 12/17/1906
William Cicero Strickland, son of John C and Ann S. Strickland 9/21/1876

ANTHONY METCALF BIBLE
Owner: Clayton G. Metcalf
405 N. Rawls Street, Enterprise, Ala. 36330

Births

Anthony Metcalf 5/20/1786
Mary Sims, wife of Anthony Metcalf, 5/12/1787
Isaac Metcalf 2/1808
Mary Ann Metcalf 12/6/1819
James Metcalf 1/31/1911
Martha Metcalf 1/3/1822
Eliza Metcalf 4/20/1813
Margaret Metcalf 8/25/1827
John Metcalf 5/4/1815
Emeline Metcalf 5/11/1830
Sarah Metcalf 6/30/1817
Synthia Metcalf 12/25/1832

(Anthony Metcalf Bible continued...)

Marriages

Anthony Metcalf to Mary 1/1810
John Reahey to Eliza Metcalf 6/1834
John Metcalf to Sarah Stroud 12/1837
Isaac Metcalf to Sarah Brown 3/1838
James W. Williamson to Mary Ann Metcalf 8/1845 James Caustin to Sarah Metcalf 7/1851

Deaths

Anthony Metcalf 3/2/1845
James Metcalf 1/19/1820
Emeline Metcalf 5/3/1843

DAVID NOAH HAMPTON AND SARAH CAROLINE KING BIBLE
Owner: Mrs. Donnie Lee Davis
207 E. Fourth Ave., Rome, Ga. 30161

Marriages

David Noah Hampton to Sarah Caroline King 1/7/1858, Polk Co., Ga. by Elder C. B. Martin
John Beard to Mollie E. Hampton 11/23/1876, Polk Co., Ga. by Rev. J. W. Pullen
L. Sutherlin to Emily F. Hampton 9/7/1879
J. W. Pullen to Mollic E. Beard 3/29/1885
Mary Shirley Sutherlin m. Spencer James Lester 5/31/1917 in Polk Co., Ga.
Marie Kathleen Sewell m. Rolfe Powell Kennard 12/24/1925 in Cave Spring, Ga.
Nellie Sue Sutherlin m. Edward E. Griffith 5/16/1913 in Haralson Co., Ga.

(David Noah Hampton Bible continued…)

Births

David Noah Hampton 11/25/1833
Noble B. Beard 11/3/1880
Sarah C. Hampton 11/3/1837
Sallie C. Sutherlin 11/1/1881
Mollie E. Hampton 11/8/1858
Myrtle C. Sutherlin 4/16/1854
Emily P. Hampton 11/13/1860
Mary Lee Pullen 7/9/1890
John A. Beard 1/15/1854
Lucile Pullen 11/20/1887
Lafayette Sutherlin 6/21/1847
Arthur Deck 6/23/1876
Zila Frances Beard 10/26/1878
Noah Hampton Sutherlin 7/3/1886
Stella Pullen 4/10/1886-5/24/1886
Nellie Sue Sutherlin 8/23/1890
Arthur Seek b. 6/23/1872 m. 9/20/1896

Deaths

John A. Beard 11/13/1771
Sarah C. King Hampton 3/3/1920
Myrtle Candis Sutherlin 7/19/1885
E. E. Griffith 5/5/1923
Noah Hampton Sutherlin 5/30/1888
Lafayette Sutherlin 11/6/1927
Ruby Sutherlin 1/3/1900
Dr. J. F. Findley 1/1929
Mary Elizabeth Pullen 11/15/1934

52

(David Noah Hampton Bible continued...)

Francis Durham Findley 6/1944
Emily Frances Sutherlin 2/13/1935
Spencer James Wester 12/5/1948
Stephen King 9/6/1892
D. N. Hampton 9/26/1911
Nobia B. Sewell 1/14/1912
Edward E. Griffith 5/6/1923

Births of Great Grand children of D. N. and Sarah C. Hampton

Francis Durham Findley 5/29/1902 -
Marie Cathleen Sewell 11/2/1902
Perry Hampton Findley 2/9/1904
Edward E. Griffith d. 5/5/1923
Isaac Sewell, Jr. 11/7/1905
Bowden Hoke Findley 7/31/1906
James Lafayette Findley 10/5/1908

Jean Connell Sutherlin, dau. of Francis Lafayette Sutherlin and Corinne Connell DeBerry b.
    12/25/1920
Francis Lafayette Sutherlin m. Corinne Connell DeBerry 5/5/1919 in Cedartown, Ga. He d.
    1/14/1954.
Jean Sutherlin m. John Harvey Norton, Jr. 9/24/1949 and had children born: John Harvey
Norton III 8/29/1950 and Corinne Sutherlin Norton 1/11/1960

Connell Snead Norton b. 12/21/1954

MILTON NEWTON SEWELL BIBLE
Owner: James S. Naugher, Rt. 2, Box 300
Leesburg, Ala. 35983

Milton Newton Sewell 6/20/1846-11/8/1925 m. Ist Nancy D. Watson 10/20/1850-2/7/1907.

Births

M. N. Sewell 6/20/1846
Watson Sewell 1/19/1879
N. D. Sewell 10/20/1850
Susie H. Sewell 10/1/1880
N. C. Sewell 2/21/1870
Thomas H. Sewell 9/7/1882
Elvira Sewell 8/25/1871
Clara Sewell 2/4/1884
Cephas Sewell 12/19/1872
Nancy Sewell 8/21/1886
Laura T. Sewell 3/22/1874
B. E. Sewell 3/4/1888
George P. Sewell 11/28/1875
Ernest C. Sewell 9/10/1889
William A. Sewell 9/19/1877
John C. Sewell 12/3/1891
Crofford N. Sewell 3/24/1893

Deaths

Nannie L. Sewell 9/11/1887
John C. Sewell 6/30/1926
 B. E. Sewell 10/6/1888
Cephas Sewell 3/14/1949
 Earnest C. Sewell 6/15/1892

54

(Milton Newell Sewell Bible, Deaths continued...)

George P. Sewell –
Watson Sewell 6/21/1911
Clara Sewell Bates 7/7/1978
Crofford Newton Sewell 8/5/1961
M. N. Sewell 11/8/1825
Norie Sewell Cartledge 1/8/1954
Laura Sewell Thornton 1/20/1851
N. D. Sewcll, wife of M. N. Sewell, 2/1907
N. E. Sewell, wife of M. N. Sewell, 7/3/1915

Marriages M. N. Sewell to N. D. Watson 1/2/1868

M. N. Sewell and Mrs. N. E. Brannen 3/1/1908
Crofford N. Sewell and Nannie D. Moon 2/22/1914

Births of C. N. Sewell's Family

Christine Sewell 5/15/1915
Clara Bo Sewell 9/22/1929
Annie Ruth Sewell 7/29/1920

Christine Sewell m. Hoyt Mackay 7/6/1935
Annie Ruth Sewell m. Bernard Naugher 8/7/1943
Clara Bolyn Sewell m. Joseph E. Carver 3/11/1949

55

GEORGE W. HALL BIBLE
Owner: John Hall, Cleburn Co., Ala.

George W. Hall 12/1/1857-5/24/1906
Nathan R. Hall 10/26/1859-5/19/1918
Sarah Jane Hall 11/26/1861-2/13/1936
John William Hall 7/12/1863-1/28/1903
James D. Hall 3/30/1866-9/13/1936
Henry A. Hall 2/25/1868-10/27/1898
Charles H. Hall 4/24/1870-3/18/1932
Samuel J. Hall b. 3/7/1873
Andrew S. Hall 5/1/1875-5/31/1941
Benjamin F. Hall b. 3/2/1879
John Hall d. 7/24/1889
Nancy Clark Hall d. 11/27/1907

JOEL DENDY-FLORENTHA HUTCHINSON BIBLE
Owner: Clark H. Dendy, Jr.
2592 Elsinore St., East Point, Ga. 30344

Marriages

Joel Dendy to Florentha Hutchinson 4/4/1833 in Laurens Dist., S. C.
Moses G. Hughs to Amanda J. Dendy 11/29/1860 in Cherokee Co.,
William A. Brown to Sarah C. Dendy 11/27/1861, Cherokee Co., Ala.
W. H. Allsup to C. H. Dendy 8/16/1867 in Cherokee Co., Ala.
Josiah E. Pridgen to Amanda J. Hughes 4/12/1865, Cherokee Co., Ala.
Joel O. Dendy to Mary C. Naugher 8/1/1869 in Cherokee Co., Ala.

Births

Joel Dendy 11/29/1810

56

(Joel Dendy Bible, Births, continued...)

John A. Dendy 3/26/1877
Florentha Hutchinson 12/3/1812
Mary Dendy 3/20/1879
Skarline? G. Dendy 1/23/1834
John Alfred Dendy 3/27/1877
Leander C. Dendy 3/27/1836
Mary Elizabeth Dendy 3/20/1879
Sarah C. Dendy 7/1/1838
Emma A. Dendy 12/24/1881
Amanda J. Dendy 12/14/1840
Lillie Mae Dendy 12/25/1898
Clara H. Dendy 5/4/1844
Clark H. Dendy 10/1/1901
Joel O. Dendy 3/19/1847
C. H. Dendy 5/12/1926
Carl V. Dendy 1/1/1928

Great Grandchildren

Margaret Jeannine Dendy-1/11/1853
Carla Ann Dendy 1/20/1859
Vernon Roy Dendy 11/25/1953
Charles Howell Dendy 12/3/1962

Deaths

Leander C. Dendy 6/12/1837, aged 1 yr., 2 mos., 16 days
S. G. Dendy was lost at Murphresborough, 12/1863, aged 29 yrs, 11 mos.
Florentha Dendy 10/17/1869, aged 56 yrs., 10 mos; 74 days
Florentha L. Dendy 10/11/1864, aged 15 yrs. 8 mos.

ANDREW JACKSON HOLLEY BIBLE

Andrew Jackson Holley b. 12/6/1914 m. Emma L. Chambliss b. 1876 (lived Coffee Co., Ala., 1880 Census.)

Births

A. C. Holley 8/16/1896
Alan Holley 10/14/1907
Hosey Holley 7/14/1898
Mae Holley 2/8/1910
Ieaman Holley 8/9/1901
Obbie Holley 8/15/1912
Randol Holley 5/21/1903
Vera Inez Holley 5/19/1915
Lela Holley 10/1/1905

URIAH NIXON AND BARDARA GAMBRILL BIBLE
Owner: Mrs. Joseph Ross McKinney
223 East 4th St., Texarkana, Ark 75502

Births

Uriah Nixon 6/30/1806
George Patrick Nixon 10/15/1842
Barbara Nixon 10/27/1810
Mary Nixon 3/21/1944
Sally Nixon 6/6/1834
Linna Ann Nixon 4/28/1945
Parthena Nixon 10/13/1835
Uriah D. Nixon 5/25/1852
Emilla Margaret Nixon 3/6/1837

(Uriah Nixon Bible, Births, continued…)

Margaret Paralee Nixon 1854
William Durrill Nixon 3/7/1839
John I. Linsey 12/8/1853
Abner Henry Nixon 10/15/1840
William H. Linsey 3/9/1858

Deaths

William Burrel Nixon 5/21/1840
Sally Nixon 7/3/1856
Mary Nixon 3/28/1844
Abner H. Nixon 4/7/1857
Uriah Nixon 9/12/1857, aged 51 yrs., 3 mos., 6 days
Margaret P. Nixon 2/16/1860
George P. Nixon 3/15/1862, aged 19 yrs., 5 mos.

Marriages:

Uriah Nixon to Barbara Gambrell 5/21/1833
William H. Nixon to Sally 8/15/1851
Thomas Linsey to Parthia Nixon 1/13/1853
John Gray to Linna Nixon 1/6/1861

Births

Lornhama Gray 9/24/1864
Henrietta Gray 1/31/1868
Emily Carry Gray 1/14/1871

JACOB BARKMAN BIBLE
Owner: June Barkman
2905 N. Kilbourne Ave., Chicago, Ill. 60641

Jacob Barkman b. 12/20/1754
Rebecca Davis 3/24/1791-1/17/1837 m. Jacob Barkman
Jacob Barkman m. (2nd wife) Mariah DIckinson 8/9/1837
Leanah Barkman 2/4/1814-9/24/1831
James E. M. Barkman b. 2/23/1819 m. Harriet E. Maddox b. 5/22/1881 Montgomery, Ala. d. 5/16/1812
V. B. Barkman b. 1/12/1842

Births

Rebecca Davis Barkman 3/24/1791
Vivian Caddo Barkman 1/11/1842
Leanah Barkman 2/14/1814
Lelia Caddo Barkman 8/31/1844
Wm. F. S. Barkman 1/26/1818
Leanah E. Barkman 4/3/1843
James B. M. Barkman 2/23/1819
Rebecca M. Barkman 9/23/1850
Harriet E. Maddox Barkman 2/22/1821
Sallie Harriet Barkman 10/8/1857
Walter Eugene Barkman 1/27/1862
James Sumner Barkman 12/14/1859

Marriages

J. E. M. Barkman to Harriet E. Maddox 3/9/1841
Leila Caddo Barkman to John D. McCabe 11/26/1863

(Jacob Barkman Bible continued...)

Deaths

Rebecca Davis Barkman 1/11/1837
Marion R. Barkman 5/2/1875
Jacob Barkman 8/23/1852
Harriet E. Barkman 5/15/1912
Valeria A. Barkman 9/11/1844
Leila Caddo Barkman 11/16/1933
McCabe Wm. F. S. Barkman 7/11/1852
James E. M. Barkman 9/13/1865
Kathleen Barkman Gates 1/19/1939
Leanah E. Barkman 7/14/1873
James Sumner Barkman 5/24/1941

HENRY BARRON BIBLE
Owner: Jack L. Barren
3200 W. 32nd, Topeka, KS 66614

Henry Barren b. 8/14/1801 m. Sarah 1/8/1824
Sarah Barron (wife of Henry) b. 1/12/1802 d. 6/28/1863, 61 yrs., 5 mos., 18 days
Henry Barron d. 4/7/1870, 66 yrs., 9 mos., 3 days
John S. Post m. Emily A. Barron 10/25/1866
John S. Post b. 1/3/1841
Henry Samuel Post, son of John S. Post, b. 11/15/1867
Amanda Elender Post b. 1870
Winney Josephine Post b. 21/5/1873
John Sidney Post, son of John S. Post, b. 2/25/1876
May Allen Post b. 5/24/1886

61

(Henry Barron Bible continued...)

Births

Zilleann F. Barro 11/7/1824
Milton Barron 2/14/1836
William J. Barron 12/24/1835
Emily Aramant Barron 5/1/1840
James D. Barron 6/3/1828
Hyram Barron 4/7/1830
Georgia Ann Elizabeth Barron 2/20/1841
Henry C. Barron 12/4/1831
Sarah Amanda Barron 11/27/1833
Benjamin Franklin Barron 1/21/1845
Lucy Barron, wife of James D. Barron S/27/1825-6/17/1850 m. 7/5/1849
William Henry Barron
J. D. Barron b. 4/16/1850
William J. Barron, son of Henry and Sally, d. 9/14/1845
Benjamin F. Barron, son of Henry and Sally, d. 8/14/1845
Infant dau. of Francis and Wilson Upshaw, stillborn 6/4/1846
M. L. Barron was killed on battlefield at Atlanta, Ga. being 28 yrs., 5 mos.
Wilson Upshaw m. Zilleann F. Barron 6/10/1847
Sarah F. Upshaw b. 6/4/1849
Sarah Emily Post m. Thomas Edwin Ballard 12/12/1859 Baskill Co., Tx.

Slaves Births:

Andrew Jack 5/2/1840; Aaron 11/3/1850; Jaccine 4/20/1855; Dock 3/5/1841;
Lanfore 3/22/1845; Mariah 8/14/1853; Luscdear 7/7/1855; Manurua Jan 11/1/1856; Ellen
5/25/1857

Emily Aramanthe Barron b. Ala. d. 11/15/1912 Haskell, Tx., buried 11/16/1912 Haskell, Tx. m.
John Sidney Post.

E. E. HOLLINGSWORTH BIBLE
Owner: Mrs. Vera Cochran, Hokes Bluff, Ala.

Marriages

E. E. Hollingsworth to Ella F. Dames 12/26/1886
E. E. Hollingsworth to Mollie Culbertson 3/25/1896
Edwin S. Cochran to Vera Hollingsworth 6/19/1917

Births:

Abel Lawrence Hollingsworth 6/18/1885
Jera Omie Hollingsworth 8/24/1890
Joseph Hollingsworth 7/19/1894
Edwin Shelton Cochran 6/10/1880
Edwin Henry Cochran 7/13/1918
Lucy Frances Cochran 6/21/1821
Vera Jo Cochran 6/13/1925
William Pershing Cochran 1/13/1928

Deaths

Ella Hollingsworth 10/7/1894
Abel Hollingsworth 1903
Joseph Hollingsworth 7/18/1896
Lucy Frances Cochran 7/1/1923
E. E. Hollingsworth 7/1/1893

W. H. AND MARY J. McELRATH BIBLE
Owner: Mrs. Mary R. Hays Stanfield

W. H.. McElrath 12/10/1839-8/16/1916
Mary J. McElrath 10/22/1848-5/2/1889
W. A. McElrath 10/11/1866-2/5/1875
John J. McElrath 3/5/1869-11/5/1936
Charlie F. McElrath 1/6/1871- 5/25/1852
Mary E. McElrath 9/2/1873-
Ella F. NcElrath Hays 12/8/1875-1/1962
H. Andrew McElrath 2/8/1879-5/31/1952
Annie R. McElrath 3/3/1881-7/19/1896
Minnie B. McElrath 6/25/1885-7/1/1866
Emma ,McElrath Harris d. 8/1930

EDMOND COFFEY BIBLE
This is April 14, 1872

Edmond Coffey b. 3/13/1810 d. near Aubry, Texas 8/29/1895
Dinah H. Coffey 1/27/1811-1893

Births

Edmond D. Coffey 6/1/1831
Betsy An Coffey, wife of E. T. Walker, 8/7/1832-5/8/1877
Lareney Coffey 3/7/1834-1/9/1894
Den Coffey 3/3/1836
Sally C. Coffey 3/16/1835
Webster G. Coffey 1/20/1840
Arrelius Coffey 3/9/1842
Thomas A. Coffey 6/27/1844

James M. Coffey 6/4/1845
Eliza Jane Coffey 6/23/1850
Martha Coffey 6/23/1850
Clarence Evergreen Coffey 12/28/1852

John Boone McKinney 12/27/1847-2/29/1866 m. 9/18/1867
Eliza Jane Coffey McKinney 10/18/1847-9/11/1915
John Thomas McKinney 6/30/1865-2/0/1891
Edmond James Archibald McKinney 11/11/2309-7/1/1935
William Webster McKinney 10/26/1871-5/1/1879
Ben Arrelius McKinney 7/20/1873-12/7/1942
Eliza Dianah Elizabeth McKinney 12/1/1878-3/8/1916
Samuel Washington Mitchell McKinney 1/28/1882-12/9/1940
Lorena Martha Evergreen McKinney 12/15/1884-10/20/1954

Marriages

Benjamin A. McKinney to Mattie Condra 4/7/1892
Edmond James Archibald McKinney to Rebecca Hinton 10/22/1895
Dianah (Ann) McKinney to Martin B. Couch 9/78/1898
S. Wash McKinney to Claudia Walker 5/27/1906
Lorena McKinney to Elrod V. Phillips 5/31/1906

ELI DANIEL BIBLE

Eli Daniel m. Milbery Puckett 11/25/1830

Births

Eli Daniel 8/13/1808
Thomas E. Daniel 1/27/1839
Milbery Daniel 10/17/1812
Martha Ann Tabitha Daniel 2/14/1841
James M. Daniel 10/20/1831
Nancy Greene Daniel 1/27/1843
John P. Daniel 12/10/1832
Francis D. Daniel 2/10/1845
Seabron F. Daniel 2/12/1835
Drusilla M. Daniel 8/14/1847
William D. Daniel 1/7/1837
Sarah C. Daniel 3/7/1849

Gains B. Daniel 12/2/1851
Jonathan Eli Daniel 1/31/1854

Deaths

Thomas Eli Daniel 12/20/1843
W. D. Daniel 6/9/1877
James Martin Daniel 9/24/1854
Milbery Daniel 3/24/1878
Tabitha Puckett 11/17/1843
Eli Daniel 7/18/1889

BENJAMIN H. AND TALITHA TYSON RODEN BIBLE
Owner: Mrs. C. D. Matthews, Attalla, Ala.

Births

Benjamin H. Roden 5/17/1814
Napoleon B. Roden 3/18/1845
Talitha Tyson 2/28/1822
Margaret Roden 4/23/1850
William F. Roden 7/16/1840
Catherine Roden 11/27/1852
Nancy R. Roden 3/18/1842
Sarah Roden 5/16/1857
Benjamin H. Roden, Jr. 12/27/1854
Louisa Roden 3/5/1844
Missouri Roden 3/13/1846
Jeremiah Roden 7/30/1859

Deaths

Louisa Roden 4/15/1855
Missouri Crump 10/10/1873
Clarinda P. Roden 7/20/1863
Sarah Melton 5/24/1882
William F. Roden, Jr. 9/21/1863
Benjamin M. Roden 11/29/1892
Talitha Stowers 11/28/1869
F. M. Roden 6/13/1871
Talitha Roden 7/7/1870
N. Roden 9/14/1904
Catherine Roden 12/6/1870
Daniel B. Roden 5/25/1949

(Benjamin H. Roden Bible continued...)

Benjamin Roden, Jr. 4/20/1878
Nancy R. Stowers 2/5/1874

Marriages

Benjamin H. Roden to Talitha Tyson 8/10/1839
William F. Roden to Clarinda P. Siniard 11/13/1961
John L. Stowers to Nancy R. Roden 11/14/1961
William D. Crump to Missouri Roden 2/24/1865
Napoleon D. Roden to Louisa J. Edwards 10/21/1869
Benjamin H. Roden, Sr. to Jane Burnett 12/29/1871
Milton Jones to Margaret Roden 3/30/1871
John Graves to Nannie J. Roden 7/31/1892
Daniel D. Roden to Nancy Gilbreath 11/15/1894

Births of Grandchildren

William F. Roden, Jr. 11/11/1862
H. Stowers 7/14/1872
William F. Stowers 11/18/1864
F. H. Roden 7/22/1870
Talitha Stowers 4/16/1867
Nannie L. Roden 9/1/1872
William H. Crump 9/8/1867
Louisa Crump 8/2/1869
Daniel D. Roden 11/18/1877
Sarah Dovie Stowers 6/14/1870
Nancy J. Roden (wife of above) 11/19/1879

Napoleon Graves Roden 4/23/1893

68

(Benjamin H. Roden Bible continued...)

Odis Roden 10/21/1800
Arizona Roden 9/4/1895
Mabel Roden 3/18/1906
General Forrest Roden 9/16/1898
Beulah Roden 6/1/1910

The following information found loose page in Bible
Jeremiah Roden b. 11/3/1764. His wife, Susana, b. 3/12/1759. They were m. 4/28/1736

Births of Children

Poly Roden 2/28/1786
Jeremiah Roden, Jr. 7/8/1792
John B. Roden 9/30/1787
Benjamin H. Roden 4/6/1795
Oega Roden 2/12/1789
John D. Roden b. 9/30/1787 m. Nancy Brassell b. 1/6/1789.

Births of Their Children

Poly Roden 10/18/1807 -
Jeremiah Roden 10/2/1820
William D. Roden 5/16/1812
Catherine Roden 4/27/1828
Benjamin H. Roden 5/17/1814
Susana Roden 4/18/1830
Martha Roden 10/16/1816
Calvin Roden 1/17/1832
Walton W. Roden 8/10/1815
Jane Roden 11/13/1816

69

CANNON BIBLE
Owner: Mrs. H. Lester Stewart
Gaylesville, Ala.

Births

Samuel Newton Dickson 8/25/1817
Elizer Miller Dickson 4/8/1858
Elizabeth Jane Wool 10/10/1831
Caleb B. Cannon 12/16/1846
Mary Ann Linton Dickson 1/22/1852
Margret Ida Cannon 2/20/1869
Katharine Wood Dickson 6/27/1856
Nannie Jane Cannon 10/6/1881
Sarah Jane Nickles Dickson 5/21/1849
Elizabeth McReynolds Dickson 12/13/1853
Thomas Linton McWhortor Cannon 2/20/1969
Willie D. Cannon 11/26/1884

Marriages

Samuel Linton Dickson to Elizabeth Jane Wood 8/1/1848
Caleb D. Cannon to Sarah J. N. Dickson 1/26/1868
T. B. Cannon to C. W. Dickson 1/16/1872
T. L. Cannon to Ella Moor 12/5/1888

Deaths

Sarah N. G. Wood 2/8/1843
Mary Ann Linton Dickson 1/18/1859
Nancy Ann Wood 8/1/1850
Andrew F. Dickson 10/27/1861
Daisy Crawford Randle 9/13/1854

(Cannon Bible continued...)

Ella Ossa Cannon 5/28/1991
C. M. Cannon 1/3/1905
C. B. Cannon 3/4/1915
Elizabeth Jane Dickson 6/13/1855

Births

Menurva Clatesta Dickson 12/13/1840
Jane Falls Wray 8/30/1799
Wiley E. Wood 12/16/1799
James W. Dickson 2/11/1821
Sarah M. G. Jordan 5/13/1806
Thomas L. Dickson 2/19/1825
John Westly Wood 10/15/1827
Ruth Jane Dickson 9/19/1827
Mary Crawford Wood 2/4/1827
Mary D. H. Dickson 5/19/1832
Rebecca Catherine Wood 5/3/1829
Nancy R. Dickson 12/10/1836
Elizabeth Jane Wood 10/10/1831
Robert Asberry Wood 4/24/1835
Nancy Ann Wood 5/11/1837
Andrew F. Dickson 3/24/1794
Sarah Ann F. Dickson 4/15/1819
Elizabeth R. Dickson 3/26/1823
Margaret M. Dickson 5/23/1830
Narcisa L. Dickson 8/17/1834
T. L. M. Cannon 2/20/1869
W. D. Cannon 11/26/1884
M. I. Cannon 8/20/1871

(Cannon Bible continued...)

M. Cannon 10/5/1887
L. S. L. Cannon 1/18/1876
E. O. Cannon 2/15/1883
C. O. Cannon 1/12/1878
R. U. Cannon 5/18/1831
N. J. Cannon 5/6/1891

J. M. WRIGHT BIBLE
Owner: Lexie T. A. Wright McCurley

Births

S. M. Wright 10/1/1849
William J. J. Wright 5/4/1850
Marthy E. Wright 10/5/1847
George Wright 10/21/1882
Robert S. M. Wright 1/15/1868
Bessie V. Wright 1/25/1885
Eliza D. Wright 10/18/1870
Marthy S. Wright 3/17/1887
James W. Wright 12/13/1872
Lexie T. A. Wright 9/12/1931
Nancy L. Wright 7/4/1875
Eliza C. Harris 2/16/1830
Samuel T. Wright 10/28/1877
John C. Miles 10/3/1861
Bobbie Lou McCurley 5/22/1917
George L. Miles 3/11/1887
Joe McCurley 8/20/1813
Sinkler McCurley 1/13/1884

Euthema McCurley 4/6/1923
Lexie McCurley 9/12/1891
Willima Jean McCurley 5/5/1926
Glee McCurley 6/30/1909
Billie Ruth McCurley 8/30/1928
Erlene McCurley 5/30/1911
Inell McCurley 4/12/1931

Claudine McCurley 4/3/1913
Martha Faye McCurley 3/22/1934
Mattie Sue McCurley 3/28/1915

Marriages

J. M. Wright to Marthy E. Dyer 4/25/1867
John C. Miles to Eliza D. Wright 2/26/1885

WILLIAM MYRICK BIBLE

Marriages

10/28/1830 William Myrick to Sarah T. Harris, Pike Co., Ga. 8/3/1862
Mary Victoria Myrick

Births:

Giles Harris 8/5/1766
William Myrick 1794
Sarah G. Myrick 10/10/1811

(William Myrick Bible continued...)

Children of above:

Giles Harris Myrick 1/2/1831
Mary Victoria Myrick 12/3/1842
Howell Augustus Myrick 183-
Albert Cicero Myrick 10/17/1844
Albert Cicero Myrick 10/17/1844
William Russell Myrick 4/26/1838
Owen Fletcher Myrick 2/20/1852
Georgia Ann Thompson Myrick 5/31/1834

Mary Lelusia Myrick 4/5/1845
Georgia Ann Myrick 3/10/1868
Osker S. Henderson 5/31/1874
Cora Let Henderson 3/1/1881
Cary Estella Henderson 3/10/1883
Howell Augustus Myrick –

Deaths

Giles Harris 10/9/1844
Giles Harris Myrick 1/20/1845
Howell Augustus Myrick 5/4/1862
John L. Myrick 12/20/1864
Sarah Giles Myrick 4/21/1875 aged 63 yrs., 7 mos, 11 days.
Guiom Houl Sanford Myrick 5/4/1858
Georgia Ann Thompson Myrick Reed

JAMES AND MARY McCULLOCH HARRIS' DIBLE
Owner: Douglas P. Home
325 East 8th St., Rome, Ga.

Births

James Harris 7/7/1766
My wife, Mary McCulloch 10/28/1771

Their Children:

Robert McCulloch Harris 1/7/1791
Adaline Harris 3/3/1803
Martha Mary Harris 10/16/1796
Mary Ann Harris 12/5/1804
Nathan Harris 10/16/1798
James Crawford Harris
Lucy Harris 1/14/1801 2/27/1812
Mary McCulloch Harris, dau. of son, Robert and Deborah, his wife, b. 7/7/1811
John McCulloch Harris, son of Robert and Deborah, b. 6/29/1813

Deaths

James Allen Harris 9/29/1816
Mary Ann Turk, dau. of said Martha who is now Martha Turk, b. Dlount Co., E. Tenn.
11/28/1819, d. 10/3/1820

Lucinda Harris, wife of said Robert, lost a fine son b. dead , at full time, 1/29/1821
Mary Ann Cobbs dau. of Richard and Lucy, b. 7/20/1820 Deborah, dau. of Robert and Lucinda,
b. 12/22/1820

Robert Turk, son of Hiram and Martha, b. 12/29/1823

75

(James Harris Bible contd....)

Sarah Upton Cobbs, dau. of Richard and Lucy, b. 5/2/1828
Lucy Jane Harris, dau. of Robert and Lucinda, b. 9/16/1826
Maria Catharine, dau. of Robert and Luclnda, b. 1/17/1830

Marriages

James Harris to Mary McCullough 1/13/1790

My son, Robert McC. Harris to Deborah McCurene of Augusta Co., 5/9/1810, said Deborah d. 12/22/1817. The said Robert m. Miss Lucinda Maupin 10/28/1819
Martha Mary Harris to Hiram K. Turk 5/25/1815
Thomas Turk, son of Hiram and Martha, b. 7/3/1826
Lucy Harris to Richard Cobbs 9/23/1819
Dr. Nathan Harris to Jane Lowry of E. Tenn.
Adaline Harris to Matthew Jouett Brason of Mason Co., Va. 2/13/1824
Mary Ann Harris to Samuel Lusk Lowry of Monroe Co., Tenn. 1/7/1827. Samuel L. Lowry d. sometime in fall of 1840
Mary Ann Lowry, formerly Mary Ann Harris to William Sandlin 2/1843

Dr. John Lowry Harris d. at Talladega, Ala. 9/25/1862, aged 37 yrs., 4 mos., 11 days.

Births

Nathan Harris, son of Hiram and Martha Turk, 1/19/1822
Patrick Henry, son of Richard and Lucy Cobbs, 12/5/1822
James Crawford, son of Nathan and Jan Harris, 2/27/1823
John Lowry Harris 5/14/1825
Mary Jane Harris 1/18/1828
Sarah Isabella Harris 1/4/1833 at Madisonville, Monroe Co.
Richard Ragland Harris 4/29/1830

76

(James Harris Bible contd....)

William Hooper Harris 8/5/1835 at Cherokee Agency, Tenn.
Nathan Crawford Harris 2/11/1838, Ross Landing, Hamilton Co., Tn.

Deaths

Richard Cobbs, husband of Lucy Harris, 6/27/1825, Monroe Co., E. Tenn.
James Harris 3/22/1830 Albemarle Co., Va., aged 63 yrs., 8 mos., 15 days
James Crawford Harris, son of Nathan and Jane 3/12/1831, aged 8 yrs., 15 days
Mary Jane Harris, dau. of Nathan and Jane, 7/21/1841
stillborn son of Lucinda and Robert Harris, 3/29/1936, Talladega Co., Ala.
Two stillborn sons of Lucinda and Robert Harris, 2/15/1838
Robert M. Harris 1/27/1845, aged 54 yrs., 20 days
Mary Harris, wife of James Harris, at house of her dau., Lucy Cobbs, in Tenn., 4/1846
Mary Ann Sandline, dau. of James and Mary Harris, 1/21/1853, aged 45 yrs., 1 mo., 14 days, at Cedar Bluff, Ala.
Nathan Harris, son of James and Mary Harris, d. 7/6/1855 at Cedar Bluff, Ala., aged 56 yrs., 8 mos., 20 days.

Births

James Crawford Harris, son of Robert and Lucinda, 2/24/1833
Martha Adaline Harris, dau. of Robert and Lucinda, 6/27/1839
Robert Thomas Harris, son of Robert and Lucinda, 5/6/1842
Virginia Adaline Harris 10/24/1840 on Chatanuga Creek, Hamilton Co., Tenn., within 1/2 mi. of Ga. Line.
James Piper Harris, son of Nathan and Janc, 2/8/1844 in Cherokee Co., Ala. (Cedar Bluff)
David Burke Harris, son of John L. and Eliza Jane Harris, 10/21/1850 at Cedar Bluff, Ala.

JOSHUA FOWLER BIBLE
Owner: Mrs. B. W. Barnes
3225 Green Tee, Apt. 122
Arlington, Tx 76013

Births

Joshua Fowler 1/3/1784 m. 9/15/1812 Elizabeth Story 12/26/1785

Births of Their Children

Mary Fowler 1/10/1813
Martha Fowler 8/19/1821
Dorothy Ann Fowler 12/1/1815
Eliza E. Fowler 1/3/1824
Nancy Fowler 11/21/1817
John J. Fowler 4/28/1826
Charity Fowler 12/17/1819
Lydia Elizabeth Fowler 5/14/1829
Charity and Elizabeth Ham 11/3/1836
Bright A. Ham 2/17/1840

Marriages

Dorothy Ann Fowler 1/17/1833
Charity Fowler 12/13/1837
Mary Fowler 12/18/1831
Lydia Elizabeth Fowler 1/4/1847
Nancy Fowler 1/13/1835
Charity Davis 2/5/1846 (2nd marr)
Martha Fowler 12/18/1836

(Joshua Bible continued...)

Births of William Thornton Family

First son 4/15/1835
Bethsheba Nancy Bethsheba 11/6/1838
Second dau. 2/13/1836
Polly Thornton 1/3/1841
Third dau., Martha Ann, 8/19/1836

The first child of Charity Davis:

Mary Loiza, 10/27/1835
Henry B. Davis 9/27/1840
John Marshel Thornton 4/4/1843
Marthy L. S. Ham 4/17/1843
William A. Harvey 12/12/1837
Henry N. Harvey 3/16/1840
James Pussley Thornton 1/39/1845
Francis Roycroft 10/13/1847
Hasel M. Roycroft 6/23/1849
Marian Roycroft 4/3/1851
W. H. Fowler 7/14/1850
Margret A. E. Fowler 12/31/1851
James S. Fowler 2/17/1854
Marthy L. J. Ham 4/17/1843
Nancy M. E. Ham 1/13/1847

Deaths

Joshua Fowler 8/26/1839
Richard Fowler 1/4/1840

Lizy Fowler 11/23/1838, aged 15
Elizabeth Fowler 8/25/1869
Benjamin Davis 9/27/1840
Nancy M. Ham 1/22/1895
Marthy Harvey 10/2/1842
Henry Ham 5/23/1883
Dorothy Ann Thornton 5/12/1847
M. E. Ward 8/21/1915
G. A. May 8/15/1900
Minnie Watkins 12/20/1915
B. A. Ham 8/4/1916
Martha Harvey 10/2/1842
Lydia Elizabeth Roycroft 6/7/1851 and her baby 6/18/1851

Births

D. M. Roycroft -/22/1865
B. N. Roycroft 1/22/1849
James W. Turner 12/8/1849
Sarah Jane 2/2/1836
Mary Caroline 1/15/1855
Francis Caroline 6/6/1836 or 1830
Martha J. Jones 5/15/1815
Newton T. 9/5/1842
Mary Ann, the black woman, d. 5/15/1847

MORRIS CLARK BIBLE
Owner: Mrs. Caroline B. Smick, Mobile, Ala.

Morris Clark m. Delilah Quay 1/22/1829

Births of Their Children

Mary Ann Clark 1/10/1830
Susanna Clark 6/23/1839
Martha Caroline Clark 8/6/1831
Morris Emery Clark 12/3/1841
William Hanford Clark 1/7/1833
Jane Mayberry Clark 3/9/1844
Caroline Clark 6/4/1935
Francis Asbury Clark 4/23/1846
Hiram Clark 7/6/1837
George DeWilton Clark 12/11/1848

Deaths

Martha Carolina Clark 1/20/1832, aged 6 mos., 5 days Hiram Clark 7/21/1838, aged 12 mos., 15 days

Jane Mayberry Clark 11/23/1852, aged 7 yrs., 8 mos. 14 days Norris Emery Clark 1019/1846, aged 4 yrs, 10 mos., 6 days

George DeWilton Clark 5/31/1855, aged 6 yrs., 5 mos., 20 days Francis Asbury Clark 1/5/1861, aged 14 yrs., a mos., 12 days William Hanford Clark 1/5/1866, aged 33 yrs., lacking 2 days

JAMES CRAWFORD CLARK BIBLE
Owner: Victor E. Clark, Jr.
14262 Southern Pines Drive
Dallas, Tx 75234

Children of James Crawford Clark who m. 11/4/1854 Dollie Adelia DeWitt, all b. in ferry Co., Ala:

Births

Hector Edwin Clark 9/23/1885
Sophia M. Clark 3/10/1897
Victor Earl Clark 11/24/1888
Dollie Adelia Clark 10/2/1899
Hugh Clifton Clark 2/10/1890
James Crawford Clark 7/2/1903
Zula Clark 9/11/1892
Robt Cunningham Clark 5/22/1909

David Tucker stayed here and taught school -- year of 1902 and returned in the summer of 1903 as a Dr.
Miss Lottie Dug taught our school in 1904

Deaths

Hugh Clark, Sr. 10/29/1898
Marcie C. Massey 7/12/1893
Cinthia M. Clark 8/8/1896
D. DeWitt 6/4/1914
Sarah Anne Clark 6/27/1900
Dollie A. Clark went to Thomasville 1/1899 and 10/1904
Mrs. T. W. Bagley was here in 1902

A. F. WILSON BIBLE
Owner: Ramon F. Wilson
524 W. Sypert St., Nashville, Ark.

"Presented to A. P. Wilson by Mary F. Wilson 1881."
A. F. Wilson of Fredonia, Ala. m.   Mary F. Phillips of Dudley's Ville, Bla. 1/20/1853 at residence of bride's mother by Rev. Samuel Marwell. Witnesses: James M. Phillips, Mrs. Dr. Gunn.

Births

Abel Fletcher Wilson 10/2/1831
Mary Lena Wilson 2/1/1875
Mary Franklin Phillips 7/28/1836
Josephus B. Echols 2/2/-Martha Ella Wilson 7/30/1855
Laura F. Biggs 2/26/1867
W. W. Wilson 2/14/1858
Lou Edwards 4/2/1874
Joseph Bush Wilson 6/12/1860
Vincent C. Thrash 1/13/1966
Edwin Fletcher Wilson 11/30/1863
Frances Haislip 2/21/1877
James Phillips Wilson 11/19/1869
S. M. Coker ---
Jesse Alonzo Wilson 8/13/1871

Marriages

Martha E. Wilson to J. B. Echols 11/18/1872
W. W. Wilson to Laura F. Biggs 12/16/1885
E. F. Wilson to Lou Edwards 12/16/1891
Lena Wilson to V. C. Thrash 1/3/1892

(A. P. Wilson Bible, contd....)

James P. Wilson to Frances Maislip 6/21/1839
Lena Thrash to S. M. Coker 3/19/--

Deaths

Joseph Bush 10/24/1863, aged 3 yrs, 3 mos., 12 days
Jesse Alonzo Wilson 3/13/1876, aged 4 yrs, 7 mos.
Vincent C. Thrash 1/17/1895, aged 23 yrs, 4 days
James P. Wilson 12/29/1902, aged 33 yrs, 1 mo., 10 days
S. M. Coker 2/7/1807 at Rock Creek, Ark.
Mary Franklin Wilson b. 7/28/1836 d. Nashville, Ark., aged 84 yrs., 5 mos., 22 days
Abel Fletcher Wilson 10/22/1922
W. W. Wilson 9/24/1932
Mrs. W. W. Wilson 8/16/1942, aged 75 yrs., 5 mos., 13 days
Forrest Wilson 11/21/1967, aged 78 yrs.
Mrs. Forrest Wilson 8/1/1960, aged 64 yrs.

REUBEN WARREN BIBLE
Owner: Mrs. Gertrude Birchfield
Oak Level, Ala.

Reuben Warren b. 12/31/1833 m. 1/12/1851 to Nancy Lott b. 12/28/1829

Births

Martha Elizabeth Wnrren 10/27/1851
Nancy Jane Warren 10/20/1853
Sarah Rebecca Warren 1/9/1856
Amanda Warren 2/7/1858
Lucinda Caroline Warren 5/28/1859

84

(Reuben Warren Bible, Births continued...)

William Smith Warren 5/11/1861
Malinda Warren 8/30/1863
Joann Warren 4/26/1865
Reuben Grant Warren 11/10/1868
Henry Clay Warren 5/24/1871

Deaths

Nancy Warren 7/18/1873
R. F. Warren 9/1875

LAWRENCE L. LIVINGSTON BIBLE
Owner: Mrs. O. J. Whitten
1720 Giles Dr., N. E., Huntsville, Ala. 35601

L. L. Livingston m. M. A. McCullough at Mooresville 1/9/1980 in presence of Father and Laura (J. H. Livingston and sister Laura Livingston). *Signed, C. Magee.*

Births

Lawrence L. Livingston 7/28/1855
M. A. Livingston 6/16/1861 (Mary Allye McCullough)

Their Children:

Lemuel Hardaway Livingston 4/20/1981
Willis Henry Livingston 4/11/1884
Lawrence Lee Livingston 7/7/1887
Bertha Mildred Livingston 4/18/1888
L. J. Livingston 9/17/1891
Loreta Fay Livingston 2/25/1898

(Lawrence L. Livingston Bible continued...)

Marriages

Lawrence L. Livingston to M. A. McCullough 1/8/1880
Tes de Graffenried to Bertha Livingston 2/27/1907
Charles T. Finley to Bertha 12/20/1915
Willis H. Livingston to Bertha Newman 4/11/1909
L. J. Livingston to Velma Torbett 11/13/1919 at Waco
C. D. Williams to Loreta Livingston 5/15/1924
J. N. Carrothers to Eloise de Graffenried 1/21/1825

Deaths

Lemuel Livingston 8/22/1882
Charles T. Wiley 2/14/1925
Lawrence Lee Livingston 1/20/1888
L. J. Livingston 6/29/1959
Gussie Marie de Graffenried 1/12/1911
Willis Henry Livingston 1850
M. A. Livingston 10/20/1940
Lawrence L. Livingston 10/10/1920
Bertha Mildred Finley 3/1/1941

Births

Eloise de Graffenried 1/4/1908
Gussie Marie de Graffenried 1/4/1908
Willis Edward Livingston 1/19/1812
Lucy Jane Livingston 11/26/1920
Jack Livingston 9/9/1924
Bertha Elizabeth Williams 4/12/1825
Howard Torbett Livingston 5/18/1926

86

ROBERT WILLIAM HOLBROOK BIBLE
Owner: Mrs. James M. Castle
2125 Cassie Lane, Mobile, Ala. 36605

Robert William Holbrook m. Irene Palmire Johnson 5/3/1905, Mobile, Ala.
James Maurice Castle m. Carmie Clark Holbrook 7/17/1940, Corinth, Miss.
Robert William Holbrook son of William Robert Holbrook and his wife, Gustavia Cox
Holbrook, b. Brownsville, Tenn. 12/15/1884
Irene Johnson, dau. of George Johnson and his wife, Alabama Revere Johnson, b. 12/21/1885 in
Mobile, Ala.

Children of George and Alabama Revere Johnson

Beulah Louise Johnson b. 1/10/1884 Mobile, Ala. m.---Schmidt, d. 4/23/1955
Irene Palmire Johnson b. 12/21/885 in Mobile, Ala. m. Robert William Holbrook, d. 3/5/1963
Mobile, Ala.
George Johnson d. 1888 Mobile, Ala.
Alabama Revere Johnson d. 1895 in Creed, Colorado

Notes: Alabama Revere had a half-bro., Douglas Merritt. When Alabama Revere Johnson died,
her sister took Beulah and Irene to rear. She was a Mrs. Clark and had two daus. that we know
of - Carmie Clark who m. Walton Sink and Nancy Clark who m. Walton Sink when her sister
died.

Children of Robert William Holbrook and wife, Irene Johnson

Robert Douglas Holbrook b. 1/29/1906 Brownsville, Tenn. d. 11/3/1909 in Mobile, Ala.
Beulah Louise Holbrook b. 2/14/1907 Mobile, Ala. m. Ist Horace Beaty, 2nd, Wesley Wilson
Castle on 9/6/1942
James William Holbrook b. 2/18/1911 in Brownsville, Tenn. m. Mary Frances Jackson 1/3/1931
Robert Gardner Holbrook b. 10/6/1913 in Brownsville, Tenn. m. Eva Mae Moore 9/8/1951
Carmie Clark Holbrook b. 7/10/1924 in Jackson, Tenn. m. James Maurice Castle 7/17/1940

(Robert William Holbrook Bible continued...)

Robert William Holbrook d. 11/6/1842 in Jackson, Tenn. and was buried 11/9/1942 in Brownsville, Tenn.
Irene Johnson Holbrook d. 3/5/1963 in Mobile, Ala., buried Mobile.
James M. Castle, son of Homer and Nancy Gladys Johnson Castle b. 11/5/1919 in Paintsville, Ky.
James Wesley Castle, son of James M. and Carmie Castle, b. 1/15/1942 in Jackson, Tenn.
Virginia Lee Castle, dau. of James M. and Carmie Castle b. 1/30/1946 in Mobile, Ala.

JOE HENRY LIVINGSTON BIBLE
Owner: Mrs. O. J. Whitten
720 Giles Dr., N. E., Huntsville, Ala. 35801

Bible presented to Miss Moley Livingston by her father, J. H. Livingston, 8/2/1882

Births

J. M. Livingston 6/3/1827
Susan C. Livingston 3/15/1886
L. L. Livingston 7/28/1855
S. O. Livingston 9/23/1874
L. J. Livingston 9/25/1857
T. L. Livingston 7/23/1876
L. A. Livingston 5/7/1860
M. O. Livingston 11/2/1879
L. L. L. Livingston 12/10/1866
M. Livingston 11/2/1881
J. H. Livingston Jr. 5/30/1862
Annie Livingston 3/18/1858
Abigail Livingston 7/21/1883

(Joe Henry Livingston Bible continued...)

Births of Children of Sarah Elizabeth Moore McDonald Livingston by her first husband:

M. A. McDonald 7/16/1866
Mary E. McDonald 8/20/1871
E. McDonald 6/27/1869

Marriages

J. H. to M. E. Livingston 12/23/1852
J. H. to Elizabeth McDonald 11/31/1873
L. J. Livingston 9/22/1878
L. Livingston 1/8/1880
Laura Drusenham 10/14/1880
Susie Livingston to Tom Walden 7/29/1908
Annie Livingston to Henry Martin 9/16/1903
Abigail Livingston to Joe L. Karr 10/16/1904

Deaths

M. O. Livingston 3/23/1873
L. L. Livingston 10/10/1920
J. H. Livingston 3/3/1914
L. J. Livingston 3/31/1931
Susie Livingston Walden 3/28/1913
Henry Livingston 12/27/1963
Ophelia Livingston Green 4/8/1925
Bobbie Livingston Karr 11/22/1935
Sarah J. Coleman 11/3/1869, aged 64 yrs., 7 mos., 23 days
D. Coleman 11/21/1868
M. E. Livingston 5/3/1872, aged 43, 4 mos. 17 days yrs., 4 mos., 17 days

(Joe Henry Livingston Bible continued...)

J. H. Livingston, Jr. 10/17/1864, aged
L. L. L. Livingston 7/25/1875
George McDonald 9/17/1872
Molsey Livingston 10/10/1882, aged 13 mos., 8 days
Lemuel Livingston, son of Lawrence Livingston, 8/22/1882
Thomas Luke Livingston 1/18/1886

A. A. AND MARY A. RIDGELL BIBLE
Owner: Mrs. Mary Anil Ridgell, Coffeeville, Ala.

Marriages:

B. R. Ridgell to Mary Dunn 2/29/1858
T. G. Dungan to Mary A. Ridgel 2/22/1871

Births

B. R. Ridgell 1/8/1838
D. Dungan 9/24/--
Mary A. Dungan 11/23/1844
C. H. Dungan 4/1/1879
T. G. Dungan 12/25/1847
Alla D. Dungan 9/24/1881
John A. Dungan 4/22/1860
David L. Dungan 10/9/1883
Sarah A. Ridgell 2/10/1859
Owen A. Dungan 3/19/1856
Francls Ridgell 10/25/1861
Lesley Dungan 3/7/1888
Isabella Ridgell 9/13/1862
Piercie B. Dungan 5/5/1891

(A. A. Ridgell Bible, Births continued...)

Willie R. Ridgell 9/11/1864
Woody G. Dungan 9/20/1893
T. A. Dungan 4/18/1873
Travis Richard Dungan 3/1896
Mary Eva Allen Dungan 3/4/1898
Daisy Gray Dungan 4/23/1902

Deaths

Francis Ridgell 11/1/1861
R. Ridgell 8/22/1866
Isabella Ridgell 7/14/1863
David L. Dungan 5/10/1900
Sarah A. Ridgell 7/15/1863

G. W. STOCKDALE BIBLE
Owner: Mrs. J. W. Corzine, 1944 Nelson Ave., Memphis, Tenn.

Births

G. W. Stockdale Sr. 1845 Talladega, Ala. - 5/1819 Memphis, Tenn. Alabama
Flavia Stockdale 1852 Mobile, Ala.
James Harold Stockdale 11/30/1873 near Birmingham, Ala. 11/30/1873 Talladega, Ala.
G. W. Stockdale, Jr. 3/7/1876 Mobile, Ala.
Colin Wesley Stockdale 5/33/1878 Birmingham, Ala.
Elinor Elizabeth Stockdale 10/31/1850 near Birmingham, Ala. Julian Levert Stockdale
2/15/188-, Talladega, Ala.
Frank Joseph Stockdale 8/7/1886 Talladega, Ala.

Marriages
G. W. Stockdale to Alabama Flavia Daughdrille 11/19/1872 in Mobile, Ala. by Rt. Rev. Richard
H. Wilmer, Bishop of the Diocese of Ala.

W. P. RICE BIBLE

On flyleaf: Greenville (Ala.) James H. Garrett, father of Prilla G. Rice 8/27/1854-1872. Eula Garrett Cook, mother of Prilla G. Rice d. 7/1941, Mobile, Ala.

Marriages

W. P. Rice- Rebecca C. Judge 12/20/1849 in Hayneville, Ala. at res. Of J. J. Judge William Rice to Charlotte Huddleston, parents of Wesley P. Rice, 3/10/1809
Mary M. Rice to Sml S. Graham 5/20/1830
Susan A. M. T. Rice to Samuel W. Meriwether 5/13/1832
James M. D. Rice to Tracy Cook 8/1833
William A. Rice to Martha P. Cook 6/28/1835
Josephine Judson Rice to Seymour N. Powell 8/24/1853
James P. Judge to Mary Ellen Sherman 2/8/1853 in Montgomery, Ala. William Rice, the 2nd time to Elizabeth C. Wheeler 9/6/1857 Willie Parks Rice to Lippie B. Reid 4/3/1872 in Ft. Deposit, Ala. Charlie Judge Rice to James Parillah Garrett 11/24/1897 in Greenville, Ala. D. F. Hardy to Ellen Lee Rice 6/28/93 in Ft. Deposit, Ala.

Births

Wesley P. Rice 8/6/1828 Autauga Co., Ala.
Rebecca G. Rice 2/11/1829 North Carolina
James Feyton Judge 5/19/1830 North Carolina
William Rice, father of W. P. Rice, 2/27/1787
Charlotte Rice, mother of W. P. Rice, 11/19/1791
Mary Maddison Rice 1/17/1811
James M. D. Rice 2/18/1813
Susan A. M. T. Rice 3/16/1815
Willie Parke Rice, lst child of W. P. and R. C. Rice 12/23/1850 in town of Hayneville, Ala.

(W. P. Rice Bible, Births, contd....)

Charlie Judge Rice, 2nd child of W. F, and R. C. Rice 5/25/1852 near Hayneville, Ala.
William A. Rice 1/3/1819
Josephus Anderson Rice 6/19/1821
Thomas Ford Rice 9/17/1823
Peyton Graves Rice 12/28/1825
Josephine Judson Rice 6/21/1833
J. J. Judge 1/3/1805
Martha P. Rice, wife of William A. Rice, 4/14/1821

Champ Terry Rice, lst child of William Rice and Elizabeth C. Rice, 7/25/1858
Lilly Dale Rice, 2nd child of William and Elizabeth Rice, 2/16/1860 in Pensacola, Fla.
Margaret M. ----, wife of Josephus Judge and mother of Rebecca C. Rice, 2/11/1812 North Carolina.
Jonathan J. Judge, father of Rebecca C. Rice, 1/3/1805, in North Carolina
infant dau. of Willie Parke Rice 10/4/1873, d. soon after, Ft. Deposit, Lowndes Co., Ala.
Charlie Judge Rice, 2nd child of Willie Parke Rice, 10/24/1875, Ft. Deposit, Lowndes Co., Ala.
Elizabeth C. Rice, 2nd wife of William Rice, 6/17/1835
Ella Lee Rice, 3rd child of Willie P. and Lippie G. Rice, 11/22/1877 Ft. Deposit, Lowndes Co., Ala.

Ann Brooks Rice, 4th child of Willie P. and Lippie G. Rice, 12/10/1879, Ft. Deposit, Ala.
Rebecca Charlotte Rice, 5th child of Willie P. and Lippie G. Rice, 4/8/1892 in Ft. Deposit, Ala.
Vessic Forester Rice, 6th child of W. P. and Lippie Rice, 10/1/1884, Ft. Deposit, Ala.
Myrtle Reese Rice, lst child of C. J. and Prilla Rice, 3/12/1899, Greenville, Ala.
Maude Hardy, lst child of E. L. and B. F. hardy, 4/2/1900, Ft. Deposit, Ala.
Charles Garrett Rice, 2nd child of C. J. and J. P. Rice, 3/12/1902 Grcenville, Ala.
Eula Dorothy Rice, 3rd child of Charles and Prilla Rice, 11/2/1905, Greenville, Ala.
Prilla Garrett Rice, 4th child of Charles and Prilla Rice, 3/5/1907 Pensacola, Fla.
William Parke Rice, 5th child of Charles and Prilla Rice, Greenville, Ala.

(W. P. Rice Bible, Births, contd....)

Jane Rice, 6th child of C. J. and J. P. Rice, 11/10/1916 Pensacola, Fla.
Margaret Lipscomb Hardy, 3rd child of B. F. and E. R. Hardy, 6/23/1908, Ft. Deposit, Ala.
Mary Frances Hardy, 6th child of Benjamin Franklin Hardy and Ellen Lee Rice Hardy, 7/26/1915
Pensacola, Fla.
Anne Elizabeth Hardy, 7th child of B. F. and E. R. Hardy, 1/22/1818 Pensacola, Fla.
Lippie R. Rice 12/22/1851-1/17/1934
Myrtle Reese Rice, Ist child of Charles and Prilla Rice, 3/12/1999, Greenville, Ala.

Deaths

Charlie Judge Rice 9/23/1855 Lowndesboro, Ala. at res. of S. N. Powell
Peyton G. Rice, son of William and Charlotte, 8/17/1827
Thomas F. Rice, son of William and Charlotte, 5/10/1834
Josephus A. Rice, son of William and Charlotte, 4/21/1843
Charlotte Rice 11/6/1855
James M. D. Rice, son of William and Charlotte, 7/4/1855
William Parke Rice, son of Wesley P. and R. C., 9/10/1923 at Pensacola, Fla,
Margaret M. Judge, mother of Rebecca C. Rice, 10/26/1852 near Hayneville, Ala.
William Rice 2/7/1867 Ft. Deposit, Ala.
Jonathan J. Judge 5/23/1868 Robinson Springs, Ala.
Annie Brooks Rice 7/8/1880
William A. Rice 1/26/1881 at Pleasant Hill, Dallas Co., Ala. Wesley Porter Rice 11/17/1902 Ft. Deposit, Ala. Rebecca Christian Rice 3/7/1910 Pensacola, Fla.
Charles Garrett Rice 5/9/1903 in Pensacola, Fla., 313 N. Wayne Street

ELIZABETH WHITE BIBLE
Owner: Mrs. Carl Hofer
1035 Carper St., McLean, Va. 22101

Births

Mary Ann White 8/6/1825 Alabama
Joseph White 9/9/1826 Alabama
William M. White 2/22/1829 Alabama
Zetha Ann White 4/23/1830 Alabama
John S. White 1/4/1831 Alabama (died in Civil War)
Berryman L. White 3/10/1832 Alabama
Rachel S. White 5/8/1835 Alabama
Catherine E. White 1/21/1833 Mississippi
Zachariah Jefferson White 12/27/1841 Mississippi

ENOCH F. PEARSON BIBLE
Owner: Dr. John Ewell Pearson
Dadeville, Ala.

Presented to Enoch F. Pearson by his father, John M. Pearson, 1843 in Tallapoosa Co., Ala.

Marriages

Enoch F. Pearson to Mary M. Pinkston 5/1/1845 in Montgomery Co., Ala.
Enoch F. Pearson to Susan J. Dunkley whose maiden name was Susan
J. Presley 12/17/1863 In Chambers Co., Ala

Births of Children of Enoch P. and Mary M. Pearson

Matilda Mosley Pearson 10/4/1846
James Ken Pearson 2/5/1854
John Marion Pearson 9/2/1848

(Enoch F. Pearson Bible, Births continued...)

Mary Clara Pearson 11/21/1858
Alice Rebecca Ann Pearson 3/13/1851
Charles Edward Pearson 7/1/1855

Children of Enoch F. and Susan J. Pearson

William Henry Pearson 7/8/1870
Emma Susan Pearson 8/10/1873
Died 1/15/1957 in LaFayette, Alabama

Deaths

Matilda Mosley Pearson, dau. of Enoch F. and Mary M. Pearson, 4/13/1856, aged 9 yrs., 6 mos., 9 days
Mrs. Mary Marcena Pearson, wife of Enoch Franklin Pearson and dau. of James K. and Matilda S. Pinkston, b. 10/10/1830 in Montgomery Co., Ala. d. 8/14/1802 in Tallapoosa Co., Ala., aged 31 yrs., 10 mos., 1 days.

JOHN STOKES PEARSON BIBLE
Owner: Theodore Bowling Pearson
Leroy, Alabama

Marriages

John S. Pearson to Annabella Beatty 10/9/1832 at Pleasant Retreat, Bladen, N. C.
John S. Pearson to Ann H. Charles 4/22/1862 in Greensboro, Ala. By Rev. R. H. Cobbs
John S. Pearson to Virginia E. Magruder 2/24/1875, second dau. of
Marion N. Greer and widow of David A. Magruder
Thomas H. Pearson to Bessie, dau. of Jessey and Carrie Arrington 8/25/1891
John C. Pearson to Annie Collier 12/16/1891

96

(John Stokes Pearson Bible, Marriages, contd....)

Thomas H. Pearson to Carrie Arrington 4/8/1901
Richmond G. Pearson to Selma, dau. of T. C. and Jennie Bowling 11/25/1903
John S. Pearson to Emma L. Deli 11/20/1903 at McEntyre, Clarke Co., said Emma being the third wife of J. S. Pearson
Richmond Greer Pearson to Selma Bowling 11/25/1903

Births

John S. Pearson 5/11/1809
Annabella Beatty 3/20/1810

Children of John S. and Annabella Pearson:

Sophia Beatty Pearson 8/11/1834 at Pleasant Retreat
William C. Beatty Pearson 4/17/1836 at Pleasant Retreat
John Stokes Pearson 5/14/1835 Payetteville, N. C.
Eliza Pearson 3/24/1841, Prospect Hill, 2 miles from Fayetteville
Sarah Croom Pearson 2/7/1844 at Prospect Hill
The above name was given to the infant child of Annabella Pearson but after the death of the mother the name was changed to that of Annabella Beatty Pearson, after the mother.

Ann H. Pearson, dau. of J. L. Charles, 7/8/1838
Virginia E. Pearson, dau. of Marion and P. E. Greer, 3/21/1849

Children of J. S. and A. H. Pearson

Minnie Pearson 9/25/1863
William Beatty Pearson 5/29/1868
John Charles Pearson 2/13/1866
Thomas Hammond Pearson 6/2/1871

97

(John Stokes Pearson Bible continued...)

Children of J. S. and Virginia E. Pearson

Richmond Greer Pearson 12/23/1875
Jonie Greer Pearson 12/22/1880
Marion Stokes Pearson 11/11/1877
Spencer J. Pearson 9/24/1892
Joseph King Pearson 2/11/1879
David Magruder Pearson 12/22/1850

John C. Pearson 9/1/1893, son of John C. and Annie, 9/1/1899
Emma Levinia, dau. of John W. Bell and C. Robinson, 8/22/1952, Clark Co., Ala.

Deaths

Sophia Beatty, eldest dau. of John S. and Annabella Pearson, 1/20/1836, aged 17 mos., 9 days.
Annabella, wife of John S. Pearson, 2/22/1844, buried Pleasant Retreat in Bladen, N. C. at her father's and left an infant dau. (named after her) only two weeks old.
Minnie Pearson, dau. of J. S. and A. H. Pearson, 9/14/1864
Ann H., wife of John S. Pearson, 12/13/1873
On 12/10/1873 gave birth to a stillborn son, was very ill until 3/2/1874 when she died near Mobile, Ala. and was buried in the new graveyard with her infant.
William Beatty, son of J. S. and A. H. Pearson, ?0/12/1887 in Burnet Co., Tx. from fall from a horse.
John Charles, son of John S. and A. H. Pearson, 9/4/1899, Selma, Ala., found unconscious in bed.
Bessie, wife of T. H. Pearson, 12/17/1900
Virginia E., wife of John S. Pearson, 4/15/1902, buried in O'Neal Graveyard in Marengo Co., Ala.

(John Stokes Pearson Bible continued...)

Births

Theodore Bowling Pearson Womack Hill, Ala. 12/15/1904 Richmond Greer Pearson 3/16/1907, Mobile, Ala.
Allen Mobley Pearson 1/14/1909 Mobile, Ala.
Giles William Pearson, bro. of John S. Pearson, d. Wilmingham Co., N. C. 4/7/1847. Left wife and five children, viz: Sarah Eliza, Sophia, Alice, Charles and John Rufus Pearson.
John Stokes Pearson d. 4/5/1949 at Pleasant Retreat.

JOEL DENDY BIBLE
Owner: Clark H. Dendy, Jr.
2592 Elsinore St., East Pt., Ga. 30344

Marriages

Joel Dendy to Florentha Hutchison 474/1833, Laurens Dist.. S. C.
Moses G. Hughs to Amanda J. Dendy 11/29/1860, Cherokee Co., Ala
William A. Brown to Sarah C. Dendy 11/27/1861, Cherokee Co., Ala.
W. H. Allsup to C. H. Dendy 8/16/1867, Cherokee Co., Ala. Josiah Pridgen to Amanda J. Hughes 4/12/1865, Cherokee Co., Ala.
Joel O. Dendy to Mary C. Naugher 8/1/1969, Cherokee Co., Ala.

Births

Joel Dendy 11/29/1810
Florentha Hutchinson 12/3/1812
Florentha Hutchinson 12/3/1812
Amanda J. Dendy 12/14/1840
Skarline? G. Dendy 1/23/1834
Clara H. Dendy 5/4/1844
Leander C. Dendy 3/27/1836

(Joel Dendy Bible continued…)

Joel O. Dendy 3/19/1847
Sarah C. Dendy 7/1/1838
Florentha L. Dendy 2/7/1849
John A. Dendy 3/26/1877
Emma A. Dendy 12/24/1881
Mary Dendy 3/20/1879
Lillie Mae Dendy 12/25/1898
John Alford Dendy 3/26/1877
Clark W. Dendy 10/1/1801
Marye Elethebeth Dendy 3/20/1873
H. Dendy 5/12/1926
John A. Dendy 3/26/1877
Carl V. Dendy 1/1/1928

Births of Great Grandchildren

Martha Jeannine Dendy 11/1/1953
Carla Ann Dendy 1/20/1959
Vernon Roy Dendy 11/25/1953
Charles Howell Dendy 12/3/1962

Deaths

Leander C. Dendy 6/12/1837, 1 yr, 2 mos., 16 days
S. G. Dendy lost at Murphresborough 12/1863, 29 yrs, 11 mos.
Florentha L. Dendy 13/11/1864, aged 15 yrs., 8 mos., 4 days
Florentha Dendy 10/17/1869, 56 yrs, 10 mos., 17 days
Joel Dendy d. 3/27/1891

100

JOHN ALEXANDER McHUGH BIBLE
Owner: Mrs. Arthur Gossett
RFD 2, Centre, Ala.

Births

John Alexander McHugh 12/8/1832
Nancy Ford McHugh 10/22/1837
Jalael Amarilous McHugh 12/14/1856
Jarety Ozelo McHugh 5/9/1877
Janeta Zaidia McHugh 7/7/1858
Joseph Benjamin McHugh 4/4/1075
John Cunagem McHugh 4/20/1861
Jeffy Mason McHugh 7/10/1878
Jenevor Margret McHugh 1/26/1864
Jeffy Lanoa McHugh 3/19/1851
Nancy Jazeleas McHugh 9/14/1866
Ethel Elisabeth McHugh 11/4/1886
Jacob Thomas McHugh 7/30/1869
Willie Johnson 11/5/1886
Ruby Johnson 11/7/1889

Deaths

Jeffy Mason McHugh 5/31/1954
Jacob Thomas McHugh 2/11/1852, aged 12 yrs., 6 mos, 17 days
Jenevor Margret Johnson 2/23/1891, aged 27 yrs, 28 days
Nancy Ford McHugh 3/1/1898
John A. McHugh 12/28/1910
Joseph D. McHugh 11/28/1936
Leila McHugh 6/25/1864

(John Alexander McHugh Bible, contd....)

Nancy Ford McHugh 3/21/1893
Margaret Pennington 8/19/1880
Almarida Aubury Pennington 3/14/1889

Births

Robert W. Johnson 4/15/1864
Willie Johnson 11/5/1886
Jenevor M. Johnson 1/26/1864
Gooby Johnson 11/7/1889

Marriages

Robert W. Johnson to Genevor M. McHugh 1/3/1886
Augustus O. Black to Nancy J. McHugh 5/19/1887
John A. McHugh to Nancy F. Pennington 3/20/1856
Wiley F. Cothern to Janetty McHugh 5/19/1875
Hiliard L. Mc---- to Jalyel A. McHugh 11/3/1875
John C. McHugh to Dora A. Ballard 11/8/1885
Robert W. Johnson to Jenevor M. McHugh 1/3/1886

JOHN ARMSTRONG BIBLE
Owner: Ira E. Armstrong, Andrews, Tx.

Births

John Armstrong 3/28/1820 Adaline Francis Hardwick 11/30/1823

John Armstrong m. Adaline Francis Hardwick 1838.
John Armstrong d. 10/10/1862.
Adaline Francis Armstrong d. 8/19/1908

(John Armstrong Bible continued...)

William O. Armstrong 9/12/1842
Lucy Viola Armstrong 5/6/1852
Sarah Elizabeth Armstrong 6/9/1833
Margaret Kiziah Armstrong 9/29/1855
Lewis J. Armstrong 12/19/1845
Garland Elisha Armstrong 8/17/1847
Louise F. Armstrong 2/11/1858
Anthony Elijah Armstrong 5/20/1850
E. I. Armstrong 5/22/1861

WILLIAM H. HARDIN BIBLE
Owner: James L. Conaway
Anniston, Alabama

Deaths

William H. Hardin 7/5/1881
Eliza L. Hardin 4/25/1901
Eli E. Hardin 8/23/1881
E. H. Hardin 2/14/1924
W. F. Neyman Hardin 5/16/1891
A. E. Hardin 5/10/1930

Marriages

G. Lehonidas Hardin to Lizzie Conaway 4/1914
Mattie M. Hardin to William Nelson 2/17/1914
Mary A. Hardin to T. A. McAbee 10/15/1885
Annis E. Hardin to W. F. Neyman 12/25/1889
Annis E. Neyman to J. B. Neyman 7/30/1891

103

(William H. Hardin Bible continued...)

Eliza L. Hardin to J. W. McAbee 12/24/1899
J. A. Hardin to Sallie M. Hester 1/13/1895
Lula P. Hardin to A. A. Hester 3/1900
Julia B. Hardin to J. A. Mobley 12/25/1900
Amos A. Hardin to Hattie Dunkin 12/25/1904

George Lehonidas to Lizzie Conaway 4/5/1914
Mattie M. to William Nelson 2/17/1914

Births

Asa Hardin b. Charleston, S. C.
Mattie M. b. 10/19/--
E. H. Hardin 7/29/1845
Julia E. Hardin 5/25/1977
A. E. Hardin 7/15/1848
Wm H. Hardin 3/17/1879
Mary A. Hardin 9/21/1866
Eli E. Hardin 6/18/1881
Eliza L. Hardin 8/9/1868
Amos A. Hardin 912/19882
James A. Hardin 11/19/1870
Lehonidas Hardin 2/14/1887
Annis E. Hardin 1/9/1873
Mattie M. Hardin 10/3/1889
Lula F. Hardin 4/10/1875

(William H. Hardin Bible, contd....)

Included in Bible (Loose Pages):

Henry Ditmore m. Abigail Holmes 12/24/1795
Martha Ditmore b. 10/1/1796
Henry Ditmore b. 2/15/1798
Henry Ditmore Sr. 4/28/1799
Thomas Holmes Sr. d. 6/29/1807
John Vernon Holmes d. 7/12/1832, aged 45 yrs., 11 mos., 7 days, leaving 7 children.
Annis Holmes, wife of John V. Holmes, 6. 10/17/1836, left 7 children.

Second Generation:

Thomas Holmes b. Piccadilly, St. James, London 12/3/1745
Sarah Peak b. Hickory Grove 10/29/1752 m. Thomas Holmes 4/6/1776 Abigail Holmes b.
1/5/1777
Thomas Holmes h. 4/4/1778
Martha Holmes 8/8/1779-1750
Elizabeth Holmes 2/4/1781-1782 (1 yr, 8 nos.)
A son stillborn 11/1782
John Vernon Holmes b, 2/15/1784
Stephen Richard Holmes 10/6/1756-1/20/1757
Sarah Holmes d. 12/27/1788, also a stillborn son, 36 yrs., 2 mos.
Thomas Holmes, son of the preceding d. 3/2/1823

Third Generation:

John Vernon Holmes m. 8/25/1811 Annis Stent by Rev. Dr. Price Infant child b. 4/26/1812, d. 2
yrs. Later
Annis Ann Holmes b. 4/5/1813
Adeline Alexander Holmes b. 4/3/1816

105

(William H. Hardin Bible, contd....)

Thomas Holmes b. 9/26/1818
John Vernon Holmes b. 2/11/1821
Howard Wyatt Holmes b. 5/27/1827
Asa A. Hardin b. 3/1814 d. 4/15/1887, aged 73 yrs., 1 mo.
Asa A. Hardin m. ---/6/1836 to Annis Ann Holmes by Rev. Poyas, Ala., Tuscaloosa Co.
Mahalah Ann Lucretia Hardin b. 1837
Mary Adeline Hardin b. --/19/1839
Annis Evilene Alexander Hardin 1/3/1841-6/8/1843
Milton Augustus Hardin b. 6/5/1843
Eli Howard Hardin b. 7/29/1845
Alxara Gordon Hardin b. and d. 3/15/1848
John Vernon Hardin b. 12/1/1849
Bethel Anderson Hardin b. 2/6/1851
William Avery Hardin b. 7/29/1855
Henry Asa Peak Hardin b. 1/4/1856

Record of Births of S. J. King's family

Samuel James King 3/14/1820
Mary Bun Houston 12/1/1822
Frances Ann Dunn 5/21/1823
Auriana Elizabeth King 7/15/1848
Ida Talulah King 12/29/1858
George Washington King 7/19/1851
R. Judson King 1/5/1803
Samuel Alonzo King 12/18/1855
James Wilson King 6/27/1857
John Robert Houston King 1/24/1861

(William H. Hardin Bible, contd....)

Marriages

Samuel James King to Frances Ann Dunn 10/29/1846
Samuel James King to Mary Ann Houston
3/1/1855 Eli H. Hardin to Auriana Elizabeth King 10/15/1865
Samuel Alonzo King to Emma E. Murdock 2/1/1851
James W. King to Mary F. Murdock 5/8/1899
J. Houston King to Fannie Meredith 11/11/1883
J. Houston King to Eva Garner 12/20/1894
R. Judson King to Minerva House 12/19/1895

Deaths

Frances Ann King 7/29/1851, aged 28 yrs., 2 mos., 9 days
Samuel James King 6/29/1864, aged 44 yrs., 3 mos., 15 days
Ida Lula King 3/12/1869, aged 10 yrs., 2 mos., 9 days
George Washington King 1882

THOMAS ASA ARMSTRONG BIBLE
Owner: Pearl Armstrong
Balmorhea, Tx-.

Marriages

T. A. Armstrong to L. V. Armstrong 11/11/1867
F. J. Armstrong 1/6/1886

Births

Thomas Asa Armstrong 1/20/1846

.

107

(Thomas Asa Armstrong Bible, Births continued…)

Lucy Viola Armstrong 5/6/1952

Feeble Jane Armstrong 11/24/1868
Etter A. Armstrong 8/15/1870
Twins 9/17/1872
Rebecca D. Armstrong 8/11/1874
Timothy Bartholomew Armstrong 12/28/1876
George Lee Armstrong 3/2/1879
Jessie Marvin Armstrong 4/20/1851
Riley Watson Armstrone 5/6/1883
James Gordon Armstrong 8/5/1884
Ira Em Armstrong 12/4/1885
Willie F. Armstrong 7/22/1889
Sherman Armstrong 9/2/1894
Robert A. Miller McAfee 7/10/1897
Maudie McAfee 3/10/1899

Deaths

Two twins 9/17 and 18, 1872
A. Armstrong 5/29/1911
Riley Watson Armstrong 8/3/1883
L. V. Armstrong 4/1/1932
W. F. Armstrong 5/26/1892
G. L. Armstrong 9/8/1941
Etter Whitty 9/18/1892
Becy Malone 9/1954
James Gordon Armstrong 9/7/1901
J. M. Armstrong 10/22/1965
F. J. Lewis 6/9/1909

(Thomas Asa Armstrong Bible continued...)

Births of G. L. Armstrong Family

G. L. Armstrong 3/2/1873
James Lee Armstrong 7/26/1917
Pearly May Armstrong 6/26/1890
Earnest R. White 1/12/1917
Etta E. Armstrong 7/23/1808
Leona White 12/7/1925
George W. Armstrong 2/22/1910
Ina Mae White 7/7/1930
Ina Mae Armstrong 1/27/1912
Ernest R. White 11/22/1934

JACKSON LAWSON BIBLE

Births

Jackson Lawson 3/17/1822
Sinder Riler Lawson 9/11/1030

Children:

James A. Lawson 10/5/1845
Joaner C. Lawson 5/10/1856
Enjayline Lawson 7/27/1850
Elmina Lawson 12/22/1853
Franklin P. Lawson 6/5/1852
Washington Lawson 2/17/1865
Mary Jane Lawson 10/7/1854
Jackson Lawson m. Cinderella Walker 10/28/1847.

JACOB BISHOP BIBLE
Owner: Jane McAfee, Box 6402, Odessa, Tx. 79762

Marriages

Jacob Bishop to Margaret J. Bishop 3/30/1846
Jacob and R. Lee Bishop 8/16/1885 (nee Willis) J.
C. Chaney and Adelfa Bishop 12/26/1906

Births

Jacob Bishop 1/23/1824
Mary J. Bishop 8/12/1855
Margaret J. Bishop 7/19/1824
Sarah A. Bishop 8/20/1857
William W. Bishop 3/6/1847
Margaret Bishop 7/2/1861
Robert C. Bishop 1/17/1849
Adelia Bold Bishop 12/26/1886
John T. Bishop 10/8/1852

Deaths

Robert C. Bishop 11/5/1851
Jacob Bishop 4/12/1912
Margaret J. Bishop 11/16/1833
R. Lee Bishop 5/30/1835

Piemoranda Harmon Willis b. 1/15/1824
Mahala (Foster) Willis b. 12/23/1822
Alexander Foster Willis b. 3/22/1857
Thurza Jane Willis b. 5/28/1844

W. W. CHANEY BIBLE

Husband, W. W. Chaney b. 1/4/1861 Carroll Co., son of Robert E. Chaney and Elizabeth Chaney
Wife, Mary Eliza Culpepper b. 6/27/1867 Barbara Co., Ala., dau. of Eliza Culpepper and Harriett Chandler Culpepper
William Wesley Chaney to Mary E. 1885

Births

Eva C. Chaney 11/3/1886
Mae K. Chaney 4/16/1894
Mattie B. Chaney 11/6/1887
Tom B. Chaney 8/8/1897
Willie P. Chaney 8/8/1889
Mamie R. Chaney 11/9/1901
Robert F. Chaney 10/23/1891
Marvel J. Chaney 6/22/1903
Ema C. Chaney 3/9/1893
Harriet T. Chaney 12/15/1906

Deaths

Mae K. Chaney 7/20/1894
Emma Calas Chaney 7/29/1894
Wm Wesley Chaney 11/25/1935
Robert E. Chaney 2/21/1895
Mary Eliza Chaney 8/26/1944
Eva C. Chaney 8/15/1908
William P. Chaney 4/12/1845
James Marvel Chaney 4/26/1955

111

MORRIS CAMPBELL BIBLE
Owner: Mrs. Ruth Gaston
Rt. 1, Talladega Springs, Ala.

Harris Campbell 3/20/1821
Jane Campbell 7/14/1823
Saphra Catharine Campbell 10/2/1844
Sophran Sarah Campbell 12/23/1845
Mary Jane Campbell 10/1/1847
Sylvester Myconiu Campbell 7/11/1849
Martha Paralee Campbell 11/22/1851
Albert Archibald Suttle Campbell 5/23/1854
Phadre Isadora Campbell 6/10/1856
Morea Emily Campbell 1/31/1859
Susan Eloise Campbell 11/18/1861
Walter H. Sawson Campbell 10/5/1064
E. L. H. Williams 18 and 78

William Walker Williams 18 and 79 in Polk Co., Ga. Lillie Mode Warren 1880

Marriages

Harris Campbell to Jane Dawson 11/26/1843
Mary Jane Campbell to H. H. Teakele 9/3/1865
Sophroney S. Campbell 12/12/1867 to M. D. Allen
Saphra Catherine Campbell 10/25/1870 to C. Durson
Sylvester Myconius Campbell 7/21/1872 to L. F. Lambert
Phadre Isadora Campbell 3/15/1874 to Robert Bailly
Morea Emily Campbell 8/19/1875 to C. A. Williams
Martha Paralee Campbell 11/13/1879 to William S. Warren
Susan Eloise Campbell 8/3/1880 to James Williams

(Morris Campbell Bible continued...)

Deaths

Harris Campbell 1/29/1895
S. M. Campbell 7/14/1833
Mary J. Teakell 4/7/1853 in Texas
Walter H. D. Campbell 8/21/1850
Albert A. Suttles Campbell 9/29/1857

Memoranda

Harris Campbell, son of Davis Campbell, the said H. Campbell b. S. C., Edgefield District.
Mother - Madinellain Sarah Gray

Births

H. H. Tekell 3/9/1845
Arthur Dewit Tekell 3/24/1870
Mary Jane Tekell 10/2/1847
M. E. Tekell 5/9/1871
H. H. Tekell 9/5/1869
Nora Lee Tekell 11/14/1879
E. L. H. Williams 1/20/1878
L. M. Warren 5/29/1880
W. W. Williams 3/19/1879

Marriages

William Campbell to Nancy McMillin 9/2/1848
Davis J. Campbell to Sarah Burk 9/12/1861
Willson Campbell to Ruth R. Roberson 12/3/1866

(Morris Campbell Bible continued...)

Births

William Campbell 11/14/1826
Nancy McMillan 11/21/1825
Davis Jasper Campbell 1/19/1839
Wilson Campbell 4/11/1845
Sarah An Campbell 10/6/1840
Ruth A. R. Roberson 9/7/1841
Martha Jane Campbell 4/17/1842

Births of Children of Wilson and Ruth Campbell

T. J. Campbell 5/24/1868
Thomas Henry Campbell 1/1884
Washington Davis Campbell 11/10/1871
Andrew Campbell 6/24/1862
Julia Margret Campbell 12/13/1873
Sarah Martha 7/5/1876
Mary Beneter Campbell 10/12/1878
S. Ida Geneva Campbell -/26/1881

Deaths

Davis Campbell 6/15/1848
Mary Beneter Campbell 10/19/1852
Maryann Campbell 4/18/1885
John Henry Campbell 4/2/1885
Davis Jasper Campbell 1/11/1863

HINTON-KING BIBLE
Owner: Frank R. King, Tuscumbia, Ala.

Marriages

G. W. Hinton to Elizabeth King, dau. of Richard King and Edith, his wife, 12/10/1822

Births

Elizabeth King, dau. of Richard and Edith King, 11/6/1806 July Souls 9/2/1807
Jeremy I. Nelms 5/12/1807
Richard King 8/20/1752-12/27/--, aged 75 yrs.
Edith King, wife of Richard King, 5/17/1767
G. W. Hinton 4/10/1802
Elizabeth Hinton, wife of George W. Hinton, 11/6/1801
Rufus K. Hinton 11/15/1826, son of George W. and Elizabeth
William Rufus Hinton, son of
George W. and Elizabeth, 1/7/1830
Lafayette Hinton 6/17/1833

Deaths

Rufus K. Hinton 7/20/1825 Richard King 12/27/1830, 78 yrs.

C. C. CHANEY BIBLE
Owner: Christopher Columbus Chaney

Births

C. C. Chaney 7/1/1853   Mary Chaney 3/31/1861
Robert W. Chaney 11/14/1878
Maudy Chanty 9/23/1885
James Chaney 2/20/1880

115

(C. C. Chaney Bible continued...)

Culbert Chaney 1/11/1890
Lillie Chaney 1/18/1852
Mirty Chaney 7/28/1892

Reney Chaney 2/16/1894
Ida Chaney 10/21/1898
Jack C. Chaney 12/12/1836

Deaths
William R. Chaney 1/11/1839
Mary Frances Chaney 11/16/1830
Culbert Chaney 5/28/1895
Myrtle Catherine Chaney 11/25/1924

Marriages

Lillie Chaney to T. L. Stephens 10/5J1902
Maud Chaney to W. 0. Martin 4/9/1918 Irene Chaney to L. V. Morris 6/10/1925 Jack Chaney to Clara Sparks 3/26/1927 Ida Chaney to L. L. Hooker 4/11/--

JAMES M. CUNNINGHAM BIBLE
Owner: Miss Linley Cuningham
1225 Ford Ave., Tarrant, Ala.

Marriages

James M. Cunningham to Sarah D. Standefer 2/9/1842
G. W. Price to Serine Woods 9/--/1865
James M. Cunningham to Elvira C. Coffey 5/8/1867
M. R. Cunningham to Florence O. Shelton 4/21/1873

(James M. Cunningham Bible continued...)

James M. Cunningham to Clorinda L. Davis 10/17/1876
F. M. Cunningham to --- 2/--/1881
Kate Cunningham to R. O. Miller 10/11/1882

Births

James M. Cunningham 12/15/1814
Nicholas M. Cunningham 3/5/1851
Sarah D. Cunningham 1/21/1825
Leonidas L. Cunningham 11/12/1853
Franklin M. Cunningham 5/9/1843
Richard Cunningham 10/30/1855
Harvey C. Cunningham 2/20/1845
Matilda Cunningham 11/23/1856
William M. Cunningham 10/17/1846
Newton A. Cunningham 12/15/1857
Madison R. Cunningham 5/8/1848
Kate H. Cunningham 12/20/1860
Henry M. Cunningham 3/17/1868
Willie V. Cunningham 5/12/1881
Sally C. Cunningham 11/3/1871
Clorinda L. Cunningham 4/26/1837
Nina Pearl Cunningham 9/30/1877

Deaths

Harvey C. Cunningham 9/28/1845
Sarah D. Cunningham 8/12/1866
Nicholas M. Cunningham 3/11/1854
Elvira C. Cunningham 3/17/1876

117

(James M. Cunningham Bible continued...)

Leonidas L. Cunningham 9/20/1854
James M. Cunningham 6/3/1883
W. M. Cunningham 10/19/1854
Kate H. Miller 3/31/1891
Richard Cunningham 12/12/1855
Lena Odel Miller 1/27/1887
Matilda Cunningham 11/24/1856
Lonnie Kate Miller 6/23/1891

WILLIAM DRISKILL BIBLE
Owner: Mrs. Sara F. Tidmore Gilbert
Rt. 1, Box 128, Collinsville, Ala. 35961

Marriages

William and Elizabeth Driskill 12/16/1813
Stephen J. and Minerva A. Tyner 10/6/1836
Warner L. Driskill and Rebecca Daty 10/17/1837
Abner McBaron and Nancy Driskill 9/21/1843
Tolliver Driskill and Elizabeth Car 6/13/1844

Births

William Driskill 3/2/1787
Nancy E. Driskill 10/28/1825
Elizabeth Driskill 6/25/1794
William Driskill 2/28/1825
Minerva A. Driskill 2/10/1815
Malissa J. Driskill 6/12/1830
Lewis W. Driskill 11/21/1816
Lucinda J. Driskill 10/15/1833
Toliver S. Driskill 3/29/1819

118

(William Driskill Bible continued...)

Andrew J. Driskill 2/13/1836
Mary C. Driskill 7/5/1821
Charles D. G. Driskill 4/19/1842
Narcissa E. Driskill 6/11/1823

Deaths

Mary C. Driskill 6/24/1822
Nancy McNaron 5/1/1855
William Driskill 3/25/1852
Malissa Wilder 1/16/1870
Elizabeth Driskill 5/13/1873
J. Driskill 4/17/1873
Minerva Tiner ?/10/1865

JAMES A. LAWSON BIBLE

Births

J. S. Lawson 10/6/1848
Pernatha Ann Lawson 5/26/1850

Children's Births:

Andrew Jackson Lawson 4/21/1869
George W. Lawson 3/15/1871
General Franklin Lawson 7/22/1873
Miney Charlotte Lawson 7/20/1876
John Hansford Lawson 8/10/1878

119

(James A. Lawson Bible continued...)

Salley Killer 7/25/1880
Lula Savanna Lawson 3/18/1882

Deaths

Pernatha Ann Lawson 7/27/1885, aged 35 yrs., 2 mos., 1 day

Marriages

J. A. Lawson to Pernatha Ann Uptain 9/17/1868
J. A. Lawson to Isabell McDee 1/15/1907

JAMES NADORS' BIBLE

Deaths

Larking Bradshaw 8/10/1884
--- Bradshaw 5/5/1833
Jane Bradshaw 1/21/1892
Nora V. Bradshaw 9/30/1896
Lillie Bradshaw b. 2/9/1875. Not living 1897, buried in Atlanta, Ga. m. Coin, m. Ed Bentley.

BENJAMIN FRANKLIN BURNS' BIBLE

Marriages

Benjamin F. Burns to Isabel C. Prickett at Ducksprings 11/20/1878

Benjamin P. Burns b. Etowah Co. 10/13/1856 d. 5/8/1939 m. 11/20/1878
Isabel C. Prickett b. Cherokee Co. 5/12/1863 d. 5/18/1943

Elsie B. Burns b. Etowah Co. 12/27/1880 m. 12/17/1897
Maudie Parilee Burns b. Etowah Co. 12/5/1882 d. 8/20/1884
Dora Ollie Burns b. Etowah Co. 9/12/1885 d. 5/1971
Edgar Franklin Burns b. Etowah Co. 5/24/1887
Claudie Mabell Burns b. Etowah Co. 4/3/1889
Lillian Viola Burns b. Etowah Co. 9/9/1891 d. 11/5/1896
Jocl Joshua Burns b. Etowah Co. 5/31/1894 m. 12/16/1916 d. 6/10/1861
Flora Ruby Burns b. Etowah Co. 7/21/1896 m. 12/?5/1918
Dewey Gurley Burns b. Etowah Co. 9/21/1898
Orion Kenneth Burns b. Etowah Co. 3/22/1902
Barbara Eler Burns b. Etowah Co. 3/13/1904 d. 7/20/1964
Choice Judson Lionell Burns b. Etowah Co. 6/15/1906 d. 10/9/1966

GEORGE MATTISON BIBLE
Owner: Mrs. James H. Strother
322 E. Columbus St., Dadeville, Ala. 36853

Births

Benjamin Franklin Mattison 12/17/1824
Ann Cordelia Mattison 2/19/1826
James Allen Mattison 2/7/1828
Penelope Lucinda Mattison 4/8/1830
Emma Mattison 2/25/1832
George Chester Mattison 10/24/1833
Urania Helen Mattison 4/8/1835
Louisa Mildred Mattison 9/9/1836
John LaFayette Mattison 4/27/1840
George Ann Clarentine Brownlee 6/21/1846

(George Mattison Bible continued…)

Marriages:

George Mattison to Nancy McDavid 2/8/1824
John Brownlee to Ann Cordelia Mattison 1/6/1845?
G. A. Brownlee to N. T. Skaggs 4/14/1863

DANIEL BUTLER BIBLE
Owner: Mrs. Drennen Smoot, Jr., Birmingham, Alabama

Daniel Butler m. B. A. Jackson 9/25/1825. Their Children:
Tyre Butler 9/20/1826-10/24/1826 Anna Butler 1/12/1828-7/3/1830 Terrsa Butler 2/28/1830-
Mary E. Butler 11/20/1831-
Philip Butler 7/31/1835-2/28/1833 Danlcl Butler 5/30/1838-11/22/1891

GEORGE CHESTER MATTISON
Owner: Mrs. Lena Mae Mattison Green, Cushing, Okla.

George Chester Mattison b. 10/24/1833 at Abbeville, S. C. d. 5/13/1908 Eutaw, Ala., m. 2/2/1859 Sarah Evins b. 7/19/1838 Bledsoe Co., Tenn. d. 1/3/1836 Eutaw, Ala.

Children:

Minnie May Mattison 4/9/1860
Arthur Lee Mattison 8/12/1962-12/12/1933
Hugh LaFayette Mattison 6/6/1864-
Crozier Evins (Bob) Mattison 7/31/1866-4/5/1947
Earl Chester Mattison 9/4/1863-
Joseph Frederick Mattison 4/26/1871-7/26/1941
Luther Andrew Mattison 3/22/1875-2/8/1943
Ellen Elizabeth Mattison 8/1/1877-9/28/1933
Sallie Lucille Mattison 4/13/1879-

ISAAC NEWTON LEETH BIBLE
Owner: W. D. Whitt, Boaz, Ala.

Marriages

Isaac N. Leeth to A. D. Chestney (Chesney) 10/5/1965 at Duck Springs by D. Smith.
Mattie Leeth to James Battles 11/13/1884
Bettie Leeth to L. W. Whitt --/13--
Ida B. Leeth to Noah Carnes 5/31/1892
R. K. Leeth to Elsie Burnes 12/14/1897
Phoebee A. Leeth to M. N. Daniel 12/13/1896

Births

Isaac N. Leeth 3/14/1842
Phoebe A. Leeth 8/18/1879
A. D. Leeth 7/29/1843
Addie M. Leeth 6/7/1852
Mattie Leeth 11/5/1866
Joe P. Leeth 10/3/1886
Bettie Leeth 5/22/1869
Neely Whitt 2/10/1891
Samuel H. Leeth 8/21/1871
Pearl Mae Whitt 3/25/1895
Ida B. Leeth 2/25/1874
Ruth Leeth 7/2/1901
Robert K. Leeth 11/30/1876
William Whitt 6/17/1906

Deaths

Mattie Battles 9/8/1887
L. W. Whitt 4/22/1928
Robert Kyle Leeth 10/23/1904

Bettie Whitt 4/2/1949
Ida B. Leeth Carnes 2/25/1914
Joe Pat Leeth 4/17/1939
Isaac Newton Leeth 7/17/1915
Samuel H. Leeth 12/23/1959
Adelinr D. Leeth 2/4/1924
Addie M. Leeth 1963

WILLIAM TAYLOR STONICHER BIBLE

Births

William T. Stonicher 3/22/1949
Nancy J. Gore, wife of W. T. Stonicher 7/23/1855
Dorah I. Stonicher 7/9/1873
Susan D. Stonicher 7/20/1980
Thomas W. Stonicher 10/30/1875
James H. Stonicher 7/7/1884
Annie May Stonicher 2/7/1878
Mary Janie Stonicher 1/11/1892

WILLIAM BANISTER BIBLE
Owner: Mrs. Ernest Johnson, Cedar Bluff, Ala. 35959

William Banister m. 2/8/1829 Prisila Humphries

Births
William Banister 11/7/1808
Savillah W. Banister 9/24/1837
Prisila Banister 5/16/1808

124

(William Banister Bible continued...)

William O. Banister 8/26/1939
John H. Banister 12/4/1829
Nancy A. Banister 9/8/1841
Sarganna Amanda Banister 6/25/1831
John W. Banister 6/6/1843
Elizabeth Banister 4/1/1833
Emeline T. Banister 12/22/1846
Whiteford S. Banister 5/29/1835
Marthin E. Banister 10/14/1848

Deaths

Whiteford S. Banister b. Chester Co., S. C., d. 10/27/1862, Jackson, Miss., aged 27 yrs., 5 mos., 26 days
Prisila Bannister 5/18/1888
William Banister 10/29/1893
John M. Banister 4/2/1837
Sarah Bannister 10/10/1831
Abraham Banister 10/10/1841

WILLIAM O. BANISTER BIBLE
Owner: Mrs. Ernest Johnson, Cedar Bluff, Ala. 35359

Marriages

William O. Banister to Amanda M. Burley 10/7/1867
Carl Banister to Johnnie Kennedy 3/20/1898
J. C. Banister to Johnnie Kennedy at the home of the bride 3/20/1895

Births

125

(William O. Banister Bible continued...)

William O. Banister 8/26/1839
William M. Banister 12/16/1872
Amanda M. Hurley 10/10/1842
John C. Banister 1/30/1877

Deaths

William M. Banister 10/10/ 1876, aged 3 yrs, 3 mos., 24 days
William O. Banister 2/7/1097, aged 57 yrs., 5 mos., 22 days Johnnie May Banister 2/18/1042

Memorandum (Births)

Gladys Leroy Bannister 8/5/1899
Vera Marie Bannister 9/7/1807
Robert Guy Bannister 3/17/1901
Jessie Carl Bannister 5/14/1913
Grace Lucile Bannister 4/26/1?04

EDMUND BEAIRD BIBLE
Owner: Oscar Carden, Rt. 4, Roanoke, Ala.

Births

Edmund Beaird 7/5/1770
Elizabeth Acok 5/15/1776, wife of Edmund Beaird
Susanna Beaird 3/2/1795
George W. Beaird 12/8/1008
Archibald Beaird 4/19/1797
Leonidas F. Beaird 1/15/1911
William Beaird 1/20/1800

(William Beaird Bible continued...)

Asenath Beaird 3/9/1813
Alexander Beaird 1/3/1802
Sally S. Beaird 3/30/1815
Anna Beaird 1/16/1804
Elizabeth Beaird 11/5/1817
Polly or Mary Beaird 7/1/1806

Marriages

Edmund and Elizabeth, his wife 6/1/1794
William Beaird to Sarah Easterburg 1/1823
Alexander Beaird to Bethean Sales 11/23/1823
George W. Beaird to Nancy Sales 12/20/1829
Thomas Bullard to Ann Beaird 5/5/1833
John Duke to Sally Beaird 1/6/1831
Lewis and Jo Anna Kilgore 11/16/1820
Archibald Beaird to Louisa Paterson 1/29/1822

Births

Elizabeth J. Beaird 1/4/1824
Susanna A. Beaird 8/3/1829
Elbert A. Beaird 8/30/1826
Edmund Beaird 4/22/1831

Mabbel Jackson, son of John F. Duke and Sally, ---/20/1832 Elizabeth W. Beaird, dau. of William and Sarah, 7/25/1830 William F. Beaird, son of George and Nancy, 10/5/1830 Ascnath, dau. of George and Nancy Beaird, 10/13/1832 William S. Beaird, son of Alexander and Bethean, 6/15/1832

Telitha C. Beaird 2/13/1834
Matilda Bullard 6/3/1834

Deaths

Asenath Beaird 9/21/1814
William Beaird, son of Edmund and Elizabeth, 2/24/1830 Anna Bullard died after 40 yrs., 4 mos., 25 days
Matilda Bullard, wife of Archibald
Edmund Beaird 11/4/1851, aged 31 yrs., 4 mos.
Elizabeth Beaird, wife of Edmund, 1/30/1863

DAVID JACKSON BEAIRD BIBLE
Owner: William Beaird, Albertville, Ala.

On flyleaf: David Jackson Beaird's Civil War Records: Private, enlisted 1/18, Talladega, Ala., 1964, Co. E, 62nd Ala., 17 yrs. of age. Captured at Blakely, Ala. 4/9/1865

Births

David Jackson Beaird 12/31/1845
Emily Charlotte (Lottie) Causey 3/24/1849

Elijah Beaird 10/8/1870
Della Beaird 7/22/1882
Dora Beaird 0/2/1872
John Beaird 1/5/1884
Jim Beaird 4/13/1876
William Charlie Beaird
Margret 2/2/1889
Cordelia Beaird 6/20/1879

(David Jackson Beaird Bible continued...)

Marriages

David Jackson Beaird to Emily Charlotte Causey, dau. of Chastford Causey 6/20/1868, Chambers Co., Ala.
Elijah Beaird to Mary Annie Carter, dau. of Micajah and Elizabeth Carter, 6/1/1887
Dora Beaird to David Burrough 7/5/1830
Jim Beaird to Dora Knight 6/12/1894, Clay Co., Bla.
Jim Beaird to Rosa 1905, Merkel, Tx.
Margret Cordelia Beaird to James Walker Burroughs 12/27/1906
Della Beaird to --- Hornsby 3/24/1907
John Beaird to Mary Hallman 4/20/1912
William Charlie Beaird to Gladys Inez Walker 12/1/1912, Ashland, Ala.

Deaths

David Jackson Beaird 5/1/1913, Marshall Co., Ala.
Lottie Beaird 8/27/1924
Dora Beaird Burroughs 6/11/1931
Elijah Beaird 4/23/1942
John Beaird 1943, Bobbs, New Plexieo
Jim Beaird 1936. Merlcel, Tx.
Margaret Cordelia Burroughs 5/23/1960

W. G. COFFEY BIBLE
Owner: Ruby Coffey, Boat, Ala.

W. G. Coffey of Edmond Coffey and L. E. Tidmore m. 1/11/---- at her residence. W. N. Chanler 1866. Rilea Coddel. Livea Coffey

Births

W. G. Coffey 1/20/1840
L. E. Coffey 1/22/1846

James Henry Coffey 10/14/1866
Fannie Luller Coffey 12/15/1877
John Adam Coffey 4/30/1863
Martha Jane Coffey 3/24/1879
William Thomas Coffey 12/27/1869
Nancy Victory Coffey 3/28/1851
Annah Elizabeth Coffey 7/20/1871
Jessie Coffey 9/9/1852
Webster Gernagin Coffey 2/2/1873
Mary Evergreen Coffey 3/28/1854
Edmond Columbus Coffey 8/13/1874
Cleariling Coffey 5/15/1886 Ruby Coffey 2/21/1876

Deaths

W. G. Coffey 2/2/1911
Mrs. Lovise E. Coffey 2/25/1835

ELIJAH BEAIRD BIBLE
Owner: Mrs. Fannie Mae Shell, Guntersville, Ala.

On flyleaf: Mr. Elijah Beaird was a Mason.

Births

Elijah Beaird 10/8/1870 Randolph Co., Ala.
Mary Annie Carter Beaird 4/3/1866, dau. of Micajah and Elizabeth Carter
Charley Webster Beaird 1/20/1889
Fannie Mae Beaird 11/10/1902
Edna Iola Beaird 5/10/1891
Cora Lee Beaird 6/13/1908
Grady Milford Beaird 4/3/1893
Arthur David Beaird 3/19/1924
Maudie Estelle Beaird 12/5/1895
Sarah Nell Beaird 3/3/1927
Ezra DeCall Beaird 11/12/1897

Marriages

Elijah Beaird to Mary Annie Carter 6/1/1887
Charley Webster Beaird to Lellia Belle Bryant 4/2/1907
Grady Milford Beard to Belle Bryant, dau. of Daniel Clayton
Bryant and Mary Melissa Terrell, 4/17/1913, DeKalb Co., Ala.
Maudie Estelle Beaird to R. S. Latham 12/31/1911, Marshall Co., Ala.
Ezra DeCal Beaird to Sarah Carrie Nelson 5/10/1913
Ezra DeCal Beaird to Minnie Bryant 3/16/1928, Guntersville, Ala.
Fannie Mac Beaird to Lee Bannister Stone 8/15/1915
Fannle Mae Beaird Stone to Arthur Newt Shell 1/2/1929
Cora Lee Beaird to Thomas Clifton Lusk 5/24/1924, Marshall Co., Ala.

(Elijah Beaird Bible continued...)

Elijah Beaird to Bertle Bodine Rhodarmer 10/1921 (and married, after
death of Mary Annie Carter Beaird, she died 8/29/1920)
Arthur David Deaird to Eddie Lee Bonds 12/21/1939
Sarah Nell Beaird to Willard Bolt 10/26/1940

Deaths

Edna Iola Beaird 1/4/1893
Elijah Beaird 4/23/1942
Charley Webster Beaird 3/6/1916
Ezra DeCal Beaird 5/25/1957
Annie Carter Beaird 8/29/1820
Grady Milford Beaird 12/27/1966
John Jr. Rhodarmer 8/15/1963

JOHN ALBERT BRANNON BIBLE
Owner: Clyde Brannon, Altoona, Ala.

On flyleaf: Reuben Walker b. 1/24/1847
John Albert Brannon m. Levicy Jane 5/4/1844

Births

John Albert Brannon 7/16/1826
Levicy Jane 2/25/1827
Mahaly Elizabeth Brannon 6/11/1845
Mary Frances Brannon 2/28/1851
James K. Poke Brannon 12/24/1847
Mahuldy Marteeny Brannon 3/1/1855
Wilbern Wesley Brannon 12/21/1850

(John Albert Brannon Bible continued...)

Deaths

Armindy Emery Line Brannon 2/27/1860
Gogy Oliver Brannon 2/1884
Malesy Whitfiel --/3/1863
Winey Lew Brannon 1886
Labern Elbury Brannon b. 7/7/1879
Iony Everline Brannon 1882
Hester Lee Harris was ? -/9/1896

GEORGE W. BEAIRD BIBLE

Births

George W. Beaird 12/8/1808
Nancy Bales Beaird 1810 in South Carolina

Their Children:

WillLam P. Beaird 10/5/1830
Elizabeth Beaird 3/7/1843
Asenath Beaird 10/13/183?
David Beaird 12/31/1845
Mary Jane Beaird 11/5/1834
George W. Beaird 2/21/1848
Louisa Deaird 12/13/1836
Johnny W. Beaird 3/18/1850
Edmund S. Beaird 3/2/1839
James Elbert Beaird –
Elijah Beaird 6/13/1841

(George W. Beaird Bible continued...)

Marriages

George W. Beaird to Nancy Dales 12720/1829
George W. Beaird to Rebecca Ann McClain 12/1/1867
Henry W. Beaird to Miss A. D. Roberts 10/22/1852

Deaths

Mary Jane Burditt, dau. of George W. and Nancy Beaird, 2/7/1860
Edmund S. Beaird, son of George W. and Nancy Beaird, 12/24/1861
James Elbert Beaird, son of George W. and Nancy, 5/2/1851
William F. Beaird, son of George U. and Nancy, 6/16/1862
A. D. Beaird, wife of H. 8., 12/8/1882
Rebecca Ann Beaird, wife of George W., 7/20/1882
Nancy Beaird, wife of George W., 9/21/1887
George W. Beaird 5/23/1830
Asenath Bassit 5/19/1908

JAMES HERRING BIBLE
Owner: Jerry B. Jones
824 Valley Drive, Attalla, Ala. 35954

Marriages

James Herring to Susannah Pool 8/29/1804
William H. Ray to Nancy Herring 12/22/1825
Asa Watt (or Wyatt?) to Delilla Herring 12/22/1835 (1836?)
Bryan Herring to Nancy Haggard 12/27/1837

(James Herring Bible continued...)

Births

James Herring Jr. 4/22/1752
Amanda Herring 11/19/1829
Susannah Herring 2/13/1787
Bryan Herring 12/4/1815
Isaac Herring Sr. 6/7/1789
Delilah Herring 3/26/1818
Lewis W. Herring Sr. 6/22/1785
James Herring Jr. 9/28/1821
Allen Herring 7/8/1805
Isaac Herring 8/90/1824
Nancy Herring 2/21/1808
William P. Herring 8/30/1824
John P. Herring 6/17/1810
Dennis T. Ray 12/17/1826
Lewis W. Herring 2/6/1813
Weyman Adare Herring 5/1/1829
Susannah H. Herring 10/25/1832
Mary Jane Herring 6/6/1835

Deaths

James Herring Sr. 7/1/1806
James Herring Jr. 1/8/1827
Asenith Herrlng 1/30/1829

135

L. F. HEFLIN BIBLE

Births:

L. F. Heflin 1829
Betty R. Heflin 10/10/1829
Hannah C. Heflin 9/14/1851
Marion R. Heflin 1/14/1853

Marriages:

L. F. Heflin to Betty Rosezella Cardin 1/5/1846
L. F. Heflin to Frances V. M. Reynolds 3/2/1871
C. M. Lentell to Hannah E. Heflin 11/7/1867
M. R. Heflin to Mattie D. Langford 12/21/1876
T. L. Heflin to Mary V. Slaughter 9/29/1895
Ora C. Heflin to J. A. Brannon 12/4/1904
Carline V. Brannon to Boss Harvey 11/8/1955
Clyde Harrington Brannon to Bessie Mae Whatley 11/23/1958

Births:

L. F. Heflin 5/5/1829
Hetta Rosezella Cardin 10/10/1828
Larkin A. Heflin 1/3/1847
Hannah E. Heflin 9/14/1851
Marion R. Heflin 6/4/1858
Frances V. M. Reynolds 4/8/1839
Hetty M. G. Heflin 1/11/1872
Thomas L. Heflin 2/23/1873
Cora A. B. Heflin 12/2/1877
Orra V. Heflin 11/7/1870
Charles E. D. Heflin 10/26/1870

(L. F. Heflin Bible continued...)

Ada Viola Heflin 10/30/1877
Albert R. Heflin 6/30/1879
Orra V. Heflin 11/7/1880
Carrie Estell Heflin 8/2/1881
Eula Lee Heflin 1/30/1897
Charles Danna Heflin 10/31/1898
Connie Franklin Heflin 11/10/1899
Thomas Guy Heflin 10/16/1900
Rex Arria Heflin 4/12/1903
Allen Norwood Heflin 6/17/1905
John Aubrey Heflin 12/2/1908
Lady Nell Heflin 3/12/1910
Clyde Harrington Brannon 6/17/1902
Virginia Carlene Brannon 3/6/1914
James Myron Harvey 11/28/1937
Carol Leune Brannon 10/1/1959

Deaths

Nancy Lentell 2/2/19/1863
Mattie D. Heflin 11/4/1887
Larkin A. Heflin 7/20/1864
Cora A. B. Heflin 7/15/1888
Hetta Rosezella Cardin 10/20/1870
L. F. Heflin 1/28/1890
Abbygail Heflin 7/6/1875
Connie Franklin Heflin 11/21/1874
Albert F. Heflin 9/5/1983
Alice E. Lentell 10/18/1886
Frances V. M. Heflin 9/3/1907
John Aubrey Heflin 10/26/1911

(L. F. Heflin Bible continued...)

Newspaper Clipping (enclosed): "Bristow's Cove. Mrs. F, W. Heflin, who was stricken with paralysis Sunday, died Tuesday at 4 p.m. Mts. Heflin had been in bad health for some months and her death, although n shozk to her many friends, was not unexpected. She had lived ;I: Aurora 18 years and was well known, She was 68 years of age. She leaves three children to mourn her loss. Interment made Wednesday afternoon In Aurora Cemetery...."

SPENCER TILLSON BIBLE
Owner: Mrs. Bill Ashleym Rt. 6, Gadsden, Ala. 35901

Marriages

Spencer Tillson to Margaret Owens 5/16/1815
Middleton Sapp to Mary Tillison 12/1838
David T. Mitchell to Mary Sapp 9/26/1950
Richard F. Nerhor to Nancy E. Tillison 3/9/1851
John Garner to Elizabeth Tillison 4/8/1844
J. W. Garner to Lucy Ann TIllson 9/11/1851
William S. Tillison to Martha A. E. McGehee 11/20/1956
F. J. Tillison to Callie Spear 10/10/1883
M. C. Tillison to Moses House 1/23/1887
T. M. Tillison to Laura McCluney 1/11/1888
Robert L. Harrison to Nannie F. Tillison 2/1/1893
Dr. J. V. Bramling to Mattie A. Tillison 2/2/1902
R. L. Tillison to Annie McCluney 12/19/1814

Births

Spencer Tillison 10/15/1791
Francis J. Tillison 9/3/1857
Margaret Tillison 3/24/1796

(Spencer Tillison Bible contd....)

Thomas H. Tillison 8/3/1859
William S. Tillison 3/7/1817
William E. Tillison 11/13/1861
Francis M. Tillison ;1/8/1820
S. P. Tillison 8/21/1865
Mary Tillison 8/20/1823
Julia M. Tillison 8/21/1865
Catharine Tillison 12/6/1825
Mary Kate Tillison 10/28/1867
Nancy E. Tillison 10/1/1823
J. B. Tillison 10/25/1869
Lucy Ann Tillison 7/17/1832
N. E. Tillison 5/13/1872
Elizabeth Tillison 5/a/1828
Charles B. Tillison 10/7/1874
Martha A. E. Tillison 6/14/1840
R. Lee Tillison 1/2/1877
Lillie Barnett Tillison 7/23/1854
Martha A. Tillison 12/5/1879
Carrie Earl Tillison 2/6/1882

Deaths

Francis M. Tillison 12/29/1845
W. E. Tillison 10/31/1891
Spencer Tillison 1/11/1852
W. S. Tillison 12/4/1891
Nancy E. Naugher 7/31/1854
Catherine Tillison 11/9/1901

(Spencer Tillison Bible contd....)

Margaret Tillison 6/13/1860
Martha Ann Eliza Tillison 12/17/1925
Lucy Ann Garner 4/28/1873
Mary Mitchell 9/22/1888
Mary Katie Tillison 3/3/1934
Frank James Tillison 2/26/1937

WILLIAM A. EDWARDS' BIBLE
Owner: Mrs. Claude Brasscale, Gadsden, Ala.

William A. Edwards d. 10/23/1827 Robert W. Edwards d. 6/29/1827
Littleton Edwards m. 3/10/1834
Lewis M. Edwards 2/2/1835-5/25/1836, aged 1 yr., 3 mos, 3 days.

JOHN EDWARDS' BIBLE
Owner: Beatrice Knight, Rt. 2, Ashville, Ala.

Marriages

John Edwards to. Rachel Edwards, his wife, 3/29/1818
Lewis David Edwards to Catherine Green 11/29.1815
John D. Edwards to Fannie N. Green 12/20/1877
Robert Lee Knight to Eugenia Edwards 3/19/1887
Eugenia Edwards Knight to John W. Talley 5/7/1896

Births

John Edwards 4/12/1787
Rachel Edwards, his wife

140

(John Edwards Bible continued…)

Their Children:

Ann Edwards 1/18/1819
Sarah Edwards 3/24/1824
Frances Edwards 1/15/1821
Louis David Edwards 8/8/1827
William Augustus Edwards 3/1/1822

Children of Lewis D. and Catherine Edwards

John D. Edwards 6/23/1850
Laura R. Edwards 12/5/1859
William A. Edwards 4/16/1853
Eugenia Edwards 5/5/186?
Emma Kitty Edwards 9/2/1856

Deaths

John Edwards 1/21/1845
Lewis David Edwards 12/20/1880
Rachel Edwards 1/13/1845
Frances Edwards 1821
Ann Edwards 9/15/1836
Catherine Edwards 5/15/1910, aged 80 yrs.
Sallie Vance 12/15/1880 (birth, death, marriage?)

CHARLEY ALLEN NORTON BIBLE

Charley A. Morton b. 3/24/1825
Melvina (Samuels) Morton b. 4/22/1829, m. 1/13/1846
Charles A. Morton volunteered 1/28/1862, mustered into service of Confederate States 2/4/1862.

Births of Children of Charley A. and Melvina Morton

Milts Morton 4/24/1847 -
MarthaChestina Morton 4/17/1856
Lucy Emaline Morton 5/5/1848
Marshall Self Morton 11/14/1860
John Colman Morton 3/7/1851
Zemiley Elizabeth Morton 7/27/1865
James Wiley Morton 1/2/1852
Cintha Lorinda Morton 2/5/1870
Sarah Louhannah Morton 2/17/1854
William Joel Morton 2/22/1076

Father and Mother:

Joel Morton b. 4/25/1786 (son of Marshall Morton) Lucy Morton b. 7/2/1789? (dau. of Charles Durham)

LITTLETON EDWARDS' BIBLE

Marriages

Littleton Edwards to Sarah A. Ahler
3/10/1834 William A. Edwards to C. C. Zeigler
6/17/1853 F. Edwards to S. R. North 6/12/1859
W. A. Edwards to Ann Helen Whltehead 5/21/1868

Births

Sara Agnes Edgar 1/1/1810-8/18/1866
Adam Edgar 3/13/1843
Ann Helen Whitehead 1/31/1849
Joseph L. Edwards 5/9/1846
Lewis a. Edvards 2/22/1835
Elizabeth I. Edwards 12/30/1841
Frances Louisa Edwards 11/23/1836
William A. Edwards

Deaths

Lewis A. Edwards 5/25/1836
Eel? E. North 7/7/1856
William A. Edwards, Sr. 10/23/1847
Ralph W. Edwards 6/22/1876
Robert W. Edwards 6/29/1827
Joseph L. Edwards 5/14/1846
Littleton Edwards 12/3/1852
Jane Edwards 3/7/1857
Elizabeth I. Edwards 1/12/1842
Frances L. North 1/17/1801
C. C. Edwards 5/27/1867, aged 27 yrs.

(Littleton Edwards Bible continued...)

Ann Helen Edwards 5/28/1902, wife of W. A. Edwards
Ralph W. Edwards 10/23/1907
William A. Edwards 4/12/1909

Written at bottom of page by S. R. North 11/18/1860:
Eugene C. Edwards b. Etowah Co., Ala. 8/7/1853 Ada M. Edwards 10/21/1884
Rex Edwards b. Etowah Co. 6/27/1908
Mildred Edwards 8/9/1910
Eugenia Edwards 11/7/1918
Eugene C. Edwards 6/5/1960
Littleton Edwards, son of A. E. and Caroline Carlton Edwards,
Eugenie Edwards m. J. P. Dodd 5/2/1836
J. P. Dodd b. 2/16/1916
Ramona Blanch Dodd b. 10/24/1937
Ramona Dodd m. William Morris Beck II 12/23/1957
W. M. Beck II b. 10/12/1936
William Morris Beck II b. 9/14/1955
Amelia Ann Dodd b. 5/26/1943
Laura Leigh Dodd b. 12/31/1953
E. C. Edwards m. Ada A. Kilpatrick 9/15/1907

JESSE EDWARDS' BIBLE
Owner: Mrs. Charles W. Shepard
320 Hollywood Rd., Gadsden, Ala.

Births

Jesse Edwards 2/20/1801
Jeptha Edwards 5/10/1828
Elizabeth Edwards 2/10/1801
Margaret Edwards 1/10/1837

(Jesse Edwards Bible continued...)

Rolen C. Crump 8/3/1808
Erie Edwards 7/19/1851
Elizabeth Edwards 2/5/1859
Essie Edwards 5/17/1876
Jeppy Edwards 10/27/1860
Ronda Dowda 11/20/1855
Jesse Edwards 4/23/1872
Maurice Edwards 3/20/1903
Ralph Williamson Edwards 2/21/1905
Jesse Carlton Edwards 10/25/1900

Deaths

Elizabeth Edwards 12/10/1857
Maurice Edwards 7/19/1903, 4 mos.
Jesse Edwards 10/27/1868
Jesse Edwards 8/7/1921
Rolen C. Crump 2/22/1901
Erie Edwards 10/25/1865
Jeppie Dowdy 4/26/1886
Jeptha Edwards 7/10/1902, 74 yrs., 2 mos.
Margaret Edwards 1/15/1906, 69 yrs., 5 days

Marriages

Jeptha Edwards to Margaret Crump 9/19/1856
O. R. Dell to Bettie Edwards 3/4/1880
R. V. Dowdy to Jeppie Edwards 3/27/1884
M. F. Stowers to Olie Edwards 6/17/1888
Samuel H. Moragne to Essie Edwards 7/30/1891
Jesse Edwards to Jessie Williamson 8/15/1897

James Jack m. Agnes McCallie 2/6/1816

Births

James Jack 8/30/1759
Agnes McCallie 10/1/1792

Macy A. Jack 11/1817
Amelia Jack 11/13/1825
Martha Jack 6/26/1818
Thomas McCallie Jack 3/4/1826
Elizabeth Jack 10/4/1819
Allen Jack 10/29/1827
John P. Jack 9/9/1821
James Jack 2/26/1831
Adaline Jack 5/1/1823
Jeremiah Montgomery Jack 12/15/1833

Deaths

Infant dau. 2/14/1829-2/23/1829
James Jack 7/10/1851
Amelia Jack Clayton 6/21/1856
Dr. Jeremiah Montgomery Jack 2/11/1884

SAMPSON CLAYTON BIBLE
Owner: Mark Clifford, Cedar Bluff, Ala.

Marriages

Sampson Clayton to Elisabeth Drain 7/20/1823
Sampson Clayton to Elisabeth Hill 1/20/1833
John Phillip Starling b. 10/15/1864
M. A. Clayton, son of Sampson Clayton, to Fannie Sheely 12/21/1873
Fannie Clayton, wife of M. A. Clayton, b. 3/11/1858

Births

Sampson Clayton 8/1/1803
Elisabeth, wife of Sampson Clayton, 1813
Palmer Clayton 9/30/1824
Permelia Clayton 2/26/1842
Daniel Clayton 4/14/1826
Easter C. Clayron 4/4/1844 J
James Clayton 2/16/1820
Manervia E. Clayton 5/2/1846 W.
H. Clayton 5/30/1830
Laura A. Clayton 10/18/1848
Perry Clayton 1/28/1834
Malinda P. Clayton 10/18/1848
Mary Jane Clayton 3/2/1836
 Nancy G. Clayton 1/22/1851
Matthew M. Clayton 4/1838
Mark A. Clayton 12/11/1853
Solomon S. Clayton 3/25/1840
William G. Clayton, son of Perry Clayton, 9/14/1857
Lucius S. Clayton 2/22/1860

(Sampson Clayton Bible continued...)

Deaths

Sampson Clayton 1/6/1865
Daniel Clayton 7/5/1875
Palmer Clayton 1842
Ferry Clayton 3/9/1864
James Clayton 6/27/1829
Solomon S. Clayton 5/24/1876
Mathew Clayton 1842
Sampson L. Clayton 10/6/1977
Fannie A. Clayton 3/5/1879
Elisabeth, first wife of Sampson Clayton, 10/8/1832
Permelia C. Sparks, wife of T. A. Sparks, 10/22/1875

GEORGE JEFFERSON WILLIAMSON
Owner: Robert Neville Mann, Cedar Bluff, Ala.

Marriages

E. W. Langston to M. J. Daniel ---
G. J. Williamson to M. J. Langston 8/29/1839

Births

David C. Langston 5/23/1837
Mary Josephine Williamson 12/29/1840
Martha McEntire Williamson 3/22/1843
Thomas J. Williamson 12/25/1844
David N. Williamson 4/7/1848

G. J. Williamson 10/4/1811
M. J. Williamson 6/22/1813

Deaths

Martha E., dau. of G. J. and M. J. Williamson, 10/17/1845
Mary J. Wiliiamson 10/9/1846
David C. Langston 1/8/1047
George J. Williamson 10/4/1859
Martha J. Williamson 2/19/1902

WARNER LEWIS DRISKILL BIBLE
Owner: Bernard E. Driskill
211 Alabama Ave., NW, Ft. Payne, Ala. 35967

Births

Warner Lewis Driskill 11/21/1816
Rebecca Emery Deary 6/7/1818
Mary Eliza Metcalf 3/10/1830
Julia Ann Louisa Driskill 8/2/1838
Elizabeth Manerva Driskill 1/2/1840
Trecey Matilda Driskill 2/7/1842
William Allison Driskill 3/27/1844
Samuel Walker Driskill 6/4/1846
Nancy Jane Driskill 6/5/1849
Sanford Carter Driskill 9/11/1853
Catharine Driskill 9/6/1855
Mary Ellen Driskill 5/27/1857
Warner Jackson Driskill 10/22/1862

(Warner Lewis Driskill Bible continued...)

Walter Scott Driskill 10/22/1862
Charles Lewis Driskill 3/15/1866
George Edwin Driskill 5/15/1868
Mattie Virginia Driskill 3/27/1871
Edgar Homer Driskill 10/3/1875

Marriages

Warner L. Driskill to Rebecca E. Beaty 10/27/1837
Warner L. Driskill to Mary E. Metcalf 11/14/1852
John D. Roden to Julia Ann L. Driskill 5/3/1857
John L. Wallace to Elizabeth R. Driskill 5/17/1857
John H. Roberts to Trecey M. Driskill 6/12/1860
William A. Driskill to Margarette Sloan 12/13/1866
James H. Hartline to Nancy J. Driskill 8/15/1868
Mastin G. Willis to Mary Ellen Driskill 8/7/1878
Sanford C. Driskill to Margarette A. Cook 12/7/1882
Warner J. Driskill to Fanny Denard 2/7/1886
Walter S. Driskill to Lucretia E. Dean 10/20/1887
Charles L. Driskill to Laura E. Dean 12/25/1889
George E. Driskill to Mattie Holcomb 11/17/1891
Richard R. Henegar to Mattie V. Driskill 3/9/1892
Wallace C. Driskill to Mattie Brasswell 11/24/1892
Samuel W. Driskill to Cynthia P. Simpson 10/6/1896
Edgar H. Driskill to Fanny A. Shankle 1/16/1899

Deaths

Rebecca Emery Driskell 9/24/1851, aged 33 yrs, 3 mos., 17 days
Catharine Driskill 10/14/1855, aged 1 mo., 8 days

(Warner Lewis Driskill Bible, Deaths continued...)

Trecey Matilda Roberts 12/6/1864, aged 22 yrs., 9 mos., 29 days
Nancy Jane Hartline 7/28/1856, aged 37 yrs., 1 mo. 20 days
William Allison Driskill 8/29/1892, aged 40 yrs.; mos. 2 days

Mary E. Driskill 2/28/1903, aged 72 yrs., 11 mos., 13 days
Sanford C. Driskill 2/15/1906, aged 52   5 mos. ;64 days, 5 mos. days
Warner L. Driskill 5/17/1907, aged 90 yrs,
Warner Jackson Driskill 4/7/1910, aged 50 yrs., 6 mos.
Samuel W. Driskill 48/1911, aged 64
yrs., 10 mos., 4 days

Deaths added from Bernard E. Driskill:

Julia Roden 3/13/1920
Ellen Willis 12/23/1928
George E. Driskill 10/17/1937
Wallace C. Driskill 11/29/1940
Charles L. Driskill 1/18/1953
Edgar M. Driskill 12/31/1963

THOMAS JACKSON CATE BIBLE
Owner: Miss Browder Cate, Niota, Tennessee

Births

Thomas Jackson Cate 12/18/1844 Lucy Ellen Cate 9/29/1855

Their Children:

Sarah Cate 12/13/1799
James L. Cate 5/16/1807
Elijah Cate 1/23/1801
Thomas Jefferson Cate 8/27/1809
Martha Cate 5/1/1802
Rachel Cate 9/8/1811
Lucy Cate 11/11/1803
William Cate 3/31/1814
Amos Cate 11/2/1805
Dalana Cate 4/28/1817

WILLIAM DUNAWAY BIBLE
Owner: Lois & Martha Kirkland, Gadsden, Ala.

William Dunaway 6/6/1800-6/9/1877
Docia Gilbert Dunaway 8/9/1805-1860

Births

Sanford Dunaway 3/22/1823 --
Tennessee Dunaway 5/29/1832
Luizy Dunaway 4/27/1825
Crittenton Serveir Dunaway 10/11/1834

(William Dunaway Bible continued...)

Natty Dunaway 8/30/1827
Amanda Dunaway 2/3/1830
Washington Marion Dunaway
Margaret Dunaway 8/12/1836
Margaret Dunaway 5/20/1839
Sanford Dunaway m. Nancy Sheffield 9/15/1826

Births

Thursey Dunaway 6/26/1843
Sarah Dunaway 12/29/1859
Docia Dunaway 1/25/1846
Nancy C. Dunavay 4/29/1863
Selcy Dunaway 10/20/1840
Una W. Dunaway 2/4/1860
Letty Dunaway 2/17/1852
Elizabeth Dunaway 8/27/1843
Nathan Dunaway 8/4/1855
Amanda Dunaway 6/15/1855
Mary H. Thompson 5/19/1882-6/18/1952
L. A. Gilbert 12/13/1839
T. W. Gilbert 8/31/1871
Isaac Gilbert 6/27/1865
J. F. Gilbert 11/25/1879

Deaths

Margaret Gilbert 1/23/1902
George Tucker 4/19/1867-7/19/1926
Una Tucker 11/28/1931

(William Dunaway Bible continued...)

Ella Lee Thompson 3/10/1926
E. Thompson 8/5/1826
Gene Lee, wife of W. L. Lee, 7/15/1927
Selia Reed 3/1824
Nancy Dunaway 6/13/1857
William Dunaway 4/12/1887
Oliver Swindall 10/5/1910
N. C. Dunaway 4/18/1938, wife of E. A. Thompson

Docie Dunaway 1/29/1864
M. W. Dunaway 2/1863
Isaac Gilbert 8/16/1875
J. Dunaway 2/26/1863
Jerry Lee 1/7/1907
Sanford Dunaway 3/13/1909
Mandy Lee 8/1/1908
Lettie Cunningham 1/31/1890
Thursey Lee 1/1/1915
Amanda Swindall 4/18/1943

DANIEL BUTLER BIBLE
Owner: Mrs. William Taylor, Springville, Ala.

Daniel Butler Jr. 1/28/1853-2/28/1859
Mary E. R. (Anna) Butler 2/15/1862-2/3/1918
Abraham Butler 8/5/1864-9/6/1875
John A. Butler 8/14/1866-12/20/1942
Son 1/10/1863-2/22/1969
Oma Butler 6/22/1870-4/25/1895
Ceney Butler 9/24/1972-10/12/1872

(Daniel Butler Bible continued...)

Henry Martin Butler 6/1/1874-7/2/1831
Joe H. Butler 7/10/1877-
Katy R. Butler 9/22/1800, bur. Lancaster, Tx.

Marriages

Oma Butler to James H. Cook 7/26/1886 Caty R. Butler to T. W.
McCalla 11/12/1893 Joe. Butler to J. H. McClendon 7/7/1897

AARON CORNELIUS BURRELL BIBLE
Owner: Ruth Clay Burrell
Rt. 3, Box 498, Amarillo, Tx. 79107

Aaron Cornelius Burrell b. 4/9/1805 Elyton, Jefferson Co., Ala.
d. 5/2/1952 Shamrock, Wheeler Co., Tx. m. Ist 12/25/1887, Trenton, Jackson Co., Ala., Martha
Jane Wilborn (sis. of James Wilborn, both orphans of George Wilborn, Trenton, Jackson Co.,
Ala.) b. Trenton, Ala. 2/24/1868-d. 2/2/1899 Brandon, Hill Co., Tx.

Their Children:

George William Burrell b. 10/13/1885 Trenton, Jackson Co., Ala. d. 3/13/1963 Shamrock,
Wheeler Co., Tx. m. 2/3/1913 Vernon, Wilbarger Co., Tx. Bonnie Mae Wright. Ch: John Baron,
George William, Jr., Harold Edward, Imogene and Robert Delano Burrell.
John Henry Burrell b.. 6/23/1991 Trenton, Jackson Co., Ala. d. 5/11/1956 Hereford, Tx., bur.
Shamrock, Wheeler Co., Tx., m. 1/29/1918 Wheeler, Wheeler Co., Tx. to Lillie Sammons.
Children: Wiley Cornelius, Bernice Marie and Hazel Oleta Surrell.
Robert Andrew Burrell b. 2/10/1894 Trenton, Jackson Co., Ala. d. 6/22/1965 Amarillo, Fetter
Co., Tx. m. 1/16/1915 Shamrock, Wheeler Co., Tx. to Geraldine Bell. Children: Gid Baron,
Mildred Estelle and Robert Glynn Burrell
Posey Lea Burrell b. 9/15/1897 Brandon, Hill Co., Tx. d. 9/28/1877, Hereford, Deaf Smith Co.,

155

(Aaron Cornelius Burrell Bible continued...)

Tx. m. 1/20/1926 Shamrock, Wheeler Co., Tx to Ola Mae Toot (d. 7/27/1933) m. 2d Estelle Williams. Child by 1st wife: Posey Lea Burrell, Jr.

Aaron Cornelius Burrell m. 2nd 11/25/1899 Sherman, Grayson Co.,
Thomas Dewey
Elvadora Ridonia (Henderson) Roberts, wid. of Thomas Dewey Roberts
and dau. of Claude 1. Henderson, o. 1/i8/1877 Birmingham,
Jefferson Co., Ala. d. 11/25/1921 Shamrock, Wheeler Co., Ala.

Their Children:

Aaron Cornelius Burrell Jr. (Nealy) b. 9/23/1900 in Bynum, Hill, Co., Tx., lives Wheeler Co., Tx.
m. Ist Cora Shirry 4/7/1928 (div), 2nd, Jewel Thomas, 3rd Louise Jones. Children by 1st wife: Jasper Earl, George and Burnece Burrell.
Elva Viola Burrell b. 1/28/1802 Brandon, Hill Co., Tx., lives Lubbock, Tx. m. 2/15/1820 Wheeler Co., Tx., Solley Norrid. Children: James Cornelius, Floyd Irvin, Mary Belle, Cecil Edward and Edna Lee Norrid.
Bertha Burrell b- 10/3/1903 Brandon, Hill Co., Tx. - d. 10/3/1903
Lela Mae Burrell b.. 8/11/1904 Brandon, Hill Co., Tx., lives panhandle, TX. m. 7/25/1923 Carson Co., Tx. Ar thur Lonnie Stovall. Kathlene (killed in wreck, 2 mos.), Arthur Lonnie, Jr., Eula Mae, Eva Ilene (d. at birth) and Allene Joyce Stovall.
Hattie Pearl Burrell b- 4/14/1906 Brandon, Hill Co., Tx. d. 2/1/1950 Amarillo, Tx., bur. Claude, Armstrong Co., Tx., m. Ist 6/30/1927 Joulious Massey, 2nd 4/15/1933 Carrol (Jack) Ivy, adopted dau., Jannie Sue Ivy.
Jimmy Burrell b. 6/1/1908 Miles, Runnels Co., Tx., d. same day.
Ethel Essie Burrell b. 5/6/1909 lives Half Oregon m. 1st, Ora
Dorothy Dean, m. Park Coker Children: Sadie Lea,
Jimmy Ray, Leon, Charles, Collene Joyce Hilderbrand.
Baby girl, unnamed, b.d. 5/9/1911 in Vernon, Willbarger Co., Tx.

(Aaron Cornelius Burrell Bible continued...)

Albert D. Burrell b. 6/19/1912, Vernon Willbarger Co., Tx., d. 6/23/1912 same place.
Ada Clara Burrell b. 6/8/1914 Shamrock, Wheeler Co., Tx.
8/9/1914 Shamrock, Wheeler Co., TX.
Dora Nell Burrell 7/1/1917-7/ 25/1917 Shamrock, Wheeler Co. TX.
Thomas Roosevelt Burrell b. 11/6/1918 Shamrock, Wheeler Co., Tx., d. 11/27/1957 same place,
m. Opal Craig.

CHARLES HAGIN BIBLE
Owner: Woodrow Boyette
Tuscaloosa, Ala. 35405

Births

Ophia Jewel Blanchard 3/12/1916
Edward Hagin, son of Charles and Sarah, 4/11/1814
Mary Hagin 12/3/1820
Elizabeth Hagin 9/18/1823
Martha Ann 7/3/1826
Lela May Blanchard 8/1898
Carlie Thomas Blanchard 10/31/1899
John David Blanchard 9/3/1908 Mallie P. Blanchard 3/29/1914

Deaths

Edward Hagin 8/23/1861
Martha Hagin 5/12/1877
Ophia Jewel Blanchard 3/14/1916
Henry Ray Blanchard 5/6/1918-7/6/1920
Tom William Tarkle 7/3/1919

DAVID ALLEN BRITT
Owner: Comdr. Grady Avant
1111 Domingo Dr., Tallahassee, Fla. 32304

D. A. Britt b. 7/5/1835
Mary E. (Eliza Pearson) Britt b. 1/16/1842   D. A. Britt m. Mary E. Britt 12/19/1858

Births

Emma C. Britt 11/27/1859
Samuel Eliot Britt 12/20/1874
Victory L. Britt 1/22/1862
Miney Zimmerman Britt 8/10/1878
Thomas Joel Britt 11/28/1867
George Barney Britt 7/13/1851
David Oliver Britt 10/7/1870
Mariah Rosannah Vernon Britt 4/6/1873
Rosannah Britt d. 5/24/1855, aged 43 yrs.
Etheldred Britt 1/30/1840-4/22/1865
Nancy Britt, sister of D. A. Britt, d. 11/8/1909
Emma Carson d. 8/28/1909, dau. of D. A. Britt
Herman Carson d. 11/12/1913
Samuel Britt, son of D. A. Britt and Mary X., d. 2/12/1900
Mary E. Britt, wife of D. S.Britt d. 6/9/1901, aged 59 yrs., 5 mos.
Mariah Vernon Britt, dau. of D. A.Britt d. 11/12/1913, aged 40 yrs.
Victoria Louisa Britt m. 11/24/1881

JESSE A. GLENN BIBLE

Owner: Comdr. Grady Avant
1111 Domingo Dr., Tallahassee, Fla. 32304

Births

Jesse A. Glenn 1/27/1809
Rosannah Glenn 1/23/1812-5/25/1855
James Glenn 6/8/1814
Mahala Glenn 1/27/1923
Mariah Glenn 9/21/1815
Jani Glenn 3/11/1825
Lucy Glenn 10/5/1817
Sarah Glenn 2/14/1827
William Glenn 5/9/1819
Nancy Glenn 8/31/1829
Washington Glenn 3/13/1821
John A. Glenn 8/15/1831
William Britt 7/12/1847
Louisa K. Britt 7/20/1842
Lemuel Britt 2/4/1843 5/20/1845
John D. Britt 7/13/1853
Nancy A. Britt 4/22/1844
J. Britt 1/25/1834-9/23/1835
Emma Britt 11/27/1859
Britt 7/8/1835
Victory L. Britt 1/22/1861
James W. Britt 6/27/1838
Nancy A. Britt 4/22/1844
Etheldred T. Britt 1/30/1840-4/22/1865
David A. Britt m. Mary E. (Eliza Pearson) Britt 12/13/1858
John M. Glenn d. 4/16/1812

ISAAC HOLLAND BIBLE
Of Smith's, Russell Co., Ala.
Owner: Mrs. Lewis C. Hanna, Columbus, Ga.

Issac Holland m. 9/1/1790 Amelia

Births
Isaac Holland 4/13/1770
Hettie Cale Holland 5/28/1793
Samuel Holland 6/21/1791
Hannah Holland 8/16/1794
John Holland 5/12/1792
Nancy Holland 3/20/1799
William Holland 3/3/1802
Amelia Brewington Holland 11/7/1800
James Holland 12/27/1804
Orlando Holland 9/30/1806
Elmina Holland 1/9/1809
Arestus Holland 4/9/1813
Julia Ann Holland 3/22/1811
Amelia Holland 9/10/1772
Sintha Holland 5/6/1816
Hettie Cale Holland 5/?8/1793

AUGUSTUS JONES DIGBY BIBLE
Owner: Mrs. Bryant Ginnett, Phenix City, Alabama

Births

Augustus Jones Digby 9/26/1823
Mary Elizabeth Digby 4/13/1861
Sophronia Webster Digby 9/22/1825

160

(Augustus Jones Digby Bible continued...)

Frances Rebecca Digby 6/2/1866
William Alonzo Digby 9/7/1843
Malissa Clementine Digby 11/7/1845
Nancy Ann Digby 4/28/1848
Sarah Caroline Digby 7/10/1851
Samuel Nathaniel Digby 5/4/1853
Caroline Columbia Digby 8/24/1856
Marjory Sophronia Digby 6/5/1859

Births of Children o: Samuel and Lydia Digby

Sallie Emmit Digby 12/30/1877
Ethel L. Digby 9/16/1936
Susan Sophronia Digby 2/29/1850
Alma L. Digby 1/28/1883
David Alonzo Digby 9/15/1882

Births of Children of James J. and Rebecca Herricks

Bessie L. Herricks 2/2/1889
Daisy Herricks 1/24/1895
Annie Lamuel Herricks 1/10/1892
Douglas Carter Herricks 8/29/1998
Bertha G. Smith 12/15/1879
Samuel Smith 3/19/1833
Maggie May Duke 7/13/1892

161

(Augustus Jones Digby Bible continued...)

Marriages

Augustus Jones Digby to Sophronia Webster 9/22/1842
Thomas M. Duncan to Malissa C. Digby 11/7/1865
William Smith to Nancy Digby 12/14/1875
Samuel Nathaniel Digby to Lydia Lunsford 3/14/1877
James Herricks to Rebecca Digby 11/12/1884
Minous Green to Carrie Digby 9/27/1857
John T. Rogers to Mary E. Digby 9/23/1890
Alonzo L. Duncan to Amelia Willis 10/7/1857
Walter Scott Duncan to Estelle Ennis 1/28/1890
Bessie Dukes to Nettie F. Duncan 6/7/1891

Deaths

Sarah Caroline Digby 5/22/1852, aged 10 mos., 12 days
Margery Sophronia Digby 9/11/1859, aged 4 mos., 6 days
William Alonzo Digby 5/3/1863 in Battle of Gettysburg, aged 19 yrs., 7 mos., 22 days
Cassie Bird Duncan 9/7/1882, aged 10 mos., 19 days
William T. Smith 12/8/1883
Augustus Jones Digby 4/5/1895, aged 72 yrs., 7 mos.
Sophronia E. Digby 7/7/1095, aged 70 yrs.
Maggie Deli Duncan 5/15/1895, aged 22 yrs.
Samuel J. Webster 1/24/1858, aged 43
Thaddeus Webster 4/6/1859, aged 39
William Webster 1/8/1833
Dawsie Duncan b. 7/3/1859
Nettie A. Duncan b. 9/30/1891
Thaddeus Duncan b. 8/24/1891?
Maggie L. Duncan b. 8/5/1896

162

WILLIAM PORCH BIBLE

Owner: Jesse Partridge Porch, Greenville, Georgia

Thomas Porch m. Tabitha 4/13/1810 Hancock Co., Ga.

Births of Children of Thomas and Tabitha Porch

William Porch 1/19/1811
Susan Porch 8/9/1822
Elizabeth Porch 9/8/1812
Julius Cesar Porch 5/8/1824
Rebecca Porch 10/12/1815
Sarah Hill Porch 1/3/1826
Alexander Porch 8/25/1816
Pleasant Bonner Porch Frances 10/25/1827
Ann Priscilla Porch 5/8/1818
Mary Louisa Porch 3/27/1830

Deaths

William Porch 8/13/1811 Rebecca Porch 7/15/1816
Henry Porch 9/27/1824, aged 15 yrs., 9 mos., 8 days
Pleasant Bonner Porch 6/1855
Thomas Porch 10/20/1860

Births

Selia Robbert? Porch 8/5/1835
John Reuben Porch 5/25/1835
Thomas J. Porch 7/25/1836
Nancy R. Porch ---
Nancy Ragland Porch 10/9/1838

(William Porch Bible continued…)

Eller G. P. Porch -/24/1052
Stiles Marshal Porch 2/27/1842
Henry Porch 12/13/1808
James Wright Porch 2/14/1820

WINSTON WOOD BIBLE
Owner: Bessie Bartlett, Bowden, Georgia

Births

Winston Wood 9/15/1800
Dicey Wood 3/22/1807
Rufus P. Wood 6/10/1825
Nancy Wood 9/7/1845
William T. Wood 7/22/1826
William Thomas Wood
Elizabeth T. Wood 4/29/1828
Nancy Ann Wood 6/18/1830
Sophia G. Wood 1/4/1830
Winston C. Wood 10/6/1848
Harmon R. Wood 11/20/1831
John Rufus Wood 8/31/1850
Martha Wood 1/23/1833
Delancy Jane Wood 2/5/1853
Wilson Bird Wood 3/15/1835
Thomas Blake Wood 3/28/1855
Levise Gay Wood 6/2/1837
Wyatt William Wood 9/4/1857
Tabitha W. Wood 6/2/1837
Dicy Elizabeth Wood 1/29/1860

(Winston Wood Bible continued...)

Wyatt H. Wood 5/15/1840
Bird Robert Wood 1/10/1964
Dosha L. Wood 8/3/1842
Nancy Tabitha Wood 10/29/1866

William T. Wood m. Nancy A. Blake 11/14/1847

WALTER SCOTT DUNCAN BIBLE
Owner: Mrs. W. L. Hobbs, Phenix City, Alabama

Births

Thomas Marion Duncan 8/29/1821 Jasper Co., Ga.
Melissa Clementine Digby Duncan 11/7/1845 Russell Co., Ala. She was 24 yrs. younger than her husband.

Davis Ennis 1832 in Georgia
Elizabeth Frances Williams Ennis 1834 in Georgia

Walter Scott Duncan 9/13/1969 at old James Duncan homestead near Mott, Ala., now in Lee Co. (formerly Russell Co.) , son of Thomas Duncan

Ida Estelle Ennis Duncan 1/16/1874 Columbus, Ga.
Thaddeus R. Duncan 8/21/1891 Columbus, Ga.
Maggie Lillian Duncan 1/17/1893 Columbus, Ga.
Walter Cecil Duncan 3/24/1894 Columbus, Ga.
Thomas Ennis Duncan 1/16/1895
Eleanor Erline Duncan 8/6/1900 Columbus, Ga. Forest Auburn Duncan 2/23/1907 Girard, Ala.
Martha Adaline Paschal Taylor Duncan 6/25/1896 Ga.
Myrtle Louise Taylor Thomason 4/12/1914

165

(Walter Scott Duncan Bible continued...)

Willis Lovic Mobbs 8/22/1893
Dorothy Jerome Pearce Duncan 11/30/1911
Walter Cecil Duncan 1/13/1919 Jacksonville, Fla.
Willis Earl Duncan 3/20/1920 Phenix City, Ala.
Frank Hayden Duncan 11/30/1923 Phenix City, Ala.
Walter Scott Duncan 1/23/1926 Phenix City, Ala.
Elizabeth Frances Duncan 7/6/1928 Phenix City, Ala.
Forest Ford Duncan 9/24/1932 Phenix City, Ala.
Eleanor Erline Duncan 10/9/1934 Phenix City, Fla.
Joel Shannon Duncan 2/23/1940 Phenix City, Ala.
Forest Auburn Duncan, Jr. 3/21/1943 Waycross, Ga.
Mary Estelle Duncan 10/27/1945 Waycross, Ga.

Marriages

Thomas Marion Duncan to Melissa C. Digby 11/7/1865 in Russell Co., Ala. by W. A. Dunn; bondsman-William Webster, Jr.
David Annis to Elizabeth Frances Williams 2/1/1855 in Muscogee Co., Ga., by Thomas D. Slade, Minister of the Gospel
David Ennis to Mattie Griggs In Columbus, Ga. 11/27/1873 by K. L. Redd, J. P., she was his second wife
Walter Scott Duncan to Ida Estelle Ennis 1/28/1990 in Columbus, Ga. by Rev. J. G. Harrison
Walter Cecil Duncan to Martha Nadine Paschal 12/1/1917 Jacksonville, Fla.
Willis Lovic Hobbs to Eleanor Erline Duncan 7/26/1924 Phenix City, Ala.
Forest Auburn Duncan to Dorothy Jerome Pearce 2/23/1842 in Columbus, Ga.
Frank Hayden Duncan to Martha Ann Chappell 1/5/1945 in Phenix City, Ala.
Joseph Aldine Maddox to Elizabeth Frances Duncan 9/14/1852 in Phenix City, Ala.
Forest Ford Duncan to Constance Lanett Whatlcy 8/6/1955 in Phenix City, Ala.

166

(Walter Scott Duncan Bible continued...)

Deaths

Thomas Marion Duncan 9/18/1895 Lee Co., Ala.
Elizabeth Frances Williams Ennis 9/28/1875 Columbus, Ga.
David Ennis 6/10/1893 Columbus, Ga.
Thaddeus R. Duncan 12/11/1891
Thomas Ennis Duncan 1/24/1898
Maggie Lillian Duncan 12/6/1833
Melissa C. Digby 4/18/1916 In Girard, Ala.
Walter Cecil Duncan, Jr. 2/6/1919 in Jacksonville, Fla.
Walter Scott Duncan 12/19/1925 Phenix City, Ala.
Ida Estelle Ennis Duncan 12/30/1832 Phenix City, Ala.
Willis Earl Duncan 2/5/1933 Phenix City, Ala.
Walter Cecil Duncan, Sr. 2/5/1941 Phenix City, Ala.
Willis L. Hobbs 7/18/1947 Phenix City, Ala.
Effie Lillian Ennis Harvey --- Eufaula, Ala.

Great Grandchildren of Walter Scott and Ida Estelle Ennis Duncan

Forest Auburn Duncan, Jr.
David Exian Duncan
Mary Estelle Duncan
Leslie Eric Szczepanski
Pamela Scott Duncan
Jessica Forest Maddox
Garry Ford Duncan

167

GEORGE DAVID LANIER BIBLE
Owner: Franklin Fleetwood Lanier, Temple, Texas

Births

George David Lanier 6/2/1862-4/22/1936
Epsy Gunn Lanier 12/23/1854
John William Lanier 7/19/1884
George Lee Lanier 8/29/1886
Henry Wheeler Lanier 9/18/1885-2/22/1923
Benjamin Davis Lanier 2/18/1891-1955
Franklin Fleetwood Lanier 8/23/1893

GREEN-OLIVER BIBLE
Owner: Miss Ethel Blackman, Eufaula, Alabama

Marriages

James W. Oliver to Susan Green 5/1/1836
J. R. Tyson to Mollie Green 10/17/1865 at res. of Mrs. Olivet by Rev. Mr. King
G. W. Oliver to Mollie J. Phelps 11/16/1865 at res. of bride's father by Rev. Mr. Teat

Births

Susan Green 1/21/1808
Jane Green 10/23/1811
Francis Green 1/4/1814
Martha Green 2/18/1817
Alsy Green 12/31/1825
George W. Oliver 3/30/1842
Maryann Green 8/17/1827
James F. Oliver 5/3/1852

(Green-Oliver Bible continued...)

Julyan Green Decatur 6/21/1829
William J. Oliver 4/22/1854
Nelly Green Culpepper 5/14/1831

Deaths

George W. Oliver Sr. 3/27/1835, aged 38 yrs.
James V. Oliver 5/25/1857, aged 52 yrs. James F.
Oliver 10/28/1858, aged 6 yrs. George W. Oliver 9/15/1887, aged 45 yrs. William J. Oliver
9/17/1930, aged 75 yrs.
Verna Oliver
Ross Leighton Oliver
Mrs. Susan Oliver 10/12/1865 aged 57 yrs.
Frances Green Oliver 3/2/1830, aged 76 yrs. Mrs. G.
W. Oliver
Joseph F. Oliver
Ida Jesse Oliver ---
Mrs. W. J. Oliver 9/24/1830
George W. Oliver Sr. 3/27/1835 Entered here by Leila Oliver Watson 1912
William Jesse Oliver b. 4/22/1854 Wife, Mary Lou Taylor b. 2/22/1863

Births of Children of William Jesse and Mary Lou Oliver

James Thaddeus Oliver 2/21/1879
Ross Leighton Oliver 1/19/1885 Leila Corinne Oliver 10/21/1880
Verna Oliver 9/2/1885
Dixie Alma Oliver 3/6/1853
James Thaddeus Oliver m. 4/1833, wife, Clyde Rogers m. 4/1899, their son: William Thaddeus
Oliver b. 3/25/1900
Lelia C. Oliver Watson m. 1/21/1898
Huddie R. Watson

(Green-Oliver Bible continued...)

Births of Children of Huddle R. and Leila Watson

Ross Oliver Watson 9/27~1900
George Florry Watson 6/9/1902
William Jesse O. Watson 12/31/1902
Dixie Alma Oliver m. 12/-- to Robert Truitt Watson
Ross Leighton Oliver 1/19/1855-3/26/1900
Verna Oliver 9/20/1885-6/8/1887

MARY DELL LANIER HAMMACK BIBLE

Father's Father - W. W. (William Washington) Lanier 3/15/1813-1/28/1802
Father's Mother - Charlotte T. Jackson 11/3/1818-10/20/1892
Father- James J. (Jackson) Lanier 10/13/1836-6/21/1902
Mother - Mary Kinard 7/ 13/1840-9/26/1910

Births Of Their Children

Emma Lanier 10/13/1866
W. L. Lanier 7/7/1868
J. T. Lanier 8/31/1869 m. Hattie Gay
M. C. Lanier 9/12/1871
B. E. Lanier 12/23/1873
J. D. Lanier 9/7/1875
H. E. Lanier 2/15/1877
A. L. Lanier 9/11/1879
M. Lanier 10/10/1881
M. Katherine Lanier 2/11/1884
William Washington Lanier and his wife, Charlotte T. Jackson Lanier, their dau., Mary E., and son, J. J. Lanier and his wife, Mary J. Knard Lanier, are all buried near New Hope Baptist Church at Fredonia, Chambers Co., Ala.

170

(Mary Bell Lanier Hammock Bible, contd....)

Father - W. W. Lanier 3/15/1813-1/28/1892
Mother - Charlotte T. Jackson 11/3/1815-10/20/1892 m. 10/22/1835

Children:

James J. Lanier 10/13/1836 m. Mary J. Kinard 6/21/1902
J. F. Lanier 11/3/1838
John D. Lanier 12/29/1840
W. W. Lanier 9/16/1844
J. S. Lanier 6/2/1847
Mary E. Lanier 3/4/1849
Sarah A. Lanier 12/19/1852
Meliza C. Lanier 5/21/1854
Susan C. Lanier 12/15/1858
Frances E. Lanier 6/12/1859
George D. Lanier 6/2/1862

Father - W. L. Lanier 7/7/1869-1/10/1931
Mother - S. S. Williams 11/5/1871- m. 11/29/1883 Langdale, Ala.

Children:

O. E. J. Lanier 10/5/1889 m. Mac Sargent
Blake Lanier 6/1/1891 m. 2/4/1721 Emma Nanners
Jim W. Lanier 10/12/1893 m. Eva Moore
Mary Deli Lanier 2/10/1896 m. J. J. Hammack 4/9/1922
Hylyard Lanier 1/20/1898 m. Maud Gilliland 5/4/1918
Cleo Lanier 2/12/1900 m. Jack Neuman
Eunice Lanier 12/12/1901
Sallie Maud Lanier 5/25/1904 m. Boyd Hollis

(Mary Bell Lanier Hammock Bible, contd....)

Osmos Lanier 11/1/1806 m. Jewel Causey
Lavonia Lanier 6/11/1909
L. P. Lanier 5/21/1912 m. Louise Blackburn

JERRY BERRYMAN ROBINSON BIBLE
Owner: Ervin Hughs Robinson, Booneville, Missouri

Marriages

Jesse Berryman Robinson to Martha Ann Carlisle 2/24/1839, 9 miles east of Lafayette, Chambers Co., Ala., by Rev. Moses Gunn

William W. C. Robinson to George Anah Turner 12/3/1857 Chambers Co., Ala. by Rev. D. H. McCoy

Thomas A. J. Robinson to Martha Holstum 4/22/1863 Meriwether Co., Ga., 3 miles west of Sand Town by Rev. William Graham

Henry C. Melton to Clara E. Robinson 10/15/1863 at Mill Town, Chambers Co., Ala. by Rev. D.H. McCoy

Eden Phillips to Malinda C. Robinson 10/15/1863 at Milltown,Chambers Co., Ala. By Rev. D. H. McCoy

Joseph W. F. Burke to Sarah V. Robinson 3/25/1869 Macan Co., Ala., 1 mile west of Notasulga by Rev. James E. Dowdle

Jesse Berryman Robinson to Helen Evelyn Cox 2/27/1871 5 miles north of Notasulga in Lee Co., Ala. by Rev. D. H. Slaton

John N. R. Burke to Martha Jane Robinson 6/9/1872, 2 miles south of Waverly, Let Co., Ala. by Rev. John Henderson

Births of Children of J. B. and Martha A. Robinson

William Whatley Carlisle Robinson, 11/27/1839 Chambers Co., Ala.
Thomas Andrew Jackson Robinson 9/3/1841 Chambers Co., Ala.

172

(Jerry Berryman Robinson Bible continued...)

Clarissa Elizabeth Robinson 1/5/1843 Chambers Co., Ala.
Jesse Berryman Robinson 12/14/1845 Chambers Co., Ala.
Malinda Christian Robinson 7/16/1847 Chambers Co., Ala.
Sarah Vandosen Robinson 5/26/1849 Chambers Co., Ala.
George Franklin Robinson 4/30/1852 Chambers Co.,
Ala. Martha Jane Robinson 5/11/1954 Chambers Co., Ala.
Mary Emma Robinson 3/7/1856 Chambers Co., Ala.
Lucy Matilda Robinson 2/10/1859 Chambers Co., Ala.
Ammarilla Robinson 2/16/1861 Milltown, Chambers Co., Ala.

Deaths

Jesse Berryman Robinson, Sr., son of Thomas and Sarah Robinson and husband of Martha Ann
Robinson, 1/21/1814-5/14/1871
George Franklin, son of Jesse Berryman and Martha Ann Robinson, 10/1/1881
Clarissa Elizabeth Melton, dau. of Jesse Berryman and Martha Ann Robinson 5/11/1975
Martha A. Carlisle Robinson 1/7/1896
Judge William Carlisle Robinson, son of J. D. R. and A. Carlisle Robinson 12121012
Mollie Evans (Emma) Robinson, dau. of J. D. and M. A. Carlisle Robinson 5/7/1915
Martha Jane Robinson Burke, dau. of J. B. and M. A. Carlisle Robinson 3/23/1899
Charity Berryman Burke, son of Joseph W. F. and Sarah V. Burke, 9/4/1873
Helen Evelyn Cox Robinson, dau. of Willis and Betsy Cox of
Notasulga, Ala. 7/29/1846-1/10/1922, Waverly, Ala.
Jesse Berryman Robinson, son of Jesse Berryman Robinson and Martha Ann Carlisle Robinson,
12/14/1845-8/19/1922 at Opelika, Ala.

RHODA BLEDSOE BIBLE
Owner: Mrs. Harvey E. Bearden, Tuskegee, Ala.

Marriages

Thomas T. Bledsoe 7/27/1856
F. P. Bledsoe 7/27/1965
Martha E. Bledsoe 1/11/1849
E. P. Bledsoe 12/31/1982
Sarah C. Bledsoe 10/24/1859?
Martha Jane Dobbs
Elbert Cleveland Bledsoe to Leola Dorom 1908
Frank Pierce Bledsoe to Mary Julia Phelps 12/20/1906 in Shotwell, Ala.
Artie M. Cottingham to Hon. W. A. Curry 12/28/1882
Jessie Bledsoe to James Cochran Phelps
Rhoda German to Bud Bledsoe in 1823, South Carolina

Births

Rhoda Bledsoe 1/23/1799
Bud Bledsoe 1803 Edgefield District, S. C.

John G. Bledsoe 8/5/1824
Sarah C. Bledsoe 2/5/1934
Thomas L. Bledsoe 1/6/1827
Franklin P. Bledsoe 5/15/1937
Martha R. Bledsoe 3/15/1829
E. P. Bledsoe 2/1/1840

Deaths

John G. Bledsoe 12/4/1868
Rhoda Bledsoe 6/27/1882, 84 yrs. Old

(Rhoda Bledsoe Bible, contd....)

T. H. Cottingham 4/2-/1892 in his 70's
W. T. Cottingham 6/17/1893 in 32nd yr.
Bud Bledsoe 1841
Elbert Pierce Bledsoe 6/5/1906
Elbert Cleveland Bledsoe 1/19/1952
Frank Pierce Bledsoe 6/17/1947
Mary Julia Phelps Bledsoe 1/24/1859
Harvey Edward Bearden 9/9/1965
Martha Jane Dobbs Bledsoe 10/3/1895
Elbert Pearce Bledsoe m. Martha Jane Dobbs 12/31/1882 Bullock Co., near Armstrong, Ala.
Elbert Cleveland Bledsoe 3/4/1854-1/19/1852 m. Leola Borom 1/22/1900 who d. 4/13/1963,
bur. Oak Hill, Union Springs, Ala. Sidney D. Bledsoe, Jr. m. Mary Nell Sweeny 5/21/1965
Teresa Lynn, dau. of Sidney B. Bledsoe Jr. and Mary Nell Bledsoe b. 2/26/1966

Frank Pierce Bledsoe 7/31/1885 Armstrong, Ala.-6/17/1947 New Orleans, La., bur. Oak Hill
Cemetery, Union Springs, Ala., m. Mary Julia Phelps 12/20/1906 Shotwell, Ala. by Rev. Isaac
Watt Chalker

Bessie Mac Bledsoe 5/1/1890-5/4/1925 at Ft. Davis, Ala. m. James Cochran Fhelps
Martha Kate Bledsoe, dau. of E. C. and Leola Bledsoe, b. 1/14/1910 m. Henry Wall Bland
7/10/1935
Sidney Borom, son of E. C. and Leola Bledsoe, b. 12/25/1921 m. Sue Downing 9/13/1942 at
Meridian, Miss. by Rev. J. L. Lane
Anne Phelps, dau. of Frank P. and Mary Phelps Bledsoe, b. 8/8/1903 Armstrong, Ala. m.
Harvey Edward Bearden 11/15/1933, Columbus, Ga., by Rev. John Frazier Chalker, St. Luke's
Meth. Church.
Mary Julia, dau. of Frank P. and Mary Phelps Bledsoe b. 6/5/1911 Armstrong, Ala. m. Daniel
Joseph Coyle 12/11/1932 Salem, Ala. (2nd husband), Dan Lamb 7/1966
Frances Lockhart, dau. of Frank P. And Mary Phelps Bledsoe, b. Birmingham Ala. m. Thomas

175

(Rhoda Bledsoe Bible, contd....)

Russell Bazzel 3/1/1847 Tuskegee, Ala. By Dr. Thomas Phelps Chalker (cou. of bride) and Rev.
Isaac Watt Phelps (uncle of bride) Tuskegee Methodist Church.
Jamie Bledsoe, dau. of James C. and Jessie Bledsoe Phelps b. 4/17/1910 Auhurn, Ala. m. Al
Powers, Los Angeles, Calif.
Philip and Phyllis, adopted twins of Martha Kate and H. W. Bland Sidney, Jr., son of Sidney and
Sue Bledsoe, b. 9/9/1946 Virginia Leanne, dau. of Sidney and Sue Dledsoe, b. 9/17/1949
Emma Suzanne, dau. of Sidney and Sue Bledsoe, b. 12/15/1850

Mary Anne, dau. of H. E. and Anne Bledsoe Bearden, b. 11/4/1934 Birmingham, Ala.
Judee Bledsoe, dau. of H. E. and Anne Bledsoe Bearden, b. 7/20/1943 Birmingham, Ala.
Mary Anne Bearden m. James Guy Patterson 12/22/1955 Highland Methodist Church,
Birmingham, Ala. by Dr. Guy McGowan
Daniel Joseph Coyle Jr., son of Dan and Julia Coyle, b. 7/11/1835 Birmingham m. Lillian
Treschel 8/3/1956 Birmingham Ala.
James Timothy, son of Dan and Julia Coyle, b. 2/3/1953 Birmingham, Ala.
Frank Bledsoe, son of Tom and Frances Bledsoe Daniel, b. 3/13/1860 Atlanta, Ga.
Thomas Russell, Jr., son of Tom and Frances Bledsoe Bazzel, b. 4/7/1962 Atlanta, Ga.
William Floyd, son of Tom and Frances Bledsoe Bazzel, b. 12/6/1956, Atlanta, Ga.

Children of Mary Anne and James Patterson

John Mitchell Patterson b. 8/6/1961 Lexington, Ky.
Carrie Anne Patterson b. 8/24/1958 Tuscaloosa, Ala.
James Grey Patterson, Jr. 5/6/1960 Tuscaloosa, Ala.

*Obituary pasted in Bible: "After a brief illness, Sister Rhoda Bledsoe departed this life, on the
27th of June 1882. She was 83 years, 5 months and 7 days old; was born in Edgefield District,
S. C. 20th of Jan. 1799; removed to Alabama in 1833 where she lived til her death. Intermarried with D.
Bledsoe in 1823, with whom she lived 18 years. After her husband's death, she battled with life 43 years in
widowhood, raising her large family of children in Great credit.*

E. C. BLEDSOE BIBLE

Owner: Sidney Boron Bledsoe, Armstrong, Alabama

On flyleaf: "This Bible given in charge of E. C. Bledsoe on Dec. 10th 1911 by Mrs. W. G. Foster, 2nd wife of E. P. Bledsoe.
E. P. Bledsoe m. M. J. Dobbs 12/31/1882
E. P. Bledsoe m. Willie A. Parks 3/17/1996 (2nd wife), no issue

Births

John B. Cottingham 3/15/1854
M. J. Bledsoe 10/6/1862
E. P. Bledsoe 2/1/1840
Elbert Cleveland Bledsoe 3/4/1884
Franklin Pierce Bledsoe 7/31/1885
Mattie Lee Bledsoe 8/27/1887
Jessie May Bledsoe 8/1/1890-5/4/1925 at Ft. Davis, Ala.
Janie Valerie Bledsoe 12/21/1893

Deaths

Mattie Lee Bledsoe 7/26/1888
Janie Valera Bledsoe 8/6/1834
Mrs. Mattie Bledsoe 10/9/1895
E. P. Bledsoe 6/8/1905
Tom Bledsoe d. in Tx. 1/5/1900, His wife, Mollie Bledsoe, 1/5/1901

HARDY BIBLE of Chambers Co., Alabama

Births

Susana Elizabeth Hardy 9/1/1821
Ethen Hardy 3/21/1836
Sarah Ann Caroline Hardy 12/29/1823
William Bland Hardy 2/9/1836
Elizabeth Malinda Hardy 3/24/1838-9/8/1908
Mary Jane Hardy 2/7/1820
George Lancelot Hardy 7/2/1841
Maria Louisa Hardy 3/27/1821
James Hardy 3/22/1832-5/10/1862
Tabitha Jane Staples 11/27/1870
Ethelbert Hardy 2/6/1834-10/28/1863
James W. Strother 1/4/1860-2/1/1938
George Hardy Strother 9/1/1861-6/30/1906
Candis Ethan Strother 5/22/1863-3/1954
Tommie Lavicil Staples 5/24/1872
Marion Elizabeth Staples 6/13/1877
Lula Pearl Hardy 8/14/1879
James Thomas Hardy 1/28/1882
Mae Olin Hardy 12/12/1888-5/8/1892
Minie Elizabeth Hardy 10/10/1890
Annie Mae - 7/24/1895
Linnie Lee Staples Cox 6/3/1891
Lou Oma Cox 7/31/1895
Lucille Elizabeth Dennis 8/4/1900
James Sylvanus Walker 1/20/1847
Sarah Elizabeth
Louisa Jane Ellen Walker 1849
John Alfred Walker 1/17/1851
Henry Hardy Walker 10/15/1853

(Hardy Bible continued…)

William Henry Harrison Hill 12/31/1872
Wayd Lindsay Hill 7/15/1893
Lois Elizabeth Hill 10/18/1895
Tommie L. Staples m. Henry Hill 10/17/1892
Mattie May Hill 9/13/1897-3/20/1902, aged 5 yrs., 7 days
William Otis Hill 3/7/1900-5/5/1903, aged 3 yrs., 3 mos., 27 days
Howard Warren Hill 2/6/1902
Strother Clive Hill 5/1904
Vester Leon Hill 2/16/1906-12/18/1906, aged 10 mos., 2 days
Mary Jane Hardy m. 12/22/1845 William B. Hardy m. 3/25/1847
James W. Hardy m. 11/11/1854
Elizabeth M. Hardy m. 2/17/1853 George Strother Marie L. Hardy m. 1/5/1862
Maria L. Willoughby m. 8/27/1865
E. M. Strother m. L. M. Staples 11/10/1867 Candis Ethan Strother m. George Weaver 11/7/1880
J. W. Strother to M. A. Gardan? 2/8/1857
Marion Elizabeth Staples to L. F. Dennis 8/3/1898

Deaths

Susan Elizabeth Hardy 2/10/1822, aged 5 mos, 16 days
Sarah Elizabeth Louisa Jane Ellen Walker 3/15/1856
Mary Jane Walker 3/6/1856
Mary Jane Walker's infant 3/5/1856
John Ashmo Walker 3/19/1856
Elizabeth Ann Hardy 1/16/1877, aged 76 yrs., 10 mos., 7 days
James McG Hardy 7/10/1888, aged 91 yrs., 5 mos., 24 days
Lindsay H. Staples 6/1/1899, aged 69 yrs., 7 mos., 21 days
George Hardy Strother 6/3/1906
Olin Hardy 5/9/1892, aged 3 yrs., 5 mos., 27 days
George Hardy Strother 6/30/1906, aged 44 yrs., 10 mos.

179

(Hardy Bible continued...)

Elizabeth M. Hardy Staples 9/8/1908
George Oscar Weaver 1/11/1942, bur. Macomb, Okla. Cemetery
Candis Ethan Strother Weaver 8/13/1954, bur. Macomb, Okla.
Tomie Lavicil Hill 6/17/1922 at Rockmart, Ga.

Births

George O. Weaver 10/25/1856
Candis Ethan Strother Weaver 5/22/1863
George William Weaver 10/13/1851-11/17/1954, bur. near Napa, CA
Hubert Earl Weaver 3/7/1854-12/6/1942, bur. Sapulpa, Okla., South Heights Cemetery
Leon James Weaver 1/26/1887
Rupert Clive Weaver 3/1/1889-/24/1927, bur. near Peublo, Colorado
Herbert Lee Weaver 6/6/1891
Strother Ivan Weaver 11/10/1892
Ina May Weaver 8/24/1896
Lillie Faye Weaver 2/1/1899
Loyal Weaver 3/17/1901-8/8/1902, bur. Old Friendship Cemetery, south of Macomb and E of Tribby, Okla.
Mona LeVesta Weaver 10/30/1903

J. M. F. HAMMACK BIBLE of Chambers County, Alabama
Owner: Cumy Mammack Butts

Marriages

J. M. F. Hammack to Sarah E.Swint 12/17/1876
Emily Elizabeth Hammack to Wiley Crowder 12/28/1899
Sarah E. Hammack to Elmer Rutland 12/30/1900
Maggie Bess Hammack to Herbert Brown 12/15/1907
J. W. Hammack to Cora Butts 3/15/1908

Cumy Hammack to Charlie Butts 12/20/1908

Births

John Millard Fillmore Hammack 5/13/1852
Sarah E. Swint 7/15/1859
Sarah E. Hammack 11/8/1877
Joe Sidney Hammack 3/11/1887
Emily Elizabeth Hammack 3/4/1879
Essie Cumy Hammock 6/21/1890
John William Hammack 5/7/1880
Freddie Hammack 3/14/1804
Mary Lou Hammack 3/26/1882
Maggie Bess Hammack 5/3/1884
Jessie Jackson Hammack 1/16/1886

Deaths

John W. Hammack 4/17/1953
Joe Sidney Hammack 9/11/1887
J. M. F. Hammack 9/16/1926
Sarah E. Hammack 8/7/1912
A. W. W. Hammack 1/7/1819-10/24/1895
E. G. Hammack 11/9/1827-12/14/1883
Willie Swint m. Martha E. Hammack 12/15/1980

Births

Charlie Butts 7/18/1890
Horace Butts 1/25/1916

(J. M. F. Hammack Bible contd....)

Cumy Butts 6/21/1890
Wade Butts 6/14/1917
Ethel Butts 1/11/1911
Kathryn Butts 10/16/1922
Clara Butts 2/3/1913
Barnard Butts 4/15/1325

Marriages

Van Sparkman to Clara Butts 3/10/1936
Burnie Williams to Ethel Butts 7/11/1939
Garvin Lepard to Kathryn Butts 9/14/1940
Barnard Lee Butts to Monteen Fitzhugh 4/29/1945
Charlie Wade to Louise Norris 3/31/1947
Horace Butts d. 2/17/1934

ROBERT B. DAVIDSON BIBLE
Owner: Mrs. Den Cubbage, DAR, John Parke Custis Chaper
Birmingham, Alabama

Duke Williams b. 2/14/1768 m. 11/4/1790 Ede Williams, his wife, b. 9/6/1775
John Williams, their Ist son, b. 1/8/1792
Betty Williams b. 10/3/1733
Robert Harris Williams b. 10/10/1795
Christopher H. Williams b. ---

182

(Robert B. Davison Bible continued…)

Births

Hugh Davidson 1/5/1767
Jane Davidson 11/30/1777
Hugh Lawson Davidson 4/17/1814
Ede H. Davidson 4/25/1821
Robert H. Davidson, son of H. L. and E. H. Davidson, 7/7/1839
Robert M. Davidson, Jr., son of R. H. and L. B. Davidson, 10/14/1861
Robert D. Davidson 3/12/1817 Narcissa L. Harrison 5/12/1829
Eliza Harrison Davidson 3/14/1849 Hugh Davidson 6/18/1852
Robert P. Harrison 10/24/1787
Julia Harrison 3/4/1825
Eliza W. Harrison 10/3/1735
Robert P. Harrison Jr. 5/21/1827
John W. Harrison 9/6/1817
Narcissa L. Harrison 5/3/1829
Ann P. Harrison 4/12/1819
Robert P. Harrison 3rd, 1831
Ede Harris Harrison 4/24/1821
Duke Williams Harrison 11/14/1833
Lucinda H. Harrison 12/14/1822
Eliza W. Harrison 3/17/1837

Marriages

Robert P. Harrison to Eliza W. Williams 9/12/1816
Hugh Davidson to Jane Vance 5/24/1796
Hugh L. Davidson to Ede H. Harrison 4/24/1838
Robert M. Davidson to Sarah A. Drame 11/27/1860
Ervin J. Frierson to Ann P. Harrison 12/17/1833

(Robert B. Davison Bible continued...)

John W. Burton to Mary A. Frierson 11/24/1852
Robert B. Davidson to Narcissa L. Harrison 8/21/1843
Robert B. Davidson to Virginia S. Buchanan 3/16/1871 by Rev. S. R. Wilson, Pastor of Ist Presbyterian Church, Louisville, Ky., at Louisville Hotel in presence of: Thomas W. Buchanan, Miss Lettie Buchanan, Mr. and Mrs. William V. Mathews, and number of strangers
Hugh Davidson to Mollie H. Thompson 1/3/1893 at home of William T. Myers, by Rev. W. C. Clark

Deaths

Hugh Davidson 9/21/1841 Jane Davidson 1/12/1858
Mrs. Angelina Morgan, dau. of above, 8/16/1848
Mrs. Mary Davidson 10/29/1848
Ede H. Davidson 3/15/1858
Robert H. Davidson 6/21/1863
Robert P. Harrison 8/5/1843
Ervin J. Frierson 12/3/1849
Ann P. Frierson 5/7/1859

ERVIN J. FRIERSON BIBLE
DAR, John Parke Custis Chapter, Ala.

Births

Ervin J. Frierson 2/12/1805
Albert Frierson 2/6/1841
Ann P. Frierson 4/12/1819
Robert P. Frierson 5/23/1843
Mary A. Frierson 12/27/1834
Ervin J. Frierson 2d 9/17/1845
Eliza H. Frierson 2/28/1837

(Irvin J. Frierson Bible continued...)

John W. Frierson 9/13/1847
William Frierson 3/14/1838
Ervin J. Frierson 3rd 11/30/1849

Lavinia M. Burton, Ist child of J. W. and M. A. Burton b. 10/3/1853
Ervln F. Burton, 2nd child of J. W. and M. A. Burton b. 6/2/1855
Ann F. Burton, 3rd child of J. W. and M. A. Burton, b. 1859

Marriages

Ervin J. Frierson to Ann P. Harrison 12/17/1833
John W. Burton to Mary A. Frierson 11/24/1852
William Frierson to Lucy T. Smith 5/19/1865
Albert Frierson to Felicia B. Cowan 12/12/1865
R. P. Frierson to Mollie Little 12/5/1867

Deaths

Eliza Harrison Frierson 11/21/1839
Ervin James Frierson 2d 6/15/1848
Ervin James Frierson Ist 12/3/1849
Ervin James Frierson 3d 1/3/1851
Mrs. Ann P. Frierson 5/7/1859
William Frierson 7/27/1882
Albert Frierson 1/2/1886
R. P. Frierson 6/26/1893 at Waukesha, Wis.
John W. Frierson 8/23/1893
Mrs. Mary A. Burton 7/12/189-, b. 12/27/1835

OLIVER-GREEN BIBLE
Owner: Miss Ethel Blackmon, Eufaula, Alabama

James W. Oliver m. Susan Green 5/1/1836

Births

Susan Green 1/21/1808
Julyan Green Decatur 6/21/1829
Jane Green 10/23/1811
Nelly Green Culpepper 5/14/1831
Francis Green 1/4/1814
George W. Oliver 3/30/1842
Martha Green 2/18/1817
James F. Oliver 5/3/1852
Elsy Green 12/31/1825
William J. Oliver 4/22/1854
Maryann Green 8/17/1827

Deaths

George W. Oliver, Sr. 3/27/1836, aged 38 yrs.
James W. Oliver 5/25/1857, aged 52 yrs.
Mrs. Susan Oliver 10/12/1865, aged 57 yrs.

CORNELIUS P. HUNTER BIBLE
Owner: John Richard Hunter
Box 44, LaFayette, Alabama

Cornelius P. Hunter 4/24/1827-1/18/1902, aged 74 yrs., 8 mos., 24 days

Deaths

Malissa Susan Hunter 2/14/1835-4/15/1900, aged 65 yrs., 1 mo., 1 day

Births

William Lucious Hunter 8/30/1870
John Richard Hunter 8/21/1877
Dora Elvira Hunter 10/10/1872

Grandparents:

Elisha Hunter 8/2/1766-10/20/1826
Rebecca Hunter b. 5/15/1780

"They were of English descent and had two brothers that served all through the Revolution War"

Woodson Beard and Mary Beard were my Mother's parents. Woodson Beard was of Irish descent. William Alston Hunter 4/16/1902-1/31/1885, baptised by Elder Jessy Mercer and ordained to the Gospel Ministry 4/11/1841
Sophrona Massy Hunter 11/20/1807-2/14/1839
W. A. Hunter m. Sophrona M. Heard 4/13/1826
Cornelius Peeples Hunter b. 4/24/1827 Columbus
Vespacius Hunter b. 8/4/1833
Eleaser Elisha Hunter 10/19/1828-11/25/1869
Mary Ann Sophrona Hunter b. 2/22/1836
William Gustavus Hunter b. 5/11/1838

187

SARAH BRAMLETT BIBLE
Owner: Mrs. Edward George Longman
1900 S. Bayshore Lane, Coconut Grove, Florida

"Sarah Bramlet's dau., Elizabeth Bramlet, m. 1st a man named Jackson and 2nd, William Harris 1785-4/2/1860. William Harris and Elizabeth Bramlet Harris moved from S. C. to Ala. where he died. She moved to Georgia in 1893."

Births

Sarah Bramlett 1/22/1789
B. F. Bramlett 1/20/1820
Eliza Beth Harris 1/26/1806
Allay C. Cannon 5/23/1825
Malinday Kilgore 4/25/1816
Sarah A. Kilgore 7/6/1840
Garlington Barksher 1/15/1818
A. A. B. Kilgore 2/23/1848
William E. Bramlett 1/20/1820

C. B. HARRISON BIBLE
Panhandle-Plains Historical Museum, Canyon, Texas

Marriages

C. B. Harrison to Nancy Towns 5/1471815. "I started to move from Georgia 1/13/1819 and arrived in Alabama 26th of said month.
W. T. Harrison to Emily T. Harrison 3/15/1859
Ada L. Matthewson to Carter D. Harrison 2/11/1904

(D. B. Harrison Bible continued...)

Births

Joel T. Harrison 9/15/1816
C. B. Harrison 2/14/1788
Benjamin Harrison 10/19/1818
Ann Elizabeth Martin 10/25/1843
William Harrison 1/5/1821
William H. Harrison 3/2/1848
Martha Ann Harrison 2/22/1823
Wiley Harrison 12/8/1849
Nancy Harrison 3/4/1825
Joseph P. Harrison 8/7/1852
Carter Braxton Harrison 8/18/1829
Ella Jane Harrison 11/4/1854
Nancy Towns 9/8/1797
Ann Elizabeth Martin 10/25/1843
Lenora Carolina Martin 6/5/1845
Charles Washington Martin 10/24/1846
Martha Peyton Martin 7/31/1848
Hicksey Hall Martin Jr. 5/7/1855
Eulalie Elizabeth Harrison 8/13/1855
Willie Harrison 7/19/1861

Deaths

Benjamin Harrison 7/12/1815
Paschal Harrison 9/16/1828
Joel Towns 12/28/1815
Young Gresham 6/1821
Benjamin Harrison Jr. 3/23/1818

(B. B. Harrison Bible continued...)

John Love 1822
Jane Harrison 6/1815
Lacy Love 1825
Albert and ---ham March and April, 1834
Patsey Booth 9/30/1817
Martha Harrison Sr.? 7/21/1831
Joel T. Harrison 8/28/1858
Anna Towns 3/26/1835
Nancy E. Bryan 5/26/1859
Hicksey Hall Harrison 12/19/1844
Martha A. Foster 8/21/1859
Nancy Harrison, consort of C. B. Harrison Sr. 2/11/1862
B. Harrison, 11/7/1848
W. T. Harrison 6/3/1889
Thomas P. Martin 7/23/1840
Charles W. Harrison 5/7/1900
Lenora? G. Martin 6/24/1849
Emily T, Harrison 1/19/1914
William Towns 7/24/1853
Carter Braxton Harrison Jr. 6/1856
N. Tallulah Harrison, dau. of William and Emily Harrison, 7/23/1877

Births

William T. Harrison 1/5/1821
Emily T. Harrison 12/13/1835

Children of William T. and Emily T. Harrison

Willie T. Harrison 7/10/1861

190

(D. B. Harrison Bible continued...)

Nancy T. Harrison 12/28/1873
Charles W. Harrison 8/13/1863
Hicksey W. Harrison 3/5/1877
Mary A. Harrison 2/18/1870

Deaths

Willie T. Harrison DeArmon 2/5/1944
Carter Draxton Harrison 8/31/1946
Mary Ann Harrison Garner 3/31/1352
Don F. Garner, husband of Mary Ann Garner, 7/23/1950

TOWERS-DUPONT-LONGWORTH BIBLE
Owner: Mrs. A. J. Trulock, Sr., Climax, Georgia

Births

Isaac Auld Towers 5/23/1818 near Cincinnati, Ohio
Robert Rumney Towers 2/26/1820 near Cincinnati, Ohio
Sophia Christianna Towers 12/31/1821 near Cincinnati, Ohio
Joseph Henry DuPont, son of Charles and Mary Ann DuPont, 10/17/-in Quincy, Gadsden Co., Fla.
Archibald Longworth, son of Edward and Eliza Longworth, 10/21/1829 in Beaufort Dist., S. C.
Eliza Frances, dau. of Charles H. and Mary Ann DuPont, 12/20/1832 at "Sweet Home", the plantation near Quincy, Fla.

Marriages

George Morton Towers to Frances DuPont 6/19/1817 in Beaufort Dist., S. C. by Rev. John Crawford of same place

191

(Towers-Dupont-Longworth Bible continued...)

Charles Henry DuPont to Mary Ann Hobson in Greene Co., Ala. 11/6/1825
Edward M. Longworth to Eliza Frances DuPont 12/11/1828 in Gadsden Co., Fla.
Joseph Marrion DuPont to Sarah T. Rains 5/1828, Twiggs Co., Ga.
N. B., Charles, Joseph and Eliza are the children of Frances DuPont or Frances Towers.

Deaths

Sophia Christianna Towers, dan. of George M. and Frances Towers, 6/24/1823 in City of Augusta, Ga.

WILLIAM VAUGHN BIBLE
Owner: Louise L. Cameron, Havana, Ark.

Marriages

William Vaughn to Hannah House 2/15/1815
Thomas P. Cameron to Martha A. Vaughn 12/27/1857

Births

William Vaughn 11/14/1783-5/11/1856
Hannah 9/26/1797-10/1/1870, 73 yrs., 5 days
Asa Vaughn 11/13/1815
 Mary E. Vaughn 4/5/1830
Willis Vaughn 1/26/1817
Nancy Vaughn 10/27/1831
Clayton Vaughn 12/7/1818
Allen J. Vaughn 9/5/1834
Jeremiah Vaughn 11/1/1820
Thomas W. Vaughn 5/25/1837

(William Vaughn Bible continued...)

Delilah Vaughn 3/13/1822
Martha A. Vaughn 11/17/1842
Sintha Vaughn 12/2/1823
Louise L. Cameron 12/24/1867
Jarret Vaughn 4/26/1826
Barnabas C. Cameron 11/23/1869
William A. Vaughn 10/24/1828

Deaths

Jeremiah Vaughn 6/7/1856
Thomas W. Vaughn 12/12/1837
Sintha Vaughn 5/21/1852
Martha A. Cameron 1/30/1831
Mary E. Molly 10/11/1856

W. S. TRIMBLE BIBLE
Owner: Mrs. Matthew Burns
2207 11th Ave., Phenix City, Ala. 36867

W. S. Trimble m. Julia J. Rollins 2/3/1870

W. S. Trimble 5/15/1850-12/23/1938
Julia J. Trimble 12/1/1853-1/30/1941
Matilda Ann Trimble 4/25/1871-12/11/1872
James Milton Trimble 2/6/1873
John Newton Trimble 4/8/1875-6/20/1903
William Franklin Trimble 3/31/1877-1/1/1933
Robert Lemuel Trimble 4/9/1879
Julia Viola Trimble 11/1/1851-2/5/1910 m. Herrin

(W. S. Trimble Bible continued...)

David Sidney Trimble 3/30/1884
Jinnia Leonia Trimble 10/20/1886
Jesey Theodora Trimble 5/20/1890
Little Albertia Trimble 3/29/1899

ADAM JORDAN FILES' BIBLE of Macon Co., Alabama
Owner: Sarah Emma Cox, Tuskegee, Ala.

Marriages

Adam Jordan Files to Mary Baskins 4/30/1790
William Baskins to Ann Reid 3/2/1769
William Franklin Wilkerson to Malissa A. Alley 11/26/1868

Births

Adam Jordan Files 3/16/1762-8/11/1840, 78 yrs., 4 mos. 26 days
Mlary Baskin Files 10/5/1769-12/25/1840, 71 yrs., 2 mos., 20 days
Ann Reid Files 9/2/1792
Elizabeth Baskin Files ---
Charlie Mitchell Wilkerson 5/18/1570-7/3/1876
Willie Zarah Wilkerson 1/8/1874-10/14/1875
William Baskins 2/14/1737
Ann Reid 12/25/1747

Deaths

Rossannah C. Bradberry 10/12/1834

MARY EUNICE YOUNG BIBLE

Births

Mary Eunice Harrison 11/2/1829, dau. of Sterling E. Harrison and his wife
Brooke William Young 10/12/1822
William Derry Young, son of D. W. and M. E. Young, 9/23/1865, Lowndes Co., Ala.
Hilda Johnson 10/21/1885

Marriages

B. W. Young to Mary Eunice Harrison 3/27/1851
William Derry Young to Hilda Johnson 11/4/1914

Deaths

Mary Eunice Young 4/26/1902 William Derry Young 4/21/1921

MARY GOODSON McKINZIE BIBLE

Mary Goodson, dau. of James and Jane Goodson, b. 8/9/1792

Births of Children of John and Mary McKinzie

Lucinda McKinzie 4/3/1814
Melvina McKinzie 1/15/1824
Elias G. McKinzie 4/29/1815
Minerva McKinzie 12/27/1825
Mary Ann McKinzie -/7/1816
Roderick McKinzie 5/7/1827
James Henry McKinzie 11/11/1817
Harriett Catherine McKinzie 1/11/1829

(Mary Goodson McKinzie Bible continued...)

Senthey Jane McKinzie 5/30/1818
John McKinzie 3/19/1820
Wm Goodson Tipton McKinzie 2/19/1831
Dianna McKinzie 1821
Charles McKinzie 7/11/1822
Polly Jane McKinzie 5/4/1833

WILLIAM LOU WYNNE BIBLE
Owner: Mrs. James Richard Batsell
824 W. Doca Chica Blvd., Brownsville, Texas

Marriages

William Lou Wynne to Helen Mary Robinson 1/21/1844 Erie, Green Co., A.a.
Edward Harper Wynne to Mazri Claire Vaughan
Mazri Vaughan Wynne to Joddie Martin Roberson
Wynne Martin Roberson to Maidel Frederick
Walter Vaughan Roberson to Janet Kerlin
Loddell Louise Roberson to James Richard Batsell 9/3/1940 at Temple, Bell Co., Texas

Births

William Lou Wynne, son of William Lou and Eleanor Wynne, 1/7/1810
Columbia Co., Ga.
Helen Mary Robinson, dau. of George and Mary M. Robinson, 1/1/1025 in Erie, Green Co., Ala.

Children of William Lou and Helen Mary Wynne

George William Lou Wynne 2/11/1846- Green Co., Ala
Walter Herndon Wynne 7/4/1849 Green Co.; Ala.
Eva Magruder Wynne 12/17/1852, Walker Co., Texas

196

(William Lou Wynne Bible, contd....)

Helen Mittie Wynne 12/16/1855, Walker Co., Texas
Edward Harper Wynne 1/7/1858, Walker Co., Texas
Eleanor Robinson Wynne 7/7/1862, Walker Co., Texas
Evline Sara Wynne 7/2/1865, Walker Co., Texas

Children of Edward Harper and Mazri Claire Wynne:

Howell Edward Harper   Edward Harper
Mazri Vaughan Harper

Children of Mazri Vaughan and Loddie Martin Roberson

Wynne Martin Roberson   Walter Vaughan Roberson 7/22/1826
Loddell Louise Roberson

Deaths

Walter Hurdon Wynne, son of William Lou and Helen M. Wynne, 9/4/1867, Green Co., Ala.
Pa 2/5/1U95
George 2/1889
Nora 8/16/1895
Alva 6/6/1906

HENRY UPSON SIMS
Protective Life Bldg., Birmingham, Ala.

Births

Guy Smith, Sr. -/19/1729-3/25/1787   Salley S. Mitchell 2/15/1781
Jacob Mitchell 5/19/1745   Zachariah Sims 7/13/1775
Mrs. Elizabeth Mitchell 11/14/1763
Zachariah Sims m. Salley S. Mitchell 9/9/1801
Willam Henry R. Sims 9/24/1802

197

(Henry Upson Sims Bible continued...)

Ann Sims 7/10/180-
James Sanders Sims 12/26/1803
John 6/9/1808-7/25/1808

Deaths

Ann D. Sims 1/7/1827
Mrs. Sarah Mitchell Sims 2/1826
Mrs. Elizabeth Swepton Molloy 8/6/1828
Joseph M. Molloy 8/15/1829, aged 30 yrs.
Joseph Moore Molloy and Elizabeth Swepton Mitchell m. 1/13/1818 by Rev. Lovick Pierce

BURWELL NORWOOD BIBLE
N. C. State Library

Births of Children of Burwell and Elizabeth Clover Norwood

John G. Norwood 1/11/1823
William Norwood 12/7/1812
Nathaniel Norwood 7/17/1824
Benjamin G. Norwood 12/22/1813
Letitia Jane Norwood 9/16/1826
Elizabeth Norwood 7/21/1815
Henry G. Norwood 2/1/1828
James W. Norwood 7/21/1816
Richard Weaver Norwood 4/8/1830
Burwell G. Norwood 12/12/1818
Joseph L. Norwood 7/28/1832
Mary Ann Frances Norwood 4/22/1820
Martha Jane Norwood 3/30/1833

(Burwell Norwood Bible, contd....)

Births

Martha C. Whits 3/7/1833
Ella T. Norwood 2/18/1865
Laura Emma Norwood 9/14/1855
Thomas E. Norwood 2/13/1868
Anna P. Norwood 2/4/1857
Susie I. Galey 3/12/1847
John William Norwood 5/25/1859
Richard W. Norwood Jr. 12/22/1862

Marriages

Richard Weaver Norwood to Martha C. White 1/19/1854 at home of Robert M. White, Moulton, Ala.
M. B. Rutherford to Ella T. Norwood 12/3/1886, Moulton, Ala.
Richard W. Norwood Jr. to Mollie Alexander 1885
Thomas E. Norwood to Minnie V. Bracken 2/22/1892, Town Creek, Ala.
Richard W. Norwood, Sr. to Susie I. Galey 9/29/1886
Mary Alice Norwood and Oscar W. Sherer 10/14/1920, Wheeler, Ala.
Burwell Norwood to Elizabeth Glover 11/10/1810
Anna P. Norwood to Thomas J. Holland 11/14/1910

Deaths

Richard Weaver Norwood 1/1906
Susie Galey Norwood 1/17/1929
Martha W. Norwood 7/17/1885
Minnie Bracken 5/22/1944
Laura E. Norwood 9/25/1857
Mack Rutherford 12/3/1999

199

(Burwell Norwood Bible, contd....)

Anna Norwood Holland 5/2/1828
John W. Norwood 9/10/1859
Richard W. Norwood Jr. 11/11/1933
Joe Lipscomb 1/1/1886
Elizabeth Glover Norwood 5/1866
Mollie Alexander Norwood 3/25/1945 in Texas
Burwell Norwood 11/1839, Trinity, Ala.

CHARLES MADISON THETFORD BIBLE
Owner: Mrs. C. M. Thetford, Columbus, Ga.

Births

Dr. Jack Norris 1805 Chambers Co., Ala.-1869 m. Kathrine Pratt 1812-1886
Y. C. Norris 1840-1914, aged 74 yrs.
Fannie Joe Lloyd, dan. of Benjamin Lloyd and Noami Cox, 8/19/1854, m. 12/1871 Y. C. Norris
Ever Morris 11/22/1872 m. 8/4/1892 Harris Co., Ga., Charles Madison Thetford b. 2/9/1869

Births of Children of Ever and Charles Madison Thetford

Louise Eunice 7/31/1892 -
Florrie Ira 8/17/1900
Zula 3/31/1895
Kathleen Zenobia 8/14/1906
Charles Maud 11/24/1996
Jeffie Elizabeth 7/17/1908

OROON DATUS WHITAKER BIBLE
Owner: Mrs. Reuben A. Garland, Atlanta, Georgia

His grandfather was - John Whitaker, and his grandmother was Olive Taylor of Virginia - and their children were: Edward, Hudson, Thomas, Samuel Taylor, Margaret Olive, and Martha

Samuel Taylor Whitaker was Oroon Datus Whitaker Sr.'s father He m. Elizabeth Williams and their children:

Winfred Mary Whitaker 1739?-9/1871
Oroon Datus Whitaker 4/14/1791-10/26/1842
Katherine B. Whitaker 12/2/1793-4/1863
Elizabeth Carr Whitaker 3/1797-7/1850

His grandfather on his mother's side was Richard Williams. He m. Elizabeth Carr. Their Children: Charles, Elisha, Lawrence, Lucy and Elizabeth

Elizabeth Williams was Oroon D. Whitaker's mother
Winfred M. Whitaker was second wire of Eli Harris, Sr. of Putnam Co., Ga.; they m. 1819. Her bro., Whitaker m.   her step-dau., Martha Rivers Harris

Katherine Boykin Whitaker m. Major John Brodnax
Elizabeth Carr Whitaker m. James Gray
John T. S. Whitaker d. unmd
The following are the ancestors of my mother - the oldest dau. of Major Eli Harris, Sr.:

Eli Harris was son of Thomas Harris and Mary Baker. They were m. in Ireland 4/20/1763

Thomas Harris b. 6/4/1739
Mary Baker, his wife, b. 5/5/1744

(Oroon D. Whitaker Bible, contd....)

Births of Children of Thomas and Mary D. Harris

Elizabeth Harris 7/3011764 1
Justus Harris 4/14-/1773
Samuel Baker Harris 7/30/1765

Eli Harris 8/18/1775
Martha Harris 9/29/1767
Thomas McCall Harris 10/10/1777
Margaret Harris 8/9/1769
Gabriel Harris 8/4/1780
Sarah Harris 2/3/1772
Laird Clark Harris 2/24/1754

JOHN PEARSON BIBLE
DAR Records, Ga. State Archives

Births

John Pearson, son of John and Mary, 5/30/1743 Sarah Raiford, dau. of Philip and Judith,
5/26/1745 Martha Pearson, dan. of John and Sarah, 11/2/1766
Mary F. Pearson (McKamle) 1/30/1768
John Pearson 3/7/1770
Sarah P. Pearson (Elkin) 3/7/1773
William Pearson 11/5/1775
Martha Pearson 3/18/1778
Philip Raiford Pearson 3/24/1780
Grace Pearson 10/2/1782
Judith Pearson 1/16/1785
Ann Pearson 2/16/1788

(John Pearson Bible continued...)

Marriages

John Pearson to Sarah Raiford 5/21/1765

Deaths

Mary Pearson McKamie 9/19/1824
Mary Pearson McKamie 11/6/1820
John Pearson 10/25/1919

DAVID LANIER BIBLE of Notasulga
(Bible burned with home in 1925)

Father's Grandparents - David Lanier 1/7/1791 Rockingham Co., North Carolina-1/6/1854 Notasulga, Macon Co., Alabama
Rachel Watt Lanier ca 1790 or 1735-1890 Notasulga, Alabama

Father's Parents - George Washington Lanier 4/27/1818 Walker Co., Alabama - 8/31/1857 Chambers Co., Alabama
Elizabeth Gordon Hutchinson Lanier 4/11/1819 Montgomery, Alabama9/10/1881 Sardis, Mississippi

Parents - George Gordon Lanier 3/24/1854 Tuskegee, Alabama 2/3/1925 Rome, Georgia
Lola May Robertson Lanier 10/4/1853 Denton, Alabama - 2/16/1811 Birmingham, Alabama

203

ROBERT AND MARGARET RANKINS' BIBLE
From: Rev. War Pension #W26365

Births of Children or Robert and Margaret Rankins

Thomas B. Rankins 5/17/1783
John K. Rankins 1/-5/1791
Elizabeth Rankins 1/27/1785
James Rankins 6/27/1792
William M. Rankins 8/24/1786
Frederick Rankins 2/15/1794
Joseph Rankins 11/4/1788
Henry Rankins 2/7/1796

Note: Robert Rankins applied for pension 7/26/1828, aged 78, Washington Co., Alabama; in 1802 lived Logan Co., Ky. Soldier d. 11/1 (or 30)/1837 Lt. Landry Parish, La. Thomas D. Rankins was killed at battle of Ft. Meus in 1813. William M. Rankins lived Montgomery Co., Texas in 1844 and Frederick Rankins in Folk Co., Texas. In 1546 William Butler testified that John K. Rankins m. 1815 or 1816 a sister of his. 3/22/1844 Margaret (Peggy) Rankins, widlw, applied from Liberty Co., Texas, stating she was b. 2/16/1756 and m. Robert Rankins 10/1/1781 in Frederick Co., Va. Her maiden name was Margaret Berry. They had 7 boys and 3 girls, six of whom are alive.

THOMAS REDMOND FOSTER BIBLE
Owner: Octavia ,Yaeffer Butt Foster, Mobile, Alabama

Thomas Redmond Foster, son of James Robert Foster and Elizabeth Fairfax, b. Occoquan, Prince William Co., Virginia 10/3/1832 m. Octavia Kaeffer, dau. of Cary Wyld and Ann Lichmael
Nicholson Forsyth Butt, b. 12/13/1835 NorEolk, Virginia m. 3/6/1860 Mobile, Alabama

(Thomas Redmond Foster Bible continued...)

Births of Children of Thomas R. and Octavia K. Foster
Little Seawell Foster 1/5/1862 Mobile, Alabama

Ann Butt Foster 12/20/1863 Mobile, Ala.-9/8/1883 Warrenton, Va.
son 2/8/1868 Mobile, Alabama
James Fairfax Foster 6/18/1874 Mobile, Alabama
Thomas Redmond Foster Sr. d. 4/7/1877 Mobile, Ala.
Mary Gaines Foster d. 4/12/1861 Mobile, Alabama
infant son d. 2/17/1861 Mobile, Alabama
James Fairfax Foster d. 7/8/1875 Mobile, Alabama

WILLIAM JONES BIBLE

Births

William Jones 12/26/1811
Sarah Rogers 11/12/1819

Their Children, all b. Monroe Co., Ala.:

Ann Eliza Jones 6/25/1841
John Thomas Jones 7/16/1849
Harrison Jones 5/16/1843
Madison Jones 5/27/1852
Sarah Jane Jones 4/16/1845
Wm Andrew Jones 10/19/1859
Abner Jackson Jones 6/21/1847
Jeremiah Davis Jones 3/24/1857

(William Jones Bible, contd....)

Marriages

William Jones to Sarah Rogers 12/19/1839
William King Booth to Ann Eliza Jones 10/7/1863 in Second Methodist Church, Montgomery, Ala.
Eugene Thomas Booth to Annie Grace Hannah of Thomaston, Ga., only dau. of Dr. G. W. T. Hannah, 7/10/1901 in Talbotton, Ga., by Rev. Morrison of Methodist Church
William King Booth to Eliza Jones 10/7/1863 in Montgomery, Ala., came to Atlanta, Ga. immediately.

Births of Children of William King Booth and Ann Eliza Jones

Julia E. Booth 7/1864 Atlanta, Ga. m. John F.Hobbs 6/4/1884 of S. C., later N. Y.
Walter Booth m. Agnes Gallagher 12/16/1891
Henry Harrison Booth 9/7/1866
Walter Henry Booth 12/19/1867
Willie Eugene Booth 7/12/1870
Lillie Booth 9/18/1872
Eugene Thomas Booth 9/18/1874

Births of Children of Thomas Booth and Annie Grace Hannah in Thomaston, Ga.

John Hannah Booth 10/8/1903
William Telford Booth 8/21/1805
William Jones and Sarah Rogers Jones refugeed from Monroe Co., Ga. to Montgomery, Ala.
William King Booth d. --
Ann Eliza Booth d. 12/31/1930, aged 90 yrs.

JOHN COLLINS' BIBLE
Owner: E. S. Drake, Ft. Gibson, MS
Births

John Collins 5/26/1786
Matthew Collins 3/8/1795
Sofia Valentine Collins 1/5/1787
Juda Collins 3/8/1795
Silas Collins 11/4/1791
Silvy Collins 5/2/1797
Mozely Collins 5/5/1795
Pat Collins 2/2/1739
James Perry Collins 9/15/1797
Sabina Collins 11/20/1800
Benjamin Michael Collins 9/11/1800
 Luci Collins 7/14/1803
William Collins 12/14/1804
Cherry Collins 7/14/1803
Edmund Collins 5/21/1807
Tamoe Collins 11/10/1805
Orrlan Collins 1/6/1755
Sam Collins 11/10/1805
James Collins 3/17/1792
Clary Collins 11/20/1811

NICHOLAS L. HOWARD BIBLE of Russell Co.
(Microfilm, Ga. State Archives)

Marriages

Nicholas L. Howard to Elizabeth Abercrombie, Russell Co., Ala. 8/5/1841, by Rev. Dr. Lovick Pierce
William Sidney Howard, son of Nicholas L. Howard to Susan J. Browning West 12/16/1850, Thomas Co., Ga.
Anderson Lee, son of William Sidney Howard to Ann Lucas Walker 10/6/1918, Cochran, Ga.

Births

Nicholas Lawrence Howard 1/24/1815 Greensboro Elizabeth, his wife, 11/30/1819 Sparta, Ga.
William Sidney Howard --/22/1842 Russell Co., Ala. ---
Elizabeth Howard -/30/1844 Columbua, Ga.
Anna Mary Howard 1/13/1846 Columbus, Ga.
John Lawrence Howard 12/31/1847 Columbus, Ga.
Anderson Howard 4/23/1850 Wynnton, Ga.
Julia Howard 4/18/1552 Wynnton, Ga.
Augustus Howard 7/6/1854 Wynnton, Ga.
Sarah Howard 3/4/1856 Wynnton, Ga.
Josephine Howard 4/13/1859 Wynnton, Ga.
Florida Howard 5/26/1862 Wynnton, Ga. Nicholas Howard 8/10/1863 Wynnton, Ga.

Births of Children of William Sidney Howard

Julia Corinne Howard 12/11/1881-5/16/1886
Anderson Lee Howard 3/14/1883
William Sidney Howard, Jr. 7/13/1856 m. 12/1920 Cora Japy
Annie Elizabeth Howard 3/11/1892 m. 10/12/1932 J. Truman Holland
Ann Walker Howard, Wife of Anderson Lee Howard, 4/27/1888

(Nicholas Howard Bible, Births, contd....)

Births of Children of Anderson Lee Howard, Jr. b. 1883)
Anderson Lee Howard, Jr. 8/25/1921 Cochran, Ga.
James Walton Howard 4/1/1923 Cochran, Ga.
Thomas Sidney Howard 1/7/1928 Cochran, Ga.
Virginia Ann Howard 2/2/1948 Cochran, Ga.
Anderson Lee Howard III 12/13/1949
Wallace Harris Howard 1/15/1952

Deaths

Nicholas, son of Nicholas L. Howard and Elizabeth, 9/10/1855

Sidney Howard 5/20/1903
Nicholas L. Howard 7/22/1879
John L. Howard 9/28/1303
Florida Howard 1/4/1881
Julia U. McGregor 2/11/1901
Augustus Howard 6/23/1858
Josephine Howard 6/2/1913
Anderson Howard 5/30/1895
Anna H. Sarelson 9/5/1927
Elizabeth Howard 11/20/1892
Mary H. Newman 2/22/1924

209

MATILDA BALEY'S BIBLE

Owner: Mrs. William Roy Holloway
Fish Pond Rd., Alexander City, 813.

Marriages

William Holloway to Matilda 7/4/1815
James Ransom to Julia Holloway 12/10/1829
James Britton to Saleta 3/26/1835
James F. Giles to Serena 7/13/1837
James Ransom to Julia 12/10/1829
Martha Holloway b. 11/11/---

Births

Julia Holloway 12/7/1813
Wm Rabon Holloway 11/4/1820
Saleta Holloway 1/7/1817
Sophronia Amanda Holloway
Surrency Holloway 8/11/1822
Surrency Holloway 12/24/1818
Sarah Ann Hendrick 2/24/1829

Deaths

Sabra Holloway, 1st wife of William Holloway, bur. 3/25/1814, d. 24th
Elbert Galeton Holloway b. 9/26/1824
Sarah A. Holloway, 1st wife of William R. Holloway, b. 8/1822 m. 2/1847, bur. 5/1847
Sarah Ann Hendrick b. 2/24/18181(1829)

(Matilda Baley's Bible contd....)

Births

James Baley 4/21/185-
Nancy Caroline Baley 6/29/1830
Eliza Baley 8/25/189-
William R. Holloway 11/4/1820-2/1/1893

Amanda Cophalia Holloway 10/11/1849
Lucien Lafayette Holloway 3/18/1851
Arbert Jarrell Holloway 1/14/1853
Lemuel Eugenius Holloway 5/7/1854
William Joseph Holloway 6/11/1856
James Marion Holloway 4/15/1858
Sarah Amanda Holloway 11/24/1859
Raburn Alonza Holloway 5/3/1564-8/6/1864

James Britton 1/3/1812
Seleta Britton 1/13/1817

Their Children:

James M. Britton 6/13/1838
William Holloway d. 1/26/1826

Births of Children of Samuel Holloway and Rebekah

Hannah Speirs Holloway 3/18/1765
Sara S. Holloway 2J27/1774
Isham Holloway 6/14/1766

211

Rebekah Holloway 2/22/1775
Samuel Holloway 12/12/1767
Nancy Holloway 9/29/1777
John Holloway 9/8/1769
Elizabeth Holloway 6/25/1779
John Holloway 3/8/1769
Joseph Holloway 3/24/1782
Jesse Holloway 3/1/1771
William Holloway 1/20/1797
Judith Holloway 12/10/1772
Polly Holloway 8/26/1791

ANTHONY W. MOSELEY BIBLE of Norrisville, Alabama

Marriages

Anthony W. Mosely of Morrisville, Ala. to Mary F. Skinner of Morrisville, Ala. 7/16/1867
W. S. Moselcy to Martha P. Bacon 1/4/1827
Elizabeth C. Moseley to William Troublefield 9/22/1849

Births

Washington Bacon, son of Richard and Mary Bacon, 11/8/1799

Martha Bacon 3/9/1805
Elizabeth C. Moseley 9/1/1827
Anthony W. Moseley 11/14/1841
Martha R. Moseley 10/2/1835
Fanny P. Moseley 10/10/1869
Thomas S. Moseley 3/19/1837

(Anthony W. Moseley Bible continued…)

Murry Smith Moseley 11/30/1871
James P. Moseley 4/17/1845
Nannie Moseley 5/3/1875
Mary T. Moseley 11/21/1842
Clara 0. Moseley -/4/1879

Deaths

Richard Bacon, son of Lyddall and Mary, 12/5/1832, aged 73 yrs.
Ann Bacon, dau. of John and Mary and wife of Richard Bacon, 7/8/1928, aged 64 yrs.
Martha P. Bacon 11/24/1851
Elizabeth C. Moseley 8/22/1850
Thomas S. Moseley 12/14/1860
Martha R. Moseley 1/3/1882
William S. Moseley 11/15/1866
Anthony Waddy Moseley 2/25/1922
Fanny P. Moseley 12/22/1869
Murry Smith Moseley 7/22/1574

CORNELIUS PEEPLES HUNTER BLBLE
Owner: Richard Hunter, Lafayette, Alabama

Cornelius Peeples Aunter b. 4/24/1829
Malissa Susan Boyd b. 2/24/1835 m. 11/28/1850
Cornelius Peeples and Malissa Susan Hunter were united with the Baptist Church of Christ at County Line 8/16/1852

Births of Their Children

Thomas Sparks Hunter 11/5/1854--
Malissa Cunny Hunter 9/5/1867

(Cornelius Peeples Hunter Bible, Births, contd....)

Cornelius Alonzo Hunter 7/5/1857
Wm Lucious Hunter 8/30/1970
Joseph Peeples Hunter 7/10/1859
Dora Elvira Hunter 10/10/1872
Emer Davis Hunter 7/6/1861
John Richard Hunter 8/21/1877

Record of Negroes:

Martha Ann 10/19/1851
Thee 2/1/1862 George 6/1/1855
Ann 5/22/1862

HUGH THOMSON BIBLE
Owner: Mrs. Margaret Hall Sturgis
Belmont, Massachusetts

"The record written by my dear father, Hugh Thomson, having been destroyed, I, their daughter, Margaret, from a smaller Bible transcribe the family record."

Margaret Boggs m. Hugh Thomson 12/1/1831

Births of Children of Margaret and Hugh Thomson

Margaret Thomson 11/25/1831
Robert Thomson 2/20/1834
James Thomson 2/20/1834-8/9/1835
Benjamin Thomson 7/1/1840-7/11/1843, aged 3 yrs., 11 days
Jane Thomson 8/8/1842
Hugh Thomson 1/4/1845-d. in few hours Emily Thomson 9/12/1847

(Hugh Thomson Bible continued...)

Deaths

Hugh Thomson 12/29/1848 in New Orleans, aged 43 yrs, bur.
Cyrpress Grove Cemetery, New Orleans, #635 is his vault
Our dear Uncle Francis W. Boggs 4/1/1859, bur. 100 miles below Eastport and abt 200 yrs. from where George Colbert sank
Jane Thomson 10/5/1898
My dear mother, Margaret Boggs Thomson, 1/13/1899
My dear sister, Margaret Thomson Brock, 7/23/1905
Emily Thomson 1915 in Ellswocth, Maine, bur Florence, Ala.
Margaret Thomson m. James Brock, M. D. 1869
Margaret Hugh Brock 2/27/1870-6/6/1945, Ellsworth Falls, Maine
James Lydian Brock 12/4/1872-12/4/1856
Margaret Hugh m. Henry Martyn Hall 8/19/1891
Henry Martyn Hall, our baby b. 8/9/1892-d. 5/13/1834
James Lydian Brock m. 1907 Norma Brown, dau. of Dr. Hardie Brown
James Lydian Brock, Jr. b. 12/10/1908
Robert Brown Brock 7/26/1910-12/23/1966
Julia Brock b. 1/24/1914
Norma Brown Brock d. 12/12/1956

JOHN SHOWELL ALLEN BIBLE
Owner: Miss Ruth Allen, Birmingham, Ala.

John Showell Allen 9/19/1788-2/7/1855 m. 6/30/1814 Miss Ruth Linton, 12/21/1795-2/4/1835, dau. of Samuel Lin ton , Esq., in Abbeville Dist., S. C., at Mt. Pleasant, at res. of Esq. Linton

Births of Their Children

Caroline Elizabeth Allen 3/23/1815, Abbeville, S. C., Rocky River
Mary Amanda Allen 8/20/1816, Abbeville, S. C., Rocky River
Samuel Linton Allen 9/15/1818, Abbeville, S. C., Rocky River
Alexander Arva Allen 5/10/1821, Abbeville, S. C. Rocky River
George Washington Allen 3/2/1823, Abbeville. S. C. Rocky River
Laurinda Clarke Allen 4/5/1825
Lewis Wardlaw Allen 2/15/1831
Ruth Linton Allen 2/4/1835

ZACHARIAH SIMS' BIBLE
Owner: Henry Upson Sims
Protective Life Bldg., Birmingham, Ala.

Births

Jacob Mitchell 5/19/1748
Amanda Swepston Sims 3/11/1819
Elizabeth Mitchell 11/11/1753
Edward Mitchell Sims 6/7/1822
Zachariah Sims 7/13/1775
David Mitchell 5/19/1748
Sally S. Mitchell 2/15/1781
Elizabeth Mitchell 4/3/1778
William Henry Sims 12/26/1803

William Mitchell 3/31/1783
Anne D. Sims 7/10/1807
Anne Mitchell 4/1/1785
John Alexander Sims 6/9/1805
John Smith Mitchell 8/22/1757
Ferdinand Sims 7/7/1809
Edward Mitchell 7/1790
Elizabeth Smith Sims 12/15/1813
Isaac Mitchell 2/5/1793
Sarah Mitchell Sims 3/5/1817
Elizab. Sweptson Mitchell 1797
William H. Sims, son of James S. and A. B. Sims, 7/31/1837
John G. Sims 2/26/1840
Sallie A. M. Sims 8/23/1850
Henry P. de Veuve 7/26/1831 in Parish of West Feliciana, La., eldest son of Julia Prentiss and Daniel de Veuve of Neufchatel, Switzerland
Laura, eldest dau. of F. Sims, 9/11/1838, Vicksburg, Mississippi
Henry Potter de Veuve 3/23/1858, eldest son of Laura Sims & Henry de Veuve 12/15/1859 Galveston, Tx.
Prentiss de Veuve 12/15/1859, son of Laura and Henry de Veuve

Marriages

Zachariah Sims to Sarah Smith Mitchell 9/9/1801
James S. Sims to Amanda B. Moore 5/24/1832
Laura Sims to Henry de Veuve 7/7/1857 in Galveston, Texas at res. of Ferninand Sims, Esq., the bride's father
"The mother of Zach Sims was Anna Howard, dau. of John Howard of N. C. 1884."

(Zachariah Sims Bible continued...)

Deaths

Mrs. Sarah S. Sims 2/18/1826
Mrs. Eliza S. Molloy 8/6/1825
Mrs. Anne B. Sims 7/7/1827
Edward M. Sims 7/13/1835-the day his father was 60 yrs. old
John Gerdine Sims 3/10/1847
Mrs. Amanda B. Sims 11/17/1878
Dr. James S. Sims 10/1880

JAMES HOBBS' BIBLE
Owner: Mrs. Homer Blankenship, Columbus, Mississippi

Births

James Hobbs 3/21/1783
Amanda Melvina Hobbs 1/3/1823
Jerusha Hobbs, his wife, 3/4/1792
Emily Antonet Hobbs 11/17/1824
Louisa Hobbs 1/8/1813
Martha Elizabeth Hobbs 7/4 /1828
Minerva Hobbs 4/12/1814
James Augustin Hobbs 9/30/1828?
May Hobbs 3/22/1816
William Rufus Hobbs 1/26/1831
Sarah A. Hobbs 2/24/1817
Angeline Hobbs 3/21/1933
Nancy Hobbs 2/3/1819
Pinnina Aleansas? Hobbs 10/7/1834
Jane Caroline Hobbs 11/16/1820
Guy Coleman 10/15/1884-8/13/1885
Mary Coleman 7/24/1883

218

(James Hobbs' Bible contd....)

Minnie Coleman 11/22/1855
Mary Frances Gunter 8/9/1841
William W. Gunter 8/12/1845
Claburn P. Gunter 5/15/1843
Jacob I. Wells 2/18/1881

Marriages

James Hobbs to Jerusha Atkinson 9/27/1810
John Nash to Louisa Hobbs 7/10/1834
William V. Nash to Mary Hobbs 10/30/1834
Elijah Moor to Minerva Hobbs 1/13/1835
James Smith to Sarah Hobbs 12/22/1835
George W. Gunter to Amanda Hobbs 2/14/1839
James A. Powers to Jane C. Hobbs 2/21/1843
Samuel Wells to Emily 7/1/1852?
Green Hilliard Gupton to Angeline Hobbs 5/11/1853?
William H.---- to Peninah A. Clayton 8/12/1855
Julia Gupton to Dolert Coleman 6/10/1854
Nina Gupton to Joe Murray 11/4/1880
Lucy Gupton to Frank Reeves 11/10/1881
Rebecca Gupton to Samuel Hedge 10/29/1987
Willie Gupton to Alice Justice 2/4/1887/97
Lillie Murray to Jessie Green 4/23/1905
Maggie A. Murray to Edd Spencer 12/23/1308
Dessle Cora Murray to John Jackson 12/11/1910/11
Virginia Jackson to Homer Blankenship 12/24/1932

219

(James Hobbs' Bible, Marriages, contd....)

Deaths

James Hobbs 3/17/1838
William C. Wells 2/27/1854?
Sarah Ann Smith 2/18/1838
James Augustin Hobbs 6/1/1864
Louisa Nash 10/29/1846

WILLIE BAKER JONES' BIBLE
Owner: Mrs. James G. Johnson, Knoxville, Tennessee

Marriages

W. H. Jones to M. O. Bass 7/17/1832
Arthur B. Jones to R. C. Swift 12/15/1852
T. B. Harris to H. M. Jones 12/14/1859
W. F. Jones to J. N. Anderson 3/2/1864
J. W. Jones to Lizzie Rives 1879
James L. Jones to Cora McManse

Births

Arthur Jones --/24/1769
Sarah Jones 1/4/1773
Willie Baker Jones 9/25/1813
Mary Fletcher Jones
4/15/1848
Mary Ohio Jones 2/7/1816
Thomas Emmett Jones 8/1/1849
J. B. Adair 9/6/1825

(Willie Baker Jones Bible continued...)

Ida Jones 10/28/1851
Arthur Baker Jones 6/21/1833
Catharine Jones 3/18/1854
Sarah Elizabeth Jones 12/17/1836
James Lockhart Jones 5/1/1856
Martha Hibernia Jones 8/3/1839
Laura Annie Jones 10/29/1863
Lucy Fletcher Jones 4/2/1840
Winston Lockhart Jones 6/14/1881
Willie F. Jones 10/25/1841
James Herbert Jones 12/27/1884
Thomas Bass Jones 7/12/1843
John Walker Jones 8/27/1846-5/1901

Deaths

Mary Ohio Jones 11/25/1898
J. N. Adair 5/3/1853
Sarah Elizabeth Jones 4/28/1877, aged 40 yrs., 4 mos., 11 days
Martha H. Harris 9/17/1878, aged 36 yrs., 1 mo., 14 days
Lucy Fletcher Jones 10/2/1847, aged 7 yrs., 5 mos.
Thomas D. Jones 9/10/1846, aged 3 yrs., 1 mo., 18 days
Mary P. Mandcock 11/27/1916
Thomas Emmett Jones 8/29/1859, aged 10 yrs., 29 days
Ida Jones 12/13/1913
Katie D. Coolidge 4/11/1916
James Lockhart Jones 6/27/1855

221

ELIJAH HEARN, JR. BIBLE
Owner: Lee Hearn, Texas City, Texas

Elijah Hearn 9/6/1776-5/5/1844 m. 1808 Sarah
Elijah Hearn, Jr. 3/10/1809-7/23/1871 Oxford, Ala. m. Freba Ann Densen 12/1836 who d. 1895 Yazoo City, Miss.

Births of Children of Elijah Hearn, Jr. and Freba Ann

Lycurgus F. Hearn 10/9/1839
Adolphus D. Hearn 6/30/1841
Leonidas B. Hearn 7/23/1843-6/14/1845
Adrianne Amelia Beam 12/3/1845
Elljah Clark Hearn 6/6/1848
Aurelius Leander Hearn 8/25/1850-6/16/1918
Leonidas Horace Beam 7/25/1853
Mirandus Fillmore Hearn 11/4/1855
Nicholas Colosthomeas F. Hearn 8/20/1859
Gustane Bertrand Hearn 11/10/1862-3/18/1937 in Texas m. Beulah Childers.
Margaret Hearn d. 12/29/1050
Densen d. 5/11/1847
George B. Williams b. 1/31/1850 m. Adrianne Amelia Hearn on 12/11/1871
Aurelius Leander Hearn m. Sarah Ann Webb 1872 (10/12/18508/20/1923), bur. at Sand Springs Church, Hickory, Miss.

Births of Children of Aurelius Leander Hearn and Sarah Ann Mary Elizabeth Hearn 5/22/1874

William Oscar Hearn 8/17/1883-8/14/1969
George Thomas Hearn 7/16/1888-1971 in New Mexico
Laura Ann Hearn 7/16/1888-1972 Hickory, Miss. m. Elm
James A. Hearn 5/8/1890 m. Sellers of Laurel, Miss.
Jesse Hearn -/18/1881-1881

222

Rob Hearn 1885-1898
Henry G. Hearn 3/28/1879-1880

Mary Elizabeth Hearn d. 1937. She m. Willie Leonard Martin

JOHN HELLUMS, SR. BIBLE
Owner: Jesse Daniel Hellums
Stark City, Arkansas

John Hellums, Sr. b. 2/24/1782 m. 7/4/1802 Margaret Prevett b. 10/6/1788

Births of Their Children

Jacob Hellums 11/23/1804
Matilda Hellums 2/20/1820
Mary Ann Hellums 12/6/1806
James P. Hellums 3/13/1822
Cyntha Hellums 2/9/1809
John L. Hellums 4/18/1824
Nancy Hellums 2/13/1811
Peninnah Hellums 8/31/1826
Anny Hellums 8/17/1813
Nathan R. Hellums 10/19/1829
William H. Hellums 11/29/1815
Elizabeth Hellums 10/12/1830
Malinda Hellums 3/17/1818
Mourning Hellums 1/6/1832

JOHN DANIEL CUNNINGHAM BIBLE
Owner: Mrs. Lelia C. Graham, Atlanta, Ga..

Marriages

John Daniel Cunningham to Cornelia Dobbins 5/8/1860
John D. Cunningham, Jr. to Mary J. Spann 10/14/1880 at res. of John D. Cunningham in West End, Ga.
William H. Graham to Lelia Cunningham 5/8/1884 at Orchid Hill

Births

John Daniel Cunningham 3/28/1842, Chambers Co., Ala.
Cornelia, eldest dau. of Miles G. and Susan J. Dobbins, 8/20/1843, Griffin, Ga.

Births of Children of John D. and Cornelia Cunningham

John Daniel Cunningham 10/16/1863, Griffin, Ga. at res. of grandfather, Miles G. Dobbins
Lelia Cunningham 3/2/1866, Montgomery, Ala.
Miles Dobbins Cunningham 8/9/1873, at res. of his grandfather, Miles G. Dobbins, West End
Ruth Cunningham 11/5/1875, West End, Ga.
George A. Cunningham 10/22/1877, West End, Ga.
Alfred Alford Cunningham 3/8/1881, West End, Ga.
Susie Mae Cunningham 12/12/1883

Deaths

John Daniel Cunningham 12/18/10927 West End, Ga., bur. Oakland Cemetery, Atlanta, Ga.
Cornelia Dobbins Cunningham, wife of John Daniel Cunningham, 2/17/1895, Atlanta, Ga., bur. Oakland Cemetery, Atlanta, Ga. John Daniel Cunningham, Jr.
Ruth Cunningham Roual
George A. Cunningham ---
Alfred Alford Cunningham ---

ZACHARIAH WHITE BIBLE of Benton Co.
Owner: Mrs. T. A. Moore, Birmingham, Ala.

Zachariah White m. 9/21/1814 Elizabeth Blackwood, Jasper Co., Ga.

Births of Their Children

Eliza Meade White 3/28/1817-
William Jackson White 5/8/1828
Elizabeth Ann White 12/27/1821
Joseph Henry White 3/21/1830
Sarah Jane White 7/19/1825
Thomas Jefferson White 4/4/1834

Births of Children of Thomas Jefferson White and Margaret

Idella White
Kelly White 7/5/1866
Eliza White 6/8/1870
Katie Aulett Gaines White 4/26/1873
Gertrude Zachariah Moore White 11/14/1875
Thomas David White 6/28/1878
Francis Blackwood, son of Rosannah Blackwood, 3/19/1760
Jane Clark, dau. of Robert and Rachel Clark, 4/17/1759
Cornelius Blackwood, son of Francis and Jane (Clark), 11/10/1787

Deaths

Francis Blackwood 1/12/1825
Joseph H. White 4/25/1861
---- Blackwood, 27th yr. of her age
Elizabeth White 12/19/1866
Zachariah White 9/5/1866, aged 73 yrs., 6 mos., 9 days

GREEN A. COLLIER BIBLE of Madison Co.

Births

Joseph Pickens 12/14/1794
Salina Braselton, his wife, 5/30/1804
Green A. Collier 1814
Hypasia A. Pickens 4/28/1820
M. G. Milligan 12/1827
Joseph Green Collier 1839
M. J. Haden, his wife, 1844
Matilda C. Church 1858
Mary H. Collier, their dau. 1878
William H. Collier, their son, 1875
R. Joseph Collier, their son, 1882
Ella Collier, their dau. 1888

Marriages

Green A. Collier to Hypasia Pickens 11/18/1835
Hypasia P. Collier to M. G. Milligan (after 1853)
Joseph Green Collier 1865 M. J. Haden
Mary H. Collier 1893 to J. Paul Neill
William B. Collier 1902 to Annie Winston
R. Joseph Collier 1903 to Texie Carter
Ella Collier 1906 to H. C. White
Mary Collier Neill 1907 to W. S. Rayburn

Deaths

Joseph Pickens 1866
Hypasia P. C. Milligan 9/19/1904
Salina B. Pickens 1893

Joseph Green Collier 1325
Green A. Collier 1853
M. J. Haden 1902

WILLIAM HENRY HUNT BIBLE
Owner: Renee Atkinson
5424 Eulace Rd., Jacksonville, Fla.

William Henry Hunt 12/15/1830 Pine Level, Autauga, Co., Ala. 9/14/1904 Prattville, Autauga Co., Ala., son of Henry Harrison Hunt and Sallie Burt, his wife
His wife, Sarah Rebecca Chambliss 10/31/1850 Old Kingston, Autauga Co., Ala.-3/25/1933 Prattville, Autauga Co., Ala., dau. of Allen Chambliss and Eliza Whitehead, his wire

Their Children:

Sallie Woodward Hunt 9/20/1871 Prattville, Ala.-11/16/1873
James Abbott Hunt 7/15/1873 Prattville, Ala.-3/13/1939
William Allen Hunt 10/10/1875 Prattville, Ala.-10/11/1923
Wade Hampton Hunt 5/14/1578 Prattville, Ala.
Arrington Julius Hunt (twin) 10/14/1880 Prattville, Ala.
Eddie Hunt (twin) 10/14/1880 Prattville, Ala.-9/12/1881
Emma Hunt (twin) 11/16/1883 Frattville, Ala.
Ella Hunt (twin) 11/16/1883 Prattville, Ala.-

Marriages

James Abbott Hunt to Cassandra McCrary 12/24/1995
William Allen Hunt to Nina Sanford 6/20/1915
Wade Hampton Hunt to Jennie Collier 11/22/1899
Arrington Julius Hunt to Nellie Maud Shafer 12/25/1906

227

WILLIAM MICHAEL BIBLE
Owner: Mrs. William M. Nichols

Births

William Michael 12/23/1739
Wm Lafayette Michael 5/4/1832
Laney Michael 6/21/1797
Jurye Anglin Michael 8/16/1835
Mary Adline Michael 7/17/1823
John Marion Michael 10/22/1840
Peney Avline Michael 9/27/1826

Deaths

Edwin Earl Michael 1/19/1904, Anniston, Ala.
William Sherwood Michael 1906
John Marion Michael 4/11/1920
Alice Sherwood Wise Michael 10/30/1930

Marriages

J. M. Michael to Alice S. Wise 7/24/1866, by Rev. John G. Gibson
W. S. Michael to Lula C. Few 12/16/1889 by Rev. W. S. Walker

Births

John Marion Michael 10/22/1840
Alice Sherwood Wise Michael 6/30/1843
William Sherwood Michael 5/23/1867
Laney Estelle Michael 3/21/1878
Moina Belie Michael 8/15/1869

(William Michael Bible, contd....)

Alice Mae Michael 8/25/1881
Annie Laurie Michael 10/21/1871
Nelle Colquitt Michael 1/16/1884
Edwin Earl Michael 12/21/1875
Nelle Colquitt Michael m. 7/17/1912, Monroe, Ga., Jere Warren Chamlee.

Births of Children of Nelle C. and Jere W. Chamlee

Nelle Sherwood Chamlee 5/8/1913
Jere Michael Chamlee 4114/1918
Alice Malinda Chamlee 8/27/1915
Moina Ann Chamlee 9/27/1923

ROBERT MANSFIELD CHAMBLESS BIBLE
Owner: Lula Chambers Dyal, Morman Library
Linda Tillman, Rt. 6, Box 393, Whistler, Alabama

Robert Mansfield Chambless 12/13/1963 Ala.-8/14/1932 Atmore, Baldwin Co., Ala., son of Wiley Chambless and his wife, Mary Anne Perry, m. 7/15/1883 in Dias, Baldwin Co., Ala., his Wife Sarah Cravey 12/7/1867-2/11/1954 Bay Minette, Baldwin Co., Ala.

Their Children:

Mary Elizabeth Chambless 1/3/1885 Lottie, Ala.
Minnle Chambless 3/14/1887 Lottie, Ala.
Dora Jane Chambless 3/28/1889 Lottie, Ala.
Pearley Chambless 12/21/1890 Lottie, Ala.
Sallie Chambless 1/12/1893 Lottie, Ala.-11/1935
Grover Cleveland Chambless 12/11/1894 Lottie, Ala.-7/25/1903
Lula Chambless 2/23/1897 Lottie, Ala.

(Robert Mansfield Chambless Bible continued…)

Robert Lee Chambless 7/22/1899 Lottie, Ala.-11/11/1948
Lelia Chambless 2/6/1902 Lottie, Ala.
Edith Mae Chambless 2/16/1904 Lottie, Ala.
Jackson Curtis Chambless 3/29/1906 Lottie, Ala.
Sadie Chambless 1/7/1911 Lottie, Ala.

Marriages

Mary Elizabeth Chambless 11/11/1899 to Joseph Milstead
Minnie Chambless to Willie Chestnut 5/21/1906
Dora Jane Chambless to Thomas Phillips 6/28/1907
Pearley Chambless to Fletcher Little 9/27/1908
Sallie Chambless to George Prestwood 7/10/1918
Lula Chambless to Walton Dahlonega Dyal 12/10/1916
Robert Lee Chambless to Bessie Arnette 3/23/1919
Lelia Chambless to Herman Howell 11/13/1927
Edith Mae Chambless to Charley Simmons 12/20/1919
Sadie Chambless to Elon W. Holt 11/9/1936

GEORGE MILLER BIBLE of Marion County

George Miller b. Spartanburg, South Carolina 8/28/1790-d. 1/10/1839 Marion, Alabama
Permelia Miller b. Greenville, South Carolina 6/6/1799-d. Marion, Alabama 9/6/1835

Ages of Children of George and Permelia Miller

Mary Missouri Miller 7/8/1819
William Eber Miller 6/11/1829
Eliza Ann Miller 1/22/1822

(George Miller Bible continued...)

Caroline Miller 9/17/1832
John Henry Miller 11/7/1825

Note: P. 306, Southern Lineages - A History of Thirteen Families Mary Missouri Miller d. ca 1880; Eliza Ann Miller m. William Newton Wyatt; William Eber Miller d. 9/6/1846 Matamoras, Mexico, soldier in Mexican War; Carolina Wycliff d. 5/1895 Aberdeen, Ms.

REV. JOHN AND EUNICE CALLAWAY MILNER BIBLE
P. 300, History of Lamar Co. (Ga.)

Rev. John Milner b. 10/17/1775 Wilkes Co., Georgia, son of Joseph Milner Sr. and Elizabeth Godwin (came to Ga. from Abington, Va.)

Births

Parents: Benjamin C. Milner 6/17/1832
Martha F. Brown 2/17/1838

Children:

Tilala Wathen Milner 2/28/1855 Barnesville, Ga.
Ida Brown Milner 3/6/1857 Barnesville, Ga.
Joseph Thomas Milner 12/13/1858 Barnesville, Ga.
Willis Justus Milner 4/8/1864 Shelby, Alabama
Benjamin Charles Milner, Jr. 11/13/1860 Barnesville,Ga

Alef Bonita Milner 7/1/1865 Autauga, Alabama
Enoch Eskew Miler 8/18/1867 Evergreen, Alabama
Lillie Ora Milner 2/10/1869 Ador Town, Ga   .
George Crossley Milner 3/12/1871 Lee Co., Alabama

(John Callaway Milner Bible continued…)

Jean Shepard Milner 9/2/1872 Dadeville, Alabama
Susana Eliaabeth Milner 3/25/1875 Dadeville, Ala.
Robert Burton Milner 12/22/1876 New Castle, Alabama
John T. Milner 9/26/1850 New Castle, Alabama

Deaths

Grandfather, mother"s side-Stephen Justus Brown Sr. 1/24/1857, 58
Grandfather, father's sidc-Willis Joshua Milner Sr. 3/15/1864, 67
Uncle, mother's side-Thomas Morton Brown 9/19/1863
All bros: Joseph Thomas Milner 8/10/1867, 8 yrs., 7 mos., 27 days
Enoch Eskew Milner 8/19/1967, aged 2 days
George Crossley Milner 7/8/1871, aged 4 mos.
John T. Mllner 12/15/1981, aged 1 yr., 2 mos., 19 days
Jean Shepard Milner 1/25/1891, aged 18 yrs., 3 mos., 23 days
Father: Benjamin Charles Milner Sr. 3/11/1902, 69 yrs., 9 mos.
Mother: Martha Brown Milner 2/10/1910, aged 72 yrs.

WILLIAM WALTER GARRETT BIBLE of Monroe County
DAR Records, Ga State Archives

Births

William Walter Garrett 10/9/1852 at Activity, Ala. m. 12/23/1900 Maggie Mae Roberts
4/17/1887 at Pineville, Ala. m. 12/22/1908, d. 10/14/1923
Vivian Boyce Garrett 8/16/1909 Dursonville, Ala.
Willie Mae Garrett 8/13/1911 at Jeddo, Ala.
William James Garrett 2/20/1913 at Uriah, Ala.
Maggie Rebecca Garrett 10/7/192? at Uriah, Ala.

(William Walter Garrett Bible continued...)

Ardis Lancaster Garrett 3/27/19V2 at Shady Dale, Ga. m. 1/16/1926 W. W. Garrett
Walter Eugene Garrett 12/3/1925 at Uriah, Ala.

Marriages

Wm Walter Garrett to Maggie Mae Roberts 12/22/1908, McWilliams, Ala.
Wits Mrs.G. L. Brantley; Mrs. G. E. Keyser.
William Walter Garrett to Ardis Lancaster 1/10/1926, Atmore, Ala.

Deaths

Maggie Mae Roberts Garrett 10/14/1923

WILSON HENRY BIBLE
Owner: Mrs. William Mason Henry, Shelby, Mississippi

Births

Wilson Henry 9/7/1834
Eliza Ann Henry 12/22/1833
Wilson Henry m. Eliza Ann McKinney 1/10/1856

Their Children:

Thomas Rolin Henry 8/7/1857
Liley Gray Verginey Henry 1/7/1859
W. Mason Henry 10/1/1861-6/18/1925 Shelby, Mississippi
          Births of Children of Thomas and Mary Ann Henry Wilson
Henry 9/7/1834
George W. Henry 1/8/1845

233

(Wilson Henry Bible continued...)

William Henry 12/24/1836
Prissley Henry 2/13/1849
John Henry 3/22/1839
James Matterson Henry 6/10/1851
Martha Ann Henry 7/14/1841
T. T. Tilday ---
R. H. McKinney 1/12/183- - 12/15/1865

Births of Children of R. H. and Merilda McKinney

T. I. McKinney 3/12/1836-3/16/1862
W. H. McKinney 11/29/1839-12/12/1862

Deaths

T. Roln Henry, son of Wilson and Lizer b. 5/7/1857
Mary Henry 5/10/1358
Wilson Henry 1/10/1863
Liley Gray Verginey Henry 1/2/1863
Eliza Ann Henry 4/3/1885
William Mason Henry 6/18/1925
Ida Wilbourn Nance m. William Mason Henry 11/20/1888
Elsie Mary Henry 9/22/1889-11/12/1889
Loula Emma Henry b. 4/30/1891
Madge Lee Henry b. 12/28/1893

234

MARCUS D. ROWE BIBLE
Owner: Mrs. W. L. Warren, Montgomery, Alabama

Marcus D. Rowe, son of Shadrack Rowe and Mary Byrum Rowe. Shadrack Rowe, Sr., father of
M. D. Rowe (Rev. War Soldier), d. 9/1853, aged 91
M. U. Rowe b. 1839
Alzada Rowe b. 1837
M. D. Rowe m. Martha F. Huling 11/19/1857

Births of Children of M. D. and Martha F. Rowe

Martha Elizabeth Rowe 7/27/1859-
Wm Mercer Rowe 12/13/1870
Alzada Imogene Rowe 11/29/1866
Mary Estelle Rowe 2/10/1874
James H. Rowe 11/29/1866
Hattie Erwin Rowe 12/14/1877

Marriages

M. Elizabeth Rowe to W. C. Moore 1/5/1882
Alzada (Genie) Rowe to S. T. Whitaker 12/12/1852
Hattie Erwin Rowe to G. P. Butler 12/27/1899
Mary Estelle Rowe to T. J. Andrews 1/16/1901
William M. Rowe to Ora Brown 7/9/1903
Deaths
William L. Bynum (uncle of M. D. Rowe) 11/24/1885
Martha K. Huling 7/4/1856 (mother of Mrs. M. D. Rowe) Andrew Huling 6/1870 (father of Mrs.
M. D. Rowe)
Martha Huling Rowe 9/28/1903
M. D. Rowe 7/17/1911, aged 72 yrs., bur. at West Point, Ga.

SHADRACK ROWE BIBLE
Owner: James Hudson Rowe, Pell City, Alabama

Shadrack Rowe 1762-9/1853, father of James Hudson Rowe
James Hudson Rowe b. 6/4/1801 m. Kathryn Moss McKloney in 1823.
Kathryn b. 4/19/1802

Births of Children of James Hudson and Kathryn Rowe

James R. Rowe 12//1825-2/28/1905
Amanda Rowe 12/10/1827
William Hughes Alexander Rowe 8/4/1829-6/1/1882
Elizabeth Jane Rowe 6/18/1831
Sarah Frances Rowe 3/11/1833
Martha Susan Rowe 7/14/1835-7/31/1837
Nancy Emily Rowe 2/16/1837
Elizabeth Ann Rowe 2/5/1838
Cynthia B. Lear Rowe 4/4/1840
Virginia Josephine Rowe 9/15/1843
Olga Ann Caroline Rowe 1/13/1840
Lydia Cathrine Dunnigan, dau. of Amanda Rowe, 1/6/1851
Alexander Morse, father of Cathrine Elizabeth Rowe, 2/24/1771-5/20/185

Grandchildren of James Hudson Rowe

James Hudson Rowe 3/27/1882 -
Luther A. Rowe 2/27/1889-6/1/1882
Samuel Oren Rowe 1/11/1893

JOHN FOUST BIBLE
Owner: J. L. Faust, Chattanooga, Tennessee

John Foust 2/22/1771-10/1/1825 m. Phoeby

Their Children:

Jacob Foust 4/18/1796
John Foust 11/29/1797-9/22/1854
Philip Foust 6/29/1800-8/28/1879 m. Catharine Poust, a cousin
Mary Foust 11/14/1802-3/8/1810
Joab W. Foust 10/1/1805
William McKendree Foust 5/4/1809-3/8/1047
James A. Foust 9/3/1811-3/20/1814
Arminda Angeline Foust 6/13/1827
Sarah Lucinda Foust 10/30/1529-6/16/1841
John Foust 11/29/1797-9/22/1822 m. Matilda Sawley who d. 6/25/1879

Births of Children of John and Matilda Foust Thomas Foust 4/27/1823

James Patrick Foust 12/15/1524-4/1/1915
Rufus H. Poust 3/30/1826-4/10/1860
Amanda M. Foust 2/23/1825
William H. Foust 12/18/1829-12/15/1903
George Foust 12/9/1831-9/20/1833
Sally R. Poust 12/27/1833
Lucinda Foust 12/27/1835-1/17/1929
Frances Marion Hawley Foust 11/20/1837-3/31/1888
John Foust 6/1840-4/14/1841
Nathan Polk Foust 7/11/1842-6/1903
Addison T. Foust 4/24/1844-8/9/1862
William H. Foust b. 12/18/1829 m. 9/19/1911 Elizabeth Wisdom

(John Foust Bible, contd....)

Births of Children of William H. and Elizabeth Foust

Addison Carey Foust 8/25/1862 m. 9/10/1901 Nina Williams. One child: Tom C. Foust, b. 10/1905
Thomas O. Foust 1/24/1864-1)/18/1905 m. 1898 Herlon Tyler
John E. Foust 9/8/1862
James Leonidas Foust 12/9/1867 m. 6/22/1910 Mina Snow
Alice P. Foust 12/2/1872-1906

Marriages

Jacob and Susannah Foust
John and Matilda Foust 9/3/1822
Phillip and Catharine Foust 2/24/1825 (cousins)
William Foust and Elizabeth Foust 7/16/1825
William Poust and Elizabeth Bright 7/10/1844

Deaths

James A. Foust 3/20/1814
William McKendree Foust 3/8/1847
Mary Foust 3/8/1816
Catherine Angeline Foust 2/28/1847
Phoeby Foust 10/1/1825
Sarah Foust 6/16/1841
Elizabeth Foust 10/31/1843
Phillip Foust 8/28/1879

HARTWELL KING BIBLE
Owner: Frank F. King, Tuscumbia, Alabama

Marriages

Hartwell King to Burchett Curtis 4/24/1805
Mary C. King to James Fennell 9/24/1829
Oswald King to Martha Rebecca Delony 1/14/1830
Susan King to Tignel Jones 5/25/1835
Robert King to Margrett Peck 2/14/1837
Martha B. King to Thaddeus W. Felton 9/5/1837
Philemon King to Eliza Wooding
Hartwell R. King to Mary H. Smith 3/1/1848
Paul H. King to Mary Cummings
Ann King to Edward Goodwin 6/18/1851
Clarence P. Goodwin to Mary 0. Jones 12/11/1878 (changed from 1877)
Susan Goodwin to John E. Delony 12/21/1880

Births

Hartwell King 3/1/1785
Burchett Curtis 2/10/1785

Births of Children of Hartwell and Burchett King

Oswald King 4/27/1806
Martha Burchett King 3/31/1818
Robert King 5/7/1803
Hartwell Richard King 3/5/1820
Mary C. King 3/4/1811
Paul H. King 9/6/1822
Susan King 5/30/1813

239

(Hartwell King Bible continued...)

Washington Lafayette King 10/5/1824
Philemon King 7/17/1815
Ann Lafayette King 3/11/1828
Ann Lafayette King 4/22/1830
Walter Reynolds Goodwin 5/28/1852
Mary Burchet Goodwin 8/13/1859
Clarence Philemon Goodwin 1/26/1854
Edith Ruth Goodwin 7/10/1861
Robert King Goodwin 10/2/1855
Annie Goodwin 6/7/1863
Susan Goodwin 2/2/1858
Edie Goodwin 6/7/1863
Edward Goodwin 9/7/1830
                    Deaths

Washington LaFayette King 10/25/1827
Ann Lafayette King 5/18/1828
Richard King 12/27/1830, aged 78 yrs., b. 1752
Edwin Goodwin 9/25/1863
Walter Reynolds Goodwin 1/16/1854, aged 13 mos., 19 days
Mary Durchet Goodwin 7/24/1860
Robert King 9/3/1841, aged 57 yrs
Hartwell King 9/3/1841, aged 56 yrs.
Burchet King 10/22/1872, aged 87 yrs., 8 mos.
Susan Jones 4/15/1866, aged 53
Hartwell Richard King 12/11/1872,
aged 52 yrs
Paul King 8/29/1871 aged 49 yrs.
Philemon King 12/14/1878, aged 63 yrs., 5 mos
Oswald King 8/15/1882, aged 76 yrs., 4 mos.

Ann Lafayette King, wife of Edward Goodwin, 2/16/1902
Martha Burchet, wife of T. W. Felton and later Tignal Jones, 9/17/1904, bur. LaGrange beside
Tignal Jones, last husband
Edith Ruth Goodwin 9/30/1875 at LaGrange, aged 14 yrs., 2 mos, 20 days

GEORGE MALONE BIBLE of Limestone County
Owner: Ruby Hamilton Triesch
3428 Flora Ave., Kansas City, Mo.

George Malone 10/13/1784 Virginia - 8/26/1847 Athens, Limestone Co., Alabama m. Ist, Essex
Co., Virginia, 12/25/1807, Martha Chamblis b. 7/15/1788, m. 2nd, 6/12/1816, Sallie Moyler

Births of Their Children William D. Malone 10/16/1808 Essex Co., Va.

Mary G. Malone 6/6/1810 Essex Co., Va.
Nathaniel Chamblis Malone 9/12/1812 Essex Co., Va. m. 1835 Martha Delilah Crenshaw

WILLIAM HENRY HUNT BIBLE of Prattville, Autauga County
Owner: Renee Atkinson, 5425 Eulace Road, Jacksonville, Florida

William Henry Hunt 12/15/1830 Fine Level, Autauga Co., Ala. 9/14/1904 Prattville, Autauga
Co., Ala., son of Henry Harrison Hunt and his wife, Sallie Burt

Sarah Rebecca Chambliss 10/31/1850 Old Kingston, Autauga Co., Ala.-3/25/1833 Prattville,
Autauga Co., Ala., dau. of Allen Chambliss and his wife, Eliza Whitehead

Births of Their Children

Sallie Woodward Hunt 9/20/1871 Prattville-11/16/1873
James Abbott Hunt 7/15/1873 Prattville-3/13/1939 m. 12/24/1895 Cassandra McCrary

(William Henry Hunt Bible continued...)

William Allen Hunt 10/10/1875 Frattville-10/11/1929 m. 6/20/1316 Nina Sanford
Wade Hampton Hunt 5/14/1878 Prattville m. 11/22/1893 Jennie Collier
Arrington Julius Hunt, twin, 10/14/1880 Prattville m. 12/25/1906 Nellie Maud Shafer
Eddie Hunt, twin, 10/14/1880 Prattville-9/12/1881
Emma Hunt, twin, 11/16/1883 Prattville Ella Hunt, twin, 11/16/1883 Prattville

JOHN LOVELESS BIBLE
Owner: John Loveless, Austin, Texas

John Loveless (son of John Loveless and Martha Daniel Loveless) m. 12/19/1866 Susan Lee,
dau. of Edward "Ned" Lee and Martha Roy Lee of Shelby Co., Alabama.

Births of Their Children

Martha Ella Loveless 10/4/1867 m. 4/20/1892 T. S. Millsap
Mary Melissa Loveless 12/6/1869 m. 2/23/1887 Thomas G. Jones
William Thomas Loveless 1/17/1873 m. 5/26/1901 Belle Parsons Missouri
Alice Loveless 11/2/1875 m. 9/27/1896 Will G. Porter
Susan Frances Loveless 8/22/1877m. Ist 2/9/1904, Frank D. Russell, 2nd, 3/12/1913, George W
DeShazo
Nancy Louvenia Loveless 4/12/1879 m. 11/3/1910 Capt. J. Robson
John Edward Loveless 12/19/1884 m. Ist Lizzie Betts, 2nd, 12/10/1920, "Topsie" Bertha Billups

John Loveless, husband of Martha Daniel Loveless, d. 9/11/1847 Martha Daniel Loveless d.
1/24/1895, bur. Pleasant Hill
John Loveless and Susan Lee Loveless bur. at Pleasant Hill William Thomas Loveless and Belie
Parsons Loveless Ezell bur. at Pleasant Hill Cemetery

William Thomas Loveless, son of John and Susan Lee Loveless, m. 5/26/1901 Belie Parsons

(John Loveless Bible, Births, contd....)

Children of William Thomas and Susan Lee Loveless

Edna Loveless b. 5/17/1905 m. 9/7/1926 Herman A. Whisenant

Clara Mae Loveless b. 3/13/1908 m. Thomas Clyde Starnes
Ralph Peyton Loveless 1/19/1912-2/8/1953 m. Inez Loveless

Children of Edna L. Whisenant and Herman A. Whisenant

Edna Jo Whisenant m. Leonard L. Lonas, Jr.
Jacquelyn B. Whisenant m. Otis D. Coston Jr.
Herman A. Whisenant, Jr. m. Joyce Leigh Diamond

PINKNEY W. AND ANNA HILSON BIBLE
Owner: Mrs. M. D. Hahn
1920-A Laurel Rd., Birmingham, Ala. 35216

Births

Cleton Hilson 3/18/1839
Hetty Hilson 11/5/1842
Milrey Hilson 10/21/1834
Aaron Henche 6/7/1844
Rutha Hilson 6/5/1836
Lency Hilson 11/25/1845
Martha Ann Wilson 10/13/1837
 H. Wilson 9/10/1847
Leborn Hilson 4 /15/1839
Lucenda Hilson 3/25/1849

(Pinkney W. Hilson Bible continued...)

Pinkney W. Hilson 6/10/1841
Sarah Nancy Adelia Hilson 10/27/1850
Anna Odom Wilson d. 10/5/1887

Marriages

P. W. Hilson t. A. E. Odom 2/7/1832
G. W. Vickry to Rutha Hilson 7/27/1854
T. J. Scale to Martha Hilson 2/29/1860
A. H. Hilson to J. E. Johnson 10/11/1865
H. T. Scale to Lucinda Hilson 1/29/1871
A. T. Sims to N. A. Hilson 12/10/1868

VINSON R. PORTER BIBLE
Owner: Mrs. M. J. Gorris
3224 Brookwood Road, Birmingham, Alabama

Births

Vinson R. Porter 8/19/1792
Amelia Beall Rees 1/3/1792

Births of Their Heirs:

Eleanor Catherine Porter 11/28/1813
Oliver Anthony Josiah Rees Porter 4/9/1823
Ann Caroline Porter 3/15/1816
Elizabeth Eveline Porter 6/10/1822
Mary Adeline Porter 2/17/1819
Ann Eliza Porter 3/5/1830

Deaths

Vinson R. Porter 12/18/1851
Amelia D. Porter 2/4/1869
Eleanor C. Lyon 4/6/1859
Ann Caroline Porter 10/9/1825
Elizabeth Eveline Porter 6/10/1822
Oliver A. J. R. Porter 8/7/1872 (or 1832)
Ann Eliza Porter 8/7/1834

Marriages

Vinson R. Porter to Amelia B. Rees 9/22/1812
Eleanor Catherine Porter to Joseph Dan Lyon 12/20/1832
Mary Adeline Porter to Pleasant Davis 12/24/1837
William Rees, our grandfather, b. 8/27/1769
Eleanor Beall, wife of William Rees, b. 5/18/1769

Children:

Leathy B. Rees m. David Lawson
Amelia B. Rees m. Vinson R. Porter
Elizabeth F. Rees m. Ist Charles Hudson, 2nd, Mr. Moreland
Thaddeus D. Rees m. Ist Rebecca
Ried, 2nd, Martha Floyd John Kees m. Ann Bracken
Abraham F. Rees m. Sallie Mathews
Nancy Walter Rees m. Daniel Hightower
Josiah D. Rees m. Elizabeth Pitts
Polly Allen Rees m. Henry Pruitt
Mary Dent Rees m. William Park
Eliza Green Rees m. Elisha Bastion
Espy Barton Rees m. Green Stephens
William Rees m. Luvancy Evans

WILLIAM ROBERTS' BIBLE
Owner: Mrs. Preston Payne
1011 Dripping Spgs Rd, Cullman, Ala. 35055

Husband - William Roberts 22/4/1863 at Penrose?-5/22nd, 48 yrs. Wife - Mary Ann Roberts b.
1863

Births of Their Children

Eliz Ann Roberts 10/13/1884 -
Catherine Roberts 1/25/1892
Mary Eliz Roberts ---
Mary Ellen Roberts 11/8/1895
Ann Roberts ---
Wm Thomas Roberts 9/11/1903
Margaret Roberts 3/17/1859

BENJAMIN F. AND EMMA F. DEVENY BIBLE
Owner: Mrs. Elizabeth Torrance

Births

Benjamin Franklin Deveny 8/1/1851
Alvin Deveny 4/17/1887
Emma Frances Deveny 4/2/1858
Emma Frances Deveny 10/13/1890
Maud May Deveny 9/12/1877
Gussie Deveny 2/26/1893
Ila Edna Deveny 10/24/1879
Lizzie Deveny 11/8/1881
Vela Deveny 2/14/1893
Viola Deveny 11/22/1884

(Benjamin F. Deveny Bible continued...)

Anna Belle Deveny 11/22/1894
Nanna Belle Deveny 11/22/1894

Marriages

Benjamin Franklin Deveny to Emma Frances Parrish 11/2/1876
Ben Beard to Maud Deveny 12/19/1879
Lucius Torrance to Lizzie Deveny 11/8/1898
Nick Morehead to Ila Deveny 12/24/1900
Austin Smith to Nannie Deveny 2/18/1912
Smith Slusher to Annie Deveny 4/7/1912

Deaths

James Parrish 2/24/1884, his res. in McLennan Co., Texas
Mrs. Elizabeth Parrish, wife of James Parrish, at her res. in McLennan Co., Texas, 11/11/1869
Bigea Parrish 2/5/1583
Viola Deveny 10/22/1886
Gussie Deveny 4/1/1893
Alvin Deveny 5/5/1907
Mrs. Emma Frances Deveny 12/2/1911
Charlotte Elizabeth Deveny 11/8/1881 at "Elm Grove", her rather's farm near Waco, McLennan Co., Texas

WILLIS AND ABIGAIL CHAMPION BIBLE
Owner: Mrs. Earle E. Warren
New McGregor Highway, Waco, Texas

Marriages

Willis Champion to Abigail Duncan 10/31/1820
William O. Williams to Sarah I. Deveny 11/2/1851
Robert B. Deveny to Frances Champion Deveny 1/2/1840
Joseph G. Deveny to Mary A. Parrish 12/15/1872
D. F. Deveny to E. P. Parrish 11/2/1876
B. D. Gambill to A. E. Deveny 9/24/1879

Births

Willis Champion 2/7/1803
Abigail Champion 11/1/1800

Ages of Children Born to Willis and Abigail Champion

William Champion 12/23/1821
James E. Champion 1/11/1832
Frances Champion 1/4/1824
Mary Ann Champion 12/15/1834
Charles D. Champion 4/15/1829
Willis Browning Champion 6/15/1836
John W. Champion 10/15/1829

Grandchildren

Sarah Deveny 11/7/1863
James Marquis Deveny 10/26/1858

(Willis Champion Bible continued...)

Mary Jane Deveny 2/13/1843
Frances Elizabeth Deveny 8/21/1862
Joseph G. Deveny 3/6/1847
Abigail Eliza Deveny 8/21/1862
Wm Duncan Deveny 3/13/1843
Sarah Isabella Deveny 11/7/1563
Benjamin F. Deveny 8/1/1851
Martha Ann Deveny 2/7/1843
Nancy Louisa Deveny 8/13/1853
Charles Seth Deveny 11/25/1855

Deaths

Willis Browning Champion 9/4/1840
William Duncan Deveny 8/23/1855
Abigail Champion 9/23/1840
Charles Seth Deveny 11/20/1858
James Estil Champion 10/1/1840
Nancy Louisa Deveny 11/27/1858
Willis Champion 10/3/1840
Mary Jane Deveny 6/30/1862
William Champion 12/29/1540
Frances Elizabeth Deveny 1/9/1863
John Woods Champion 2/16/1847
Robert B. Deveny 1/22/1873

GEORGE W. RUSH BIBLE
Owner: Rosa Lee Newman, 3120 SE 41 Place, Ocala, Fla. 32671

"Grandpa G. W. Rush (George W.) 9/3/1929-3/14/1911, son of William Lassiter Rush and Lucy R. Teagle. He was b. Coweta Co., Ga., moved to Coosa Co., Ala. and settled on the Rush Place on Hatchett Creek. His mother and father were buried on the place. His mother was Lucy Teagle of Coweta, Ga. She died of cancer. There were ten children born to them. Five of whom still survive."

Births

John Allen Rush 3/1/1855-d. 2 yrs. old
Henry Miles Rush 11/3/1867
William Renton Rush 7/2/1856
Tony Parker Rush 6/1/1870
Thomas Levi Rush 4/13/1858
Sim Hilliard Rush 3/10/1872
Rufus Teagle Rush 3/6/1860   F
Felix Austin Rush 11/7/1874
Harris Walter Rush 4/18/1865

Deaths

T. L. Rush 2/12/1935
Tony P. Rush 9/26/1941
Sim H. Rush 2/21/1935
Henry Miles Rush --
Felix A. Rush 3/2/1936

250

(George W. Rush Bible, contd....)

Grandma M. Rush's Family. Eleven children were born to them

Sarah Margaret d. 1/1/1904
Mack Knight went to war - killed
Pryor Nabors
Thomas Harrison d. in about '30
Rebecca Anna drowned at 7 yrs. from school Reuben Arnold went to war - killed
John William d. with measles, child
Isaac Asa d. in Texas
James Allen d. in Miss.
Essie Nancy d. 10/28/1938
Marcus Lafayette d. 7/7/1940

Loose Pages in Bible:

Marriages

John Thomas to July Ann Billingsby 9/1858
John Thomas to Nancy A. Rush 10/31/1871

Births

John Thomas 7/28/1795-8/12/1873, aged 78 yrs, 15 days
Nancy A. M. C. Thomas 10/29/1836
Henry Thomas 1843
John Thomas 5/7/1848?
William L. Rush 3/22/1804
Nancy A. M. C. Rush 10/29/1836
Lucy Rush 11/31/1806
Delila E. Rush 1/16/1839

251

James F. Rush 12/7/1825
William A. Rush 5/4/1841
John O. H. Rush 1/12/1828
Lucy J. Rush 1/19/1843
George W. Rush 9/3/1823
Tabitha A. Rush 12/20/1844
Warren R. Rush 8/14/1834

Deaths

William R. Rush 8/3/1843, aged 2 yrs, 3 mos.
T. A. Rush 12/4/1883, aged 3 yrs, 1 lack 11 days
D. E. Rush 7/2/1872, aged 32 yrs, 16 days
Lucy Rush 8/28/1878, aged 71 yrs, 8 mos., 28 days
William L. Rush 12/5/1878, aged 74 yrs., - mos., 17 days

Births

James M. Murphy 7/31/1857
John W. Murphy 9/21/1859
Printis Murphy 10/28/1861

JAMES H. CHAMBERS' BIBLE of Russell County
Owner: C. A. Myers, 3460 Wellington Road, Montgomery, Ala. 36106

Births of Children of James H. and Mary F. Chambers

James McCoy Chambers 8/26/1870, Russell Co., Alabama
Charles A. Chambers 9/12/1871, Russell Co., Alabama
William Henry Chambers 11/12/1873, Russell Co., Alabama
Gordon Llewellen Chambers 3/1/1875, Russell Co., Alabama
Josiah Flournoy Chambers 2/7/1877, Montgomery, Alabama

252

(James H. Chambers Bible, Births, contd....)

Mary Chambers 10/27/1878, Russell Co., Alabama at "Greenwood"
Julian Sydney Chambers 3/16/1893, Russell Co., Alabama

Marriages

James Henry Chambers, Ist son of William and A. L. Chambers of Columbus, Ga., 11/16/1869, by Rev. J. H. Nail, to Minnie Flournoy Albecrombie, 2nd dau. of C. S. and V. G. Albecrombie of Grcenwood, Alabama
James McCoy Chambers, Ist son of James H. and Mary F. of Oswiche, Alabama, 10/14/1836 by Rev. Alonzo Monk, to Florence Bloom
Nesbit, only dau. of Robert A. Nesbit of Macon, Georgia

Deaths

Charles Albecrombie Chambers, 2nd son of James H. and Mary F.
Chambers, 9/4/1875 in Mary Chambers, only dau. of James H. and Mary P., 9/16/1873, Columbus, Georgia

NATHANIEL RAY BIBLE
Owner: Mrs. Leroy Riddick
915 Newell, Memphis, Tennessee

Marriages

Benjamin Rosser to Elizabeth Ray 11716/1843
Jefferson Dominick to Catharine H. Ray 1/9/1845
William M. Spencer to Permely Ray 1/13/1848
William A. Ray to Martha Glass 8/29/1850
James Ray to M. E. Freeman 1/14/1856 J
J. H. Ray to Mary A. D. Avery 12/5/1855

(Nathaniel Ray Bible continued...)

Births

Nathaniel Ray 12/15/1793
Margaret Ray 9/5/1797
Elizabeth Ray 11/7/1822
William A. Ray 8/13/1828
Catharine Ray 2/8/1824
Permely Ray 3/23/1830
James Ray 2/18/1826
Jackson Ray 11/3/1837

Deaths

Nathaniel Ray 5/12/1876
Jefferson Dominick 2/16/1884
Margaret Ray 3/30/1883 (or 1889)

LEE CAMPBELL ECHOLS' BIBLE
Owner: Mrs. Annie Eliza Giles
1004 Cottrell St., Mobile, Alabama

L. C. Echols 8/31/1868 Tallasee, Alabama-11/16/1944 Atlanta, Ga. m. 8/31/1868
Katherine V. Brand 2/21/1873 Maplesville, Alabama-11/30/1959 m. 11/12/1898
James Lee Echols 9/21/1891 Randolph Co., Alabama m. 5/8/1917
Oliver C. Echols 9/16/1892 Randolph Co., Ala. m. 12/9/1916
Annie E. Echols 8/7/1895 Randolph Co., Alabma m. 9/10/1913
Willie A. Echols 10/28/1897 Chepultapec, Alabama m. 8/9/1914
Catherine V. Echols 6/12/1900 Birmingham, Alabama m. 5/5/1929
Hattie L. Echols 4/12/1903 Birmingham, Alabama m. 7/20/1919
Maggie M. Echols 12/9/1905 Birmingham, Alabama (twin) m. 7/16/1926

(Lee Campbell Echols Bible continued...)

Gaston T. Echols 12/9/1905 Birmingham, Alabama (twin)-11/11/1906
Mattie L. Echols 6/16/1908 Birmingham, Alabama m. 9/1/1930
   Births of Grandchildren of Mr. and Mrs. L. C. Echols
William H. Giles 7/5/1914, Montgomery, Alabama Geraldine Echols 7/28/1917, Montgomery, Ala.
Cathleen C. Echols 5/23/1918, Atlanta, Georgia
Catherine L. Echols 5/23/1918, Atlanta, Georgia
Milton A. Mensinger, Jr. 6/11/1920 Atlanta, Georgia - 1/17/1936
Charles Lee Mensinger 8/12/1921 Atlanta, Georgia m. 2/2/1940

MILO BARRETT BIBLE
Owner: Dr. Marion Barrett Clisby, Starkville, Mississippi

Marriages

Milo Barrett to Eugenia C. Blue 4/24/1856 in Montgomery, Ala. by Rev. T. W. Dorman
Augustua Masillon Allen II to Marjorie H. Horner 6/9/1921 in Montgomery, Ala. by Rev. M. H. Holt
Montgomery, Ala. Ralph Gordon Williams to Mary Adelaide Freeman 10/19/1909 In Birmingham, Ala.
Marion Barrett Clisby to Gladys Virginia Reid in Houston, Miss.
by Rev. W. C. Stewart 12/4/1940
Davis Clisby to Sally Chapman 6/1954, Chattanooga, Tenn.
Lorenzo Clisby to Clara Barrett by Rev. O. R. Blue in Verbena, Ala. 7/16/1879
George Mortimer Williams to Kate Barrett by Rev. O. R. Blue in Montgomery, Ala. 4/6/1881
Adolphus G. Bunkley to Ellen Barrett by Rev. A. D. Woodfin in Montgomery, Ala. 2/8/1883
William Lowell Smith to Clara Frances Clisby by Rev. James A.
Stewart in West Point, Miss. 11/1/1941
Augustus Massillon Allen to Minnie Rosa Barrett by Rev. O. R. Blue In Montgomery, Ala.
4/6/1887

255

William Bostwick Howard to Ellen Barrett Bunkley by Rev. O. R. Blue in Montgomery, Ala.
12/13/1832
Eugene M. Barrett to Sallie B. Deli by Rev. O. R. Blue in Montgomery, Ala. 6/8/1892
Barrett Jerome Clisby to Beverly Ann Parker at State College of Miss. by Rev. Gammill
12/24/1970
Gates Thomas Ivy to Clara Clisby by Rev. R. A. Meek, West Point, Miss. 12/6/1905
Rowland H. Moody to Ethel Clinton Clisby by Rev. R. A. Meek, West
Point, Miss., 12/3/1902
Floyd J. Olson to Ethel C. Moody by Rev. A. R. Willett, West
Point. Miss., 6/28/1919
Milo Barrett Clisby to Pearl Anna Davis by Rev. Herman Stone in Newberry, S. C., 10/18/1916

Births

Milo Barrett 9/10/1829 in Ossian, Alleghany Co., New York
Eugenia C. Blue 1/20/1837 in Montgomery, Alabama
Clara Barrett 3/10/1857 in Montgomery, Alabama
Albert Chester Barrett 11/10/1858 in Montgomery, Alabama
Kate Barrett 11/1/1860 in Montgomery, Alabama
Ethel Clinton Clisby 5/15/1883 in Eufaula, Alabama
Milo Garrett Clisby 9/2/1584 in Eufaula, Alabama
Clara Mortimery Williams 2/13/1982 in Montgomery, Alabama
Ralph Gordon Williams 7/1/1884 in Verbena, Alabama
Ellen Barrett 11/14/1863 Montgomery, Alabama
Minnie Rosa Barrett 9/28/1565 Montgomery, Alabama
Eugene Mile Barrett 5/13/1867 Montgomery, Alabama
Katie Clisby 5/15/1880 Montgomery, Alabama
Clara Clisby 8/5/1881 Montgomery, Alabama
Mary Freeman Williams 8/8/1911 in Flat Creek, Alabama
Eula Frances Williams 10/6/1915 in Flat Creek, Alabama

Kate Barrett Williams 8/6/1913 in Flat Creek, Alabama
Ralph G. Williams, Jr. 11/11/1918 in Birmingham, Alabama
Minnie Franklin Bunkley 11/22/1883 in Montgomery, Alabama
Adolphus Gerald Bunkley 6/26/1886 in Montgomery, Alabama
Virginia Keene Howard 3/5/1994
William John Howard 3/13/1896
Mile D. Howard 10/22/1897
Eugenia Blue Howard 12/10/1899
Ellen Howard 1/5/1903
William D. Howard, Jr. 9/22/1907

Augustus Massillion Allen II 12/14/1887 Montgomery, Alabama
Augustus M. Allen III 9/8/1922 Montgomery, Alabama
Harry Lee Allen 8/30/1925 Montgomery, Alabama
Lydia C. Allen 5/14/1927 Montgomery, Alabama
Barbara Ann Allen 2/11/1932 Montgomery, Alabama

Catherine Price Ivy 2/17/1911 West Point, Mississippi
Gates Thomas Ivy, Jr. 8/23/1912 West Point, Mississippi
Clara Frances Clisby 10/10/1917 Newberry, South Carolina
M. Barrett Clisby 7/1/1921 Newberry, South Carolina
Edward Davis Clisby 11/26/1932 West Point, Mississippi

William Lowell Smith 11/9/1943 in Chattanooga, Tennessee
Barrett Jerome Clisby 9/10/1946 West Point, Mississippi
Charlotte Ann Smith 10/27/1946 Chattanooga, Tennessee
Michael Gene Clisby 2/16/1953 Starkeville, Mississippi

257

(Milo Barrett Bible continued...)

Deaths

Albert Chester Barrett 4/30/1860, Montgomery, Alabama
Milo Barrett 6/24/1888 in Verbena, Alabama
A. G. Bunkley 2/1/1887 in Montgomery, Alabama
A. M. Allen I 3/27/1893 in Monteomery, Alabama
Eugenia C. Barrett 7/9/1896 in Birmingham, Alabama
Sallie B. Barrett in Montgomery, Alabama
G. M. Williams 3/23/1912 in Birmingham, Alabama

Elisa Blue Allen 11/8/1932 in Montgomery, Alabama
Eugene Milo Barrett 5/7/1934 in Colorado Springs, Colorado
Kate Barrett Williams (Mrs. G. M. Williams) 5/24/1958 in Newcastle, Alabama
Pearl Davis Clisby 10/26/1941 in West Point, Mississippi
A. Massillon Allen II 3/29/1946
Minnie R. Barrett Allen 10/31/1948 in Montgomery, Alabama Gates
Thomas Ivy 12/28/1954 in
Meridian, Mississippi
Clara Clisby Ivy 12/24/1956 in West Point, Mississippi

Clara Mortimer Williams 7/11/1883 in Montgomery, Alabama
(Edward Davis Clisby 7/31/1971, Melbourne, Fla., bur. Melbourne cemetery)

Clara Barrett Clisby 11/1/1931 in West Point, Mississippi
Lorenzo Clisby 10/6/1933 in West Point, Mississippi
Milo Barrett Clisby 3/27/1957 in Chattanooga, Tennessee
Kate Clisby 2/7/1959 In West Point, Mississippi

Births

W. M. F. Downs 7/5/1853
M. E. Downs 6/10/1854
And they were married 3/9/1871
Lula Loretta Downs 2/19/1872
Cora Florence Olena Downs 12/23/1873
Willis Shelly Downs 2/7/1876
Rhoda Evie Green Downs 12/16/1877 Infant b. and d. 3/3/1850
Elizabeth Ellen Downs 3/26/1881
Tinsy Ann Downs 1/18/1884
Talmage Lowery Downs 7/20/1886
Leroy and David Downs 11/7/1888
Martha Agnes Downs 4/24/1892
Era Cleo Downs 10/22/1896

Deaths

W. M. F. Downs 7/20/
Rhoda Evie G. 5/23/1904
Willis Shelly Downs 7/25/1929
Lee Roy 5/22/1966
Martha E. Downs 5/8/1944
Talmage L., Sr. 6/24/1866
Lula Loretta 8/1/1349
David 2/11/67
Cora Florence O. 10/10/1351
Martha Agnes 9/30/69
Tinsy Ann 2/7/1956
Elizabeth Ellen 10/66

RICHARD LEE JUDGE BIBLE
Owner: Mrs. T. J. Judge, Dauphine Island, Alabama

Births

Nancy W. Judge 4/20/1821
Thomas Judge 9/10/1813

Their Children:

James Simeon Judge 3/9/1842
Nancy W. Judge 2/6/1850
Thomas Anthony Judge 11/21/1843
Bryan Write Judge 4/21/1852
Litha Ana Judge 9/2/1846
Chas Fletcher Judge 5/17/1855
Andrew Jackson Judge 5/7/1848
John Robert Brantley 4/30/1858
Judge Mary Elizabeth Judge 2/6/1850
Richard Lee Judge 6/29/1860

Deaths

Thomas Judge 8/24/1864 A. J. Judge 10/10/1874
Nancy W. Judge 6/12/1886
Bryan Write Judge 2/6/1895
Richard Lee Judge 11/15/1945 at Hiwannee, Wayne Co., Miss., interred at Mexia, Alabama
Thomas Judge m. Nancy W. Taylor 6/30/1840

DANIEL ARINGTON BIBLE
Owner: Mrs. Lynda Eller
P. O. Box 249, Lanett, Ala. 36863

Marriages

J. A. Arington to N. A. Johnson 9/19/1876 at bride's res. by S. M.
Lipscomb, J. P. Witnesses: David Johnson, Sarah A. F. Johnson
Daniel Arlngton to P. J. Vowell Arington 10/3/1854
Marvin E. Arington 8/12/1902
M. L. Arington to S. G. Nichols 11/12/1905
Pearly J. Arrington to R. J. Breed 6/20/1909
Anna P. F. Arrington to Truit Rowe 1/8/1911
Willie B. Arrington to John Rice 4/23/1911
Dora I. Arrington to S. T. Barfield 11/6/1917 Note: sp. changes

Births

Daniel Arington 1/10/1830
P. J. (Jane) Arington 6/14/1928
Madorah I. Arington 12/20/1877
Pearlly J. Arington 1/10/1891
Anner P. F. Arington 3/17/1880
Willie Deli Arington 6/16/1893
Marvin E. Arington 10/22/1882
J. A. Arington 11/17/1855
Mary L. Arington 7/11/1886
Nancy A. Jonston Arington 10/19/1850
Olly May Arington 5/15/1859

(Daniel Arington Bible contd....)

Deaths

Parmcaly J. Arington 7/10/1592, aged 64 yrs.
Daniel Arington 12/7/1891, aged 62
Ollie May Aringtoon 11/7/1889, aged 5 mos., 22 days
John A. Arington 5/9/1924, aged 68 yrs, 5 mos., 22 days
Nancy A. Arington 1/6/1925, aged 67 yrs, 2 mos., 17 days
Pearley J. Breed Arington 9/6/1933
S. G. Barfield 8/10/1934, aged 75 yrs., 6 mos., 8 days
Marvin Arington 4/27/1942
Dora I. Arington Barfield 6/2/1953
M. Lula Arington Nichols 6/8/1953
James Truit Rowe 4/8/1955
R. J. Breed 7/29/1956
Sam G. Nichols 10/4/1958

JACOB B. DICUS BIBLE
Owner: John M. Sheftall
2517 Northwoods Drive, Macon, Georgia 31204

Births

Jacob B. Dicus 3/25/--
Morrison B. Dicus 10/4/1837
Haner Dicus 6/---
Rebecca Ann Dicus 11/11/1839
William C. Dicus 12/27/1828
Kayziah Dicus 5/17/1842
James E. Dicus 2/14/1830
Milton Dicus 8/26/1844

(Jacob Dicus Bible continued...)

Elisey Jain Dicus 2/14/1833
Winfield Dicus 9/2/1847
America Dicus 3/27/1835
James E. Dicus m. Rhoda L. Hicks 2/24/1853

PLEASANT CRENSHAW BIBLE of Clark County

P. Crenshaw of Clark Co. m. S. McClinton of Clark Co. 9/4/1863 at S. McClinton's by M. E. King, J. P. Wits: John Harrison and J. M. Ferry

Births

Pleasant Crenshaw 6/4/1838
Susan Crenshaw 3/12/1837
Willie Crenshaw 6/2/1866
George M. Crenshaw 1/3/1873
Annie E. Crenshaw 10/22/1867
Una M. Crenshaw 1/27/1875
M. Eliza Crenshaw 5/6/1869
J. Whit. Crenshaw 4/17/1876
John M. Crenshaw 4/15/1871
Emmit R. Crenshaw 11/30/1877
Annie May Day 6/29/1836

Deaths

Emmit R. Crenshaw 8/1878
Annie E. Crenshaw 7/14/1947
Willie Crenshaw 3/15/1897
M. Eliza Crenshaw 8/7/1954

(Pleasant Crenshaw Bible continued...)

Pleasant Crenshaw 5/7/1904
George M. Crenshaw 8/9/1964
John M. Crenshaw 1/12/1909
Una M. Crenshaw 7/14/1962
Susan Crenshaw 1/20/1909
J. Whit. Crenshaw 8/14/1869

E. S. HOLTAM BIBLE

E. S. Holtam, son of Spencer and Nancy, b. 8/3/1783

Deaths

Jeff Holtam 10/8/1864
Emeline Hedrick, dau. of E. S. Holtam, 12/16th, aged 77 yrs., 10 mos., 29 days

Births

Dolly James 3/13/1788
Sarah James 7/13/1790
Mary Ann Muncrief 2/24/1844
James Muncrief 11/28/1848
Caleb U. Muncrief 8/21/1846

Deaths

Spencer Jackson Holtam 1/20/1841
Malinda C. Moncrief, dau. of E. S. Holtam, 3/29/1850
Mary C. Flinn, dau. of E. S. Holtam, 2/9/1851

(E. S. Holtam Bible continued…)

Sarah A. Holtam 3/27/1867, aged 77 yrs, 2 mos., 13 days
William M. Merrell b. 11/30/1811

Births

Spencer J. Holtam 1/7/1810
Sarah Ann Holtam 12/14/1827
Abner S. Holtam 6/27/1820
Emily Jane Holtam 1/18/1830
Thomas J. Holtam 1/21/1823
Mary C. Holtam 2/27/1833
Malinda C. Holtam 2/3/1826

Deaths

Elijah S. Holtam 8/17/1868, aged 85 yrs., 14 days

Marriages

Abner S. Holtam 3/2/1843
Sarah Ann Holtam 3/20/1845
William M. Merrell 1/9/1833
Emeline Jane Holtam 1850
Thomas J. Holtam 7/4/1844
Mary Caroline Holtam 4/17/1849
Malinda C. Holtam 2/17/1842

265

CHESTER SLAPPEY BIBLE of Salem, Alabama

Births

Susie Elizabeth (Janner) 8/27/1868
Eva Lee Slappey 8/4/1888
Carrie Mae Slappey 1892
Chester Slappey 6/3/1905
Susie Elizabeth Hanners m. William Eli Slappey 11/4/1886
Fannie's Ist baby, Irma Francis Gulatte, b. 12/21/1904 in Lee Co., Beat 9.

GIDEON JOHNSON BIBLE
Owner: Edwin Brown, Rt. 3, Box 213
Evergreen, Alabama 30401

Births

Gideon Johnson 4/18/1786
Mary (Redding) Johnson 4/20/1790
William A. Johnson 8/2/1811
Gabriel M. Johnson 9/2/1820
Lieueazer Ann Johnson 5/14/1812
Mary D. Johnson 3/5/1823
Martha E. Johnson 8/30/1815
Rebeckah L. Johnson 9/23/1826
Gideon T. Johnson 2/3/1818
Sarah M. Johnson 9/1/1833

Deaths

Rebeka G. Slocumb 4/18/1892
Gid (Slocumb) 11/11/1929

Births

Rebecca G. Mims 9/11/1851
Ida Virginia Mims 7/14/1853
Our Ist boy b. 10/20/1855
Rebecka G. Slocumb 9/11/1851
James W. Mims 6/12/1858
Fletcher M. Slocumb 12/13/1868
James Dickinson Slocunb 2/1/1880
Willie Martial Slocumb 4/18/1873
Rudy Melvin Slocumb 11/13/1881
Charlton McTyeire Slocumb 5/25/1854
Percy Lee Slocumb 9/12/1875
Our little baby 5/3/1986-5/17/1886
Robert Gideon Slocumb 7/5/1877
Robert E. (Edwin) Slocumb 12/6/1845
Edwin Virgil Slocumb 3/13/1891

Marriages

Gideon Johnson to Mary 11/1/1810
Robert E. Slocumb to Rebecka G. Mims 10/25/1866
William H. Johnson to Emily 9/15/1831
Louisa H. Johnson 9/28/1831
Martha E. Johnson 12/13/1833
Sarah M. Johnson Mims 11/20/1850

Deaths

Gideon Johnson, aged 52

267

(Gideon Johnson Bible, Deaths contd....)

Rebecca L. Chambliss, dan. of Gideon G. and Mary M. Johnson, 2/7/1841
James Mims, son of W. (Williamson) and C. (Cynthia) Mims 5/17/1861
Sarah Mims Wood 4/26/1921, aged 83 yrs.
Gabricl M. Johnson 5/1/1864 in defense of his country
Percy Lee Slocumb 10/24/1879, aged 4 yrs., 1 mo. 12 days.

JAMES PATE BIBLE
Owner: Fannie Sue Pate, Smiths, Alabama

Births

James Pate 3/5/1800-7/23/1856
Riney A. Pate 12/15/1802-6/16/1876
William H. Pate 5/10/1521-12/4/1908
Gilbert G. Pate 7/20/1823-6/1897
Mary Ann Pate 1/6/1826-3/10/1856
James M. Pate 11/18/1827-7/1848
Thomas F. Pate 3/3/1829
Martha Jane Pate 11/28/1831-d.
Louisa Elizabeth Pate 9/23/1833
Emily Ezibeler? Pate 7/23/1833-5/12/1873
Williamson H. G. Pate 7/23/1838-d. Ft. Delaware during was Balus E. Pate 7/18/1840
Robert S. Pate 3/23/1842-9/10/1917
Rufus Pate 5/6/1847-fall of 1847
W. W. Pate d. 12/3/1906

ZEBEDEE AND MYRTLE ANDREWS' BIBLE
Owner: Mrs. Jewel Davis
1307 Martindale Dr., Phenix City, Ala. 36867

Births

Zebedee Andrews 8/26/1889, son of Zebedce and Myrtle
Wife, Myrtle Andrews 7/1/1893, dau. of Lydia and Samuel Bradley
Marriages
Zebedee. and Myrtle Andrews 4/24/1918 at N. Penobscot, Me.
Max. Holt Andrews, only child, b. Ellsworth, 5/9/1923 First child (son) stillborn at Franklin, Me. 3/3/1922

HENRY GAITHER HARRIS' BIBLE
Owner: C. Arthur Harris
Rt. 4, Box 50, Alexander City, Ala. 35010

Births

Henry Gaither Harris 3/24/1843, Newton Co., Ga.-4/18/1930 Clay Co., Ala., buried Macedonia Cemetery
Mary Amanda Phillips 9/20/1843, Newton Co., Ga.-1/16/1923, bur. Macedonia Cemetery, Clay Co., Ala.
Thomas Henderson Harris 10/21/1866, Newton Co., Ga.-9/16/1919, bur. Macedonia Cemetery, Clay Co.
William Deaton Harris 7/8/1868, Newton Co., Ga.-1946 Griffin, Ga.
Leola A. Harris 1/8/1870, Clay Co., Ala.-8/26/1964, bur. Providence Cemetery, Clay Co., Ala.
Edward Henry Harris 4/28/1871, Clay Co., Ala.-6/7/1957
Susan Estell Harris 3/3/1873, Clay Co., Ala.-10/19/1924, bur. Macedonia Cemetery, Clay Co. Ala.
Joseph Bennett Harris 6/29/1876, Clay Co., Ala.-S/18/1932 Muscogee, Oklahoma
John Leroy Harris 6/2/1878, Clay Co., Ala.-5/23/1956, bur. Macedonia Cemetery, Clay Co., Ala.

(Henry Gaither Harris Bible continued...)

Mary Elizabeth Harris 5/9/1880, Clay Co., Ala.-11/18/1918 Fla.
Christopher Columbus Harris 12/13/1882 Clay Co., Ala., twin 4/12/1962, bur. Ashland City
Cemetery, Clay Co., Ala.
Robert Lee Harris 12/13/1882, Clay Co., Ala., twin-5/26/1977 Tifton, Ga., bur. Ty Cemetery
Charles Blair Harris 2/8/1885, Clay Co., Ala.-6/3/1960 Alexander City, Ala., bur. Hillview
Cemetery

Marriages

H. G. Harris to M. A. Phillips 10/19/1865, Newton Co., Ga.

Deaths

M. E. Harris nee Burnett 11/18/1918, Fla.
T. H. Harris 9/16/1919
M. A. Harris 1/16/1923
H. G. Harris 4/18/1930
J. B. Harris drowned 8/18/1932
J. L. Harris 5/23/1956
E. H. Harris 6/7/1957
Charles Blair Harris 6/9/1960

CHARLES BLAIR HARRIS' BIBLE
Owner: C. Arthur Harris, Rt. 4, Box 50
Alexander City, Alabama 35010

Charles Blair Harris of Yates, Ala. m. Minnie I. Mathis of Yatcs, Ala. 10/15/1905 at W. C.
Mathis' house, by Rev. John N. Moore

Births

Charles Blair Harris 2/8/1885

270

(Charles Blair Harris Bible contd....)

Minnie Iula Harris 10/9/1883
William Thomas Harris 11/26/1906
Stacie Edna Harris 11/11/1917
Charles Arthur Harris 2/1/1809
Edith May Harris 3/28/1920
Katie Irene Harris 4/28/1911
Thelma Estelle Harris 7/16/1922
Carlton Lorenza Harris 8/2/1913
Mary Ruth Harris 10/17/1925
Woodrow Wilson Harris 8/27/1915
Joseph Edward Harris 7/26/1927
Mrs. Izie Mathis 4/24/1865

Marriages

William T. Harris to Ezell Pope 612611924
Katie Irene Harris to Herschel Yates 7/7/1327
Carlton L. Harris to Lula Monroe 3/7/1931
Woodrow W. Harris to Irene Yates 9/12/1931
Charles A. Harris to Deryal Hart 8/15/1932
Stacy Edna Harris to William Otto Vickers 7/8/1933
Edith Mae Harris to Marcus Black 5/19/193-
Thelma Estelle Harris to Thomas Ellis 8/3/1940
Mary Ruth Harris to J. Lawrence Nolen 2/7/1946
Joseph Edward Harris to Nancy Kate Dixon 6/23/1951

Deaths

William Thomas Harris 3/2/1948
Minnie Iula Harris 3/17/1979

(Charles Blair Harris Bible, Deaths contd....)

Charles Blair Harris 6/9/1960
Mrs. Izie Mathis 5/19/1938

WILLIAM AND MARGARET HOPE BIBLE
Owner: Mrs. Mary Gullatte
Rt., 2, Box 264B, Salem, Ala. 36574

Births

William Hope 3/15/1799 m. Margaret Miles 1/22/1801
Margaret Hope 6/21/1773
Hannah Hope 10/23/1801
Benton Hope 1/25/1812
Elizabeth Hope 8/2/1803
John Hope 3/28/1813
Thomas Hope 8/5/1805
William N. Hope 9/13/1815

Aquila M. Hope 8/29/1807
Catherine Hope 2/23/1818
Anna Hope 11/8/1809
Almira Hope 12/30/1820
James David Hope 10/7/1824
William Edwin Hope 10/15/1849
John Everett Hope 1/14/1857
Robert Emmett Hope 4/12/1851
Fannie S. Hope 12/28/1867
Winford Thomas Hope 5/31/1853

(William and Margaret Hope Bible continued...)

Deaths

Margaret Hope 12/13/1836
William Edwin Hope 10/28/1859
William Hope 5/19/1842

WILLIAM MOSS AND SARAH JANE CAPPS' BIBLE
Owner: Mrs. Mary Gullatte
Rt. 2, Box 2640, Salem, Ala. 36874

On flyleaf: Rev. W. M. Capps, bought of his nephew, J. M. Greene, 11/11/1879

Marriages

William Moss Capps of Lee Co., Ala. to Sarah Jane Sykes of Lee Co., Ala. 2/28/1850 at res. of
Josiah Sykes by Rev. John Talley. Wits: William Haley, Wesley Sykes

Births

William Moss Capps 7/6/1826
Sarah Jane Sykes 12/31/1833

Their Children:

Martha Jane Capps 1/1/1852
Margaret Ann Capps 2/20/1856
William Wesley Capps 10/9/1854

(William Moss and Sarah Jane Capps' Bible, contd....)

Grandchildren:

Wesley Moss Harrison 9/18/1876
William Oscar Capps 11/10/1878-11/24/1959
Maud Olivia Capps 12/18/1880
Margaret Thomas Harrison 12/29/1881
Raleigh David Capps 12/27/1882
Robert Tolliferro 12/27/1882
Young Milton Capps 6/12/1885
John Clinton Capps 1/14/1855-2/23/1960
Minnie Capps 3/1/1890
Mattie Lillie May 9/29/1892
Sarah Rebecca 11/13/1895
Luline Dillard 12/21/1906

Marriages

Thomas Harrison to Martha Jane Capps 11/23/1871
William Wesley Capps to Ella Olivia Edwards 1/6/1875
William Oscar Capps to Mary Morton 12/15/1901
Mamie Lee Capps, dau. of Oscar and Mary, b. 1/16/1903 J
John Clinton Capps to Lizzie Dudley 8/6/1911
Sarah Rebekah Capps to Paul A. Jones 11/20/1913
Maud Olivia Capps to Cullen Gordon Durkes 4/22/1918
Lillie Mae Capps to Edgar Harrison 4/25/1920
Annell Jones ---
Lou Ella Capps to John Edward Coppedge 3/6/1939
Sarah Rebekah Capps Jones to William Larry Pickard 4/4/1942

(William Moss and Sarah Jane Capps' Bible, contd....)

Deaths

Margaret Ann, 2nd dau., 4/3/1860, funeral by W. B. Neal
Flora Capps, our venerable mother, 1/4/1878. Funeral by W. B. Boswell
Rev.James Wesley Capps, our venerable father, 8/3/1848. Funeral by J. W. Roper
Margaret Thomas, our 2nd grdau, 4/2/1883
Rev. William M. Capps, 6/11/1897, Funeral by J. M. Creen
Mrs. M. J. Harrison 3/10/1909
W. W. Capps 11/8/1910
Mrs. Ella O. Capps 4/25/1915
Minnie Capps 5/5/1918
Mrs. Emma Lou Capps 6/15/1917
Young Milton Capps 10/6/1942
Robert Tolliferro Capps 1/21/1930
Raleigh David Capps 11/27/1940
Sara Pauline Jones, dau. of Sara Capps, 11/21/1944
Richard C. Aldinger, son of Eleanor Harrison, 10/21/1949
Cullen Burkes, Jr., son of Maud and Cullen G., 8/20/1957
Maud Capps Burke 3/26/1959
Ada Lulline Dillard Berry 5/3/1959
Edgar Harrison, father of Eleanor and Billy Harrison, 7/11/1964

Memoranda Cullen

Gordon Burkes, Jr. b. 9/22/1919
Eleanor Madelyn Harrison b. 7/13/1923
Sara Pauline Jones b. 8/29/1921
Lou Ella Capps b. 7/21/1915
Annelle Jones, dau. of Sara Capps, b. 9/29/1924
William Wiley Harrison, son of Lillie Capps, b. 10/19/1926

(William Moss and Sarah Jane Capps' Bible, contd....)

William Young Coppedge, son of Louella Capps, b. 11/4/1940
Robert Eroll Burkes, son of Cullen Burkes, Jr., b. 9/3/1942
Jessie Burges Haralson, son of Annel Jones, b. 6/4/1942
Richard Charles Aldinger, son of Eleanor Harrison, b. 2/1/1940
David Christian Aldinger, son of Eleanor Harrison, b. 11/7/1350
Beverly Lane, dau. of Cullen Burkes, Jr.
Sara Paul Haralson, dau. of Annell Jones H., 1/21/135-
Debroh Blanchard Aldinger, dau. of Eleanor and Richard Aldinger, b.3/14/1956

SUSIE GODWIN BIBLE
Historical Room, Lewis Cooper, Jr., Memorial Library, Opelika, Ala.

On flyleaf: "Miss S. E. Godwin, presented by her father - 1867"
Mrs. A. E. Godwin, our dear mother, d. 6/26/1882 Mr. A. K. Harrison d. 6/17/1885
Mrs. Martha Harrison d. 6/20/1890

DAVENPORT GRAVES REEVES' BIBLE of Macon County
Owner: Mrs. Margaret R. Donaghey
500 Village Lane, Minter Park, Pla. 32792

Births

Davenport G. Reeves 2/9/1822 (Josper Co., Ga., d. 1859 Macon Co., Alabama) m. 1844 in
Chambers Co., Ala., Mary Ann G. (Garnett) Lee Reeves 12/28/1825, dau. of Charles Henry Lee
Jonathan Leonadas Reeves 3/22/1845 (Russell Co., Alabama) Eliza Clarinda Reeves 11/6/1846
Ella Occanna Reeves 11/7/1848
Henry Powel Reeves 4/27/1851
Charley Sherwood Reeves 8/31/1853
Davenport Dowdell Reeves 5/29/1856

(Sanford Graves Reeves Bible continued...)

Births of Children of C. S. and Annie E. Reeves

Clyde Reeves 5/23/1880
Charles Reeves 10/1988
Garnett Davenport Reeves 5/9/1883
Helen Reeves 7/1591
Gussie Reeves 9/7/1885
Henry Thomas Reeves, son of Henry P. and Nora, 8/30/1878

Births of Children of D. D. and L. E. Reeves

Mabel Lee Reeves 12/2/1886 - - -
Ella Ruth Reeves
Garland Graves Reeves 1887
Mary Reeves --
Dowdell Reeves 1831

Births of Children of J. D. and Eliza Reeves Sentell

Claudia Roberta Sentell 9/1/1866
Ella Sentell 1878
John D. Sentell 9/1863
Clam Sentell 1880
Eugenia H. Sentell 1873
Nellie Sentell
Richard Lee Sentell 11/1874
Edna Sentell 1889
Mary Sentell 1875
Jane, a servant, 1849

(Sanford Graves Reeves Bible continued...)

Births of children or B. L. and Minnie Eddins Reeves

Cleno E. C. Reeves 7/15/1868
Mary C. Reeves 8/9/-
Ella M. Reeves 3/9/1870
Hurd Lee Reeves 11/23/1880
William D. Reeves - d. infancy
Charles D. Reeves 3/21/1877-1926
J. L. Reeves m. 2nd, Mary J. Warthin

Births of Children of J. L. and Mary J. Reeves

James N. Reeves 3/1 -- -
Edwin H. Reeves 10/19-7
Edwin H. Reeves 10/1887
John W. Reeves 1890

J. L. Reeves m. 3rd, Ellie Browning Sanford, and had one son, Neil Reeves, b. 190-.

Davenport G. Reeves to Mary A. G. Lee
John D. Sentell to Eliza C. Reeves 9/21/1865
Jonathan T.. Reeves to Minnie A. Eddins 10/16/1867
R. A. Sentell to Lila O. Reeves 2/4/1869
Henry P. Reeves to Nora Warthen 1874
Charles S. Reeves to Annie Justiss 3/13/1879
Dowdell D. Reeves to Leila E. Blanks 12/23:1885

(Danford Graves Reeves Bible continued...)

Births

Dowdell D. Reeves 4/1/1930, aged 73 yrs., 10 mos.
D. G. Reeves 2/16/1859, aged 37 yrs., 7 days, 2 hrs.
Mary, wife of D. G. Reeves, 3/1836, aged 70 yrs., 7 mos.
H. P. Reeves 8/4/1878, aged 27 yrs., 3 mos., In days
Garnett D. Reeves, son of of C. S. and A. E. Reeves, 9/12/1886
Minnie A. Reeves, wife of J. L. Reeves, 7/1882
Eliza, wife of J. D. Sentell, 8/1894, aged 48 yrs.
Ella, wife of R. A. Sentell, 12/1916, aged 68 yrs.
Charles Sherwood Reeves 1907
Jonathan L. Reeves 1/11/1929, aged 34 years, 9 mos.

JOHN W. AND CORDELIA A. ORR BIBLE
Owner: J. Herbert Orr, Opelika, Alabama

Births

John M. Orr 1/6/1846
Cordelia A. Pickard, wife of J. H. Orr, 9/13/1861

Births of Their Children

John Orr, Jr. 11/23/1880
George Mitchell Orr 6/13/1891
Fannie Helen Orr 10/16/1882
Ethel Love Orr
James Dawson Orr 1/27/1885
Robert Sylvester Orr 10/5/1888

279

(John W. Orr Bible continued...)

Marriages

Fannie Helen Orr to Robert D. Foster 2/13/1901
Robert Sylvester Orr to Almer Moline Bishop 8/1/1908
George Mitchell Orr to
Cumi Freeman 12/1/1912
Ethel Love Orr to John A. Capps 1/23/1913
James Dawson Orr to Ermine Hardin 6/10/1914

Deaths

John Orr, Jr. 11/9/1886
Cordelia A. Orr, wife of John H. Orr 7/4/1895
John H. Orr, Sr. 1/14/1931
George Mitchell Orr 4/25/1930
James Dawson Orr 2/11/1956
Robert Sylvester Orr 10/8/1956
Fannie Helen Foster 10/31/1942
Ermine Orr 1/30/1968
Elizabeth Orr, wife by 2nd marriage of J. H. Orr, 8/20/1906
Alma Moline Bishop Orr 11/28/1963

GEORGE IRVIN WILSON BIBLE
Owner: Brady Wilson, Columbus, Ga.

George Irvin Wilson b. 6/25/1815, son of Elias and Martha Wilson, Sumter Co., S. C. and Henry Co., Ala. to Grimes Co., Texas m. Effie F. Outlaw b. 4/3/1821, dau. of Silas and Flora Outlaw, Chesterfield Co., S. C. and Henry Co., Ala., on 6/18/1840, Henry Co., Alabama

Births of Their Children

James Riley Wilson 4/26/1841
Mary Adaline Wilson 5/30/1856
Nancy Lucinda Wilson 9/3/1843
David Alexander Wilson 8/9/1858
Flora Louisa Wilson 6/27/1846
Frances Margaret Wilson 12/14/1861
John Wesley Wilson 5/14/1853

Marriages

Nancy L. to Louis M. Robertson 2/14/1871
Flora L. to James Henry Day 6/7/1869
George H. M. to Ist Martha Ellen Young 6/2/1870, 2nd, Oleha Allsup
Anna I. to Robert A. Anderson
Mary A. to George Washington Newson
David A. to Elizabeth Gooch 1/17/1884

(George Irvin Wilson Bible continued...)

Deaths

James R. 10/23/1861 Camp Moore,Confederate Soldier
George I. 7/14/1878, Texas
Effie F. 2/10/1892, Texas
James, Confederate Soldier, Camp Moore
Flora L. 5/6/1893, Texas
Anna I. 6/7/1928, Alabama
John W. 7/1954, Barbour Co., Alabama
Mary A. 11/3/1930
David A. 2/24/1923, Central America
Frances 12/7/1869, Texas
George M. 8/28/1948, Texas

C. C. HODGE BIBLE
Owner: Mrs. C. C. Gullatte
Rt. 2, Box 2640, Salem, Ala. 36574

Marriages

C. C. Hodge to M. F. Meadows 1/9/1866
Maude Thomas Hodge (2nd) to Samuel Price Hamilton 12/17/1927 by Rev. Clide Bobo
J. P. Hodge to Maude Thomas (Ist marr.) 11/22/1900
Robert Prince to Alice Hodge 12/14/1893
Mamie Hodge to John Lillie 6/3/1802
Will Poole to Emma Hodge 12/13/1894

(C. C. Hodge Bible continued...)

Births

C. C. Hodge 9/21/1841
Charlie Hodge 10/9/1866
John Porter Hodge 9/12/1870
Mary C. Hodge 10/19/1868
Emma Wiley Hedge 5/14/1878
Alpha C. Hodge 2/1/1876, tw;n
Columbus C. Hodge 5/30/1880
Alice Belle Hodge, twin, 2/1/1876
Mamie Lee Hodge 7/28/1887
M. F. M. Hodge 2/5/1845

Deaths

Charlie Hodge 7/3/1888
C. C. Hodge 9/21/1841-1/24/1892

M. F. M. Hodge 2/8/1845-3/10/1920
John Porter Hodge 5/28/1922
Helen Maude Thomas Hodge, Hamilton Hodge 3/8/1931
S. P. Hamilton, 2nd husband of Maude Hodge, 9/21/1940
C. C. Hodge 12/3/1945, 3rd husband of Maude Hodge
Emma Hodge Poole 5/14/1878-1/25/1903

ABEL FLETCHER WILSON BIBLE

Abel Fletcher Wilson b. 10/2/1831, Jasper Co., Ga., son of Joseph Armstrong Wilson m. Mary Franklin Phillips, b. 7/281836, dau. of Jesse Bush and Martha Talbot Phillips of Greene Co. Ga., on 1/20/1853, Dudley's Ville, Alabama

Births of Children

Martha Ella Wilson 7/30/1855 -
James Phillips Wilson 11/13/1869
William Walker Wilson 2/14/1858
Jesse Alonzo Wilson 8/13/1871
Joseph Rush Wilson 6/12/1860
Mary Lena Wilson 2/1/1875
Edwin Fletcher Wilson 11/30/1863

Marriages

Martha E. Wilson to J. B. Echols 11/18/1872
William W. Wilson to Laura F. Biggs 12/16/1885
Edwin F. Wilson to Lou Edwards 12/16/1891
Mary L. Wilson to V. C. Thrash 1/3/1892
James P. Wilson to Frances Haislip 6/21/1099

Deaths

Joseph D. Wilson 10/24/1563
Abel F. Wilson 10/22/1922

(Abel Fletcher Wilson Bible, Deaths continued...)

Jesse A. Wilson 3/13/1876
William W. Wilson 9/24/1332
James P. Wilson 12/29/1902
Mary F. Wilson 2/6/1920, Nashville,

WASHINGTON JEFFERSON WILSON BIBLE of Coosa County
Owner: Brady Wilson, Columbus, Ga-

Washington Jefferson Wilson b. 7/27/1826 m. Sarah A. Elizabeth Mann b. 4/1831

Births of Their Children

Margaret Wilson 1851
Clement Wilson 3/3/1861
Calvin Wilson 3/3/1861
Benjamin Wilson 1855
Whitman Wilson 1853
Charlie S. Wilson 8/22/1865
Mary Jane Wilson 5/5/1857
Elizabeth Frances Wilson 8/30/1867
Laura Josephine Wilson 2/12/1859
Andy Jackson Wilson ---
Mittie Ann Wilson 7/5/1871
Levi Wilson 5/22/1870

Deaths

Washington J. Wilson 11/1/1915
Levi Wilson 1/10/1952
Sarah A. E. Wilson 1918

(Washington Jefferson Wilson Bible, Deaths, contd....)

Elizabeth F. Wilson 2/14/1968
Clement Wilson 9/10/1901
Calvin Wilson 8/2/1937
Mittie A. Wilson 12/10/1946
Charlie S. Wilson 4/19/1948
Mary J. Wilson 7/19/1934
Laura J. Wilson 9/2/1939

ISAAC ROWELL BIBLE
From: Rev. War Pension #W9634

Births

Isaac Rowell 9/20/1759
Susanna Morris 8/21/1760
Isaac and Susanna m. 1/11/1782

Births of Their Children

Elizabeth Rowell 6/23/1783-8/30, aged 20 mos., 7 days
Keziah Rowell 9/6/1784-5/2/1785, aged 10 mos., 20 days
Polley Rowell 11/8/1785
Rowena Rowell 4/25/1787
Jeremiah Rowell 12/13/1788
Priscilla Rowell 12/24/1790
Benjamin Rowell 9/11/1792
Betty Shelton Rowell 3/14/1794
Tempy Rowell 12/25/1795
Alexander Rowell 5/29/1738
Susan Rowell 2/17/1801

JAMES M. ORR BIBLE
Owner: J. Herbert Orr, Opelika, Alabama

Marriages

James M. Orr to Anna T. Orr 1/14/1891
Emery M. Orr to Aleese Clements Orr 6/15/1946
Robert H. Orr to Ethel Mae Dykes 12/23/1926
Robert H. Orr (2/26/38) to Violet Y. Roberts (7/17/16) on 6/20/1979, Judge William C. Barbour officiating

Births

James M. Orr 10/6/1847
Anna T. Orr, wife of James M. Orr, 3/12/1869
James L. Orr 11/24/1891
William C. Orr 10/19/1893
Roy J. H. Orr 5/29/1896
Robert Homer Orr 2/26/1898
Emery Marcus Orr 11/23/1901

Deaths

James M. Orr 1/24/1902
Anna T. Orr 5/4/1956
William C. Moore 9/8/1956
Emery M. Orr 1/5/1957 James L. Orr 2/7/1977
Ethel G. Orr, wife of Roy J. Orr, 11/14/1977
Ethel M. Orr, wife of Robert H. Orr, 11/26/1977
Roy J. Orr 5/5/1979

WILLIAM C. GERMANY BIBLE
Owner: Mrs. Joe Nichols, Langdale, Alabama

William C. Germany 5/10/1860 Chambers Co., Ala.-1/14/1945 Lafayette, Ala. m. 1/20/1885 at home, Stewart Co.. Ga., by Rev. M. F. Hurst, minister, Nora L. Armor 10/4/1866 Stewart Co., Ga. 11/20/1839 Lafayette, Ala.

Father's Father: R. C. Germany 5/1/1837 Chambers Co.,
Father's Mother: S. E. Germany 12/9/1840 Chambers Co., Ala.-
12/1/1928 Lafayetta, Ala.

Mother's Father: James M. Armor 8/5/1829 Putnam Co., Gs.-6/21/1867, Stewart Co., Ga.
Mother's Mother: Frances E. Armor 10/2/1835 Wilkinson Co., Ga.-2/5/1905 Stewart Co., Ga.

Births of Children

Robert Armor Germany 10/31/1866 Chambers Co., Ala. m.. Annie Pope Robinson 10/4/1916
Charlie Brooks Germany 6/12/1891 Chambers Co., Ala.-9/12/1891
Lizzie Mae Germany 6/22/1892 Chambers Co., Ala. m. Carl Q. Wilson 6/10/1914
Annie Ruth Germany 10/27/1897 Chambers Co., Ala. m. Joe T. Nichols 11/20/1919

Miscellaneous

Carl Wilson, Jr., grandson of William C. and Nora L. Germany, b. 8/13/1920, Lakeland, Fla.
James Marion Wilson b. 11/24/1922 Lakeland, Fla.
Mary Elinor Wilson b. 7/11/1924 Lakeland, Fla.
Mildred Lavinia Wilson b. 7/14/1925 Lakeland, Fla.
Herbert Clopton Wilson b. 9/19/1926 Lakeland, Fla.

JOHN RUTHERFORD BIBLE
Ower: Mrs. C. H. Gunter, Phenix City, Alabama 36967

Marriages

John Rutherford to Lucy Ann Stroud 1/7/1841
Reuben Pitts to Lizzie Rutherford 6/2/1859
Eli Rutherford to Jacquenine McCoy 11/15/1868
Walter Vaughan to Ida Rutherford 12/3/1872
Orion Rutherford to Emma Richards 6/2/1872
Henry Neill West to Mattie Rutherford 11/27/1878
Amasa John Pitts to Mattie Slay Zuber 3/26/1903

Births

Lucy Ann Rutherford, wife of John Rutherford, 1/1/1823
Eli Stroud 6/4/1789
Elizabeth Stroud, 2nd wife of Eli Stroud,
Tinsey Stroud, dau. of Eli and Elizabeth Stroud, 9/15/1809
Mark Stroud, son of Eli and Elizabeth Stroud, 1/31/1812
Martha Stroud, dau. of Eli and Elizabeth Stroud, 3/2/1814
Aplin Bib Stroud 12/20/1820
Lucy Ann Stroud 1/1/1823
D. Lafayette Stroud 12/24/1824
Eunice Stroud 12/24/1827
Cranford Howard Collier 7/11/1915
Elizabeth H. L. Rutherford 11/7/1841
Georgia Ann M. Rutherford 2/10/1843
Eli Stroud Rutherford 10/3/1846
M. Luther Rutherford 6/4/1849
Unice Ida Rutherford 7/25/155?
John A. Rutherford 2/2/1855

289

(John Rutherford Bible, Births, contd....)

Mattie Rutherford 5/12/1859
Lafayette D. Rutherford 7/16/1861
Walter Henry Vaughan 2/2/1874
Willie John Harrison West 11/4/1879
Niellie Maud West 11/13/1880
Ira Miller Pitts 10/29/1913
A. J. Collier 10/23/1906
Lucy Clay Collier 1/15/1913
Homer Rutherford 9/27/1869
Viola Rutherford 6/22/1872
Amasa Rutherford Pitts 10/3/1904
Martha Bernice Pitts 10/16/1906
Georgia Kathryn Pitts 10/1/1910
Catie Lou Pitts 10/23/1875
Amasa John Pitts 3/4/1878
Georgia Emma Hendrick Collier 7/31/1901
Reuben Andrew Howard Collier 3/12/1904

Deaths

John Rutherf'ord 11/18/1860
Elizabeth H. L. Pitts 11/19/1878
M. Luther Rutherford 7/27/1880
Lucy Ann Rutherford 5/5/1899
Reuben Pitts 6/21/1904
Georgia Ann M. Pitts 11/17/1907
Georgia Kathryn Pitts 10/8/1910
Walter W. Vaughan 1/8/1874
WIllie John Harrison 10/15/1881
Reuben Howard Collier 8/24/1910

290

DR. B. F. WILSON BIBLE
Owner: Brady Wilson, Columbus, Georgia

D. F. Wilson b. 5/15/1822, son of William and Martha Clements Wilson m. Elizabeth A. Bostick, dau. of F. W. Bostick

Births of Children

William Francis Wilson 12/3/1844
Julia Sue Wilson 1/15/1553
Claudius Wilson 1/13/1847
Ben F. Wilson 1854
Mary Ellen Wilson 9/28/1849
Elizabeth Gertrude Wilson

Marriages

William F. Wilson to Sarah Burnside 12/3/1869
Julia Wilson to Dr. A. E. Hill 1/24/1875
Mary E. Wilson to Silas Durham
Ben P. Wilson to Emma Ferguson
Elizabeth G. Wilson to Charles E. Gilbert

JAMES FRANKLIN WILSON BIBLE

James Franklin Wilson b. 1/18/1873, son of Meredith Asa and Mary Elizabeth Burks Wilson, Crenshaw Co., Ala. m. 12/22/1901, Bradleyton, Alabama, Carry Estelle Dorman (b. 10/11/1856), dau. of Ezikias Bates and Love De Ann (Best) Dorman, Crenshaw Co., Ala.

Births of Children

Bessie May Wilson 11/28/1902 -

(James Franklin Wilson Bible, contd....)

James Meredith Wilson 12/27/1915
Ruthie Estelle Wilson 6/3/1904
Archie Ray Wilson 1/15/1918
Lyman Albert Wilson 2/11/1906
Lillie Odelle Wilson 5/2/1920
Mary Love Wilson 12/1/1907
Woodrow Wilson 6/15/1922
Charles Moroni Wilson 4/2/1909
Lady Grace Wilson 9/9/1925
Irvine Nephi Wilson 3/15/1911
Datha Roberta Wilson 8/7/1928
Rosa Belle Wilson 12/14/1913

Marriages

Bessie May Wilson to O. B. Stewart
Ruthie Estelle Wilson to Leon Emmett Short
Lyman Albert Wilson to Archie Ethelene Berry
Mary Love Wilson to George Julian Norris
Charles M. Wilson to Florelle Duck
Irving N. Wilson to Fletcher S. Courtrey
Rosa Belle Wilson to C. L. Mellon
Archie R. Wilson to Voncille Rowell
Lillie O. Wilson to W. R. Holley
Woodrow Wilson to Velma Collins
Lady Grace Wilson to Glen Parkam

YOUNG D. AND TALITHA HARRINGTON BIBLE
Of Tallasee County
Owner: Young Drew Harrington
16 Davis Dr., Montgomery, Ala. 36105

Marriages

Young 0. Harrington to Talitha G. Emfinger 11/8/1839 (Russell Co., Alabama)
James Howard to Martha A. S. Harrington 2/10/1861
Young J. Harrington to Marry M. Oliver 11/9/1865
William F. Harrington to Nancy A. Oliver 11/19/1868
James L. Oliver to Matilda C. Harrington 11/3/1870
H. J. Harrington to Sarah C. Turner 12/1/1872
G. M. Harrington and Amelia Lancaster 11/21/1872

Births

Y. D. Harrington 6/4/1818
Talitha G. Emfinger 5/3/1816
Martha Ann Sophroney Harrington 10/12/1840
James Harvey Harrington 1/1/1842
Drewry Hamilton Harrington 1/10/1844
Jeptha Harrington 11/27/1845
William Franklin Harrington 11/3/1847
Henry Jasper Harrington 2/3/1850
Matilday Caroline Harrington 6/24/185
George Miles Harrington 10/12/185-
John R. Harrington 10/3/1856
Mary Frances E. Harrington 1/3/1860
M. Harrington 1855
Mary Jane Howard 12/27/1861
Drury Anna Howard 7/21/1865

(Young D. Harrington Bible, continued…)

Martha Penelope Howard 6/3/1867
Talitha Caroline Howard 2/3/1869

Deaths

James R. Harrington 9/10/1865
Mourning Emfinger 11/17/1866
D. Harrington 7/9/1868
Talitha G. Harrington 9/10/1889
Henry G. Harrington 2/3/1850
Sarah C. Turner 1/24/1856
Young Preston Harrington 11/9/1874
Charley Bartis Harrington 5/1/1876
Samma James Harrington 12/1/1877
Henry Hamilton Harrington 2/3/1880
Mary Jane Harrington 4/7/1881
Willey Lenord Harrington 3/30/1858

Marriages

William G. Johnson to Mary F. E. Harrington 12/19/1875
John R. Harrington to Sophronia Osburn 2/20/1879

Deaths

Madie Catherine Lyles Harrington, wife of Charlie Dartis
Harrington, 10/17/1970
Nina P. Johnson 8/14/1881
Samma J. Harrington 10/16/1901
M. J. Harrington 12/29/1911
Sarah C. Harrington 8/3/1920

294

(Young D. Harrington Bible, continued...)

Young Preston Harrington 7/4/1928
Charlie D. Harrington 8/7/1943
Henry H. Harrington 12/24/1951
Mary Jane Harrington 5/27/1911

Births

Cora Lee Harrington 5/8/1869
William Harvey Oliver 9/18/1871
Nina Perkins Johnson 11/1/1879
Lula May Johnson 9/30/1881
Thelma Harrington 1/7/1897
Thelma Dunn Harrington 1/13/1932

ELLIS CROWDER BIBLE
Owner: Charles H. Crump, Lanett, Alabama

Marriages

John Ellis Crowder of Randolph Co., Ala. to Cassie Let Tomlin of Randolph Co.. Ala. 1/10/1903
at John Henderson's. Wit: Edgar L. Holladay, Mary E. Holladay
James Gordon Crowder to Ellene Beaird 10/15/1332
Lillie Agnes Crowder to James Floyd Brown 11/9/1935
Catherine Janet Crowder to Alfred L. Aubrey 4/27/1942

Births

John Ellis Crowder 3/25/1087
Cassie Lee Crowder 3/23/)992
James Gordon Crowder 1/27/1910, son of John E. and C. L. Crowder
Lillie Agnes Crowder 11/9/1912

(Ellis Crowder Bible continued...)

Annie Evelyn Crowder 1/31/1918
Catherine Janette Crowder 3/27/1820

Deaths

James Gordon Crowder, Jr., son of James Gordon, Sr. and Eilene Crowder, 6/9/1949
Joyce Izora Crowder, dau. of James Gordon Crowder, Sr. and Eilene, 4/15/1919

JAMES DANIEL POE BIBLE
Owner: Mrs. J. W. McClendon
Rt. 3, Box 227A, Lafayette, Ala. 36862

Births of Children of James Daniel and Sarah Gardner Poe

Martha Ann Poe 9/19/1839
James William Poe 4/4/1859
Mary Jane Poe 10/26/1840
Josephine Poe 4/22/1861
Lucinda Frances Poe 8/9/1842
Henrietta Poe 3/4/1864
Nancy Elizabeth Poe :/27/1844
Mary L. Poe 2/20/1879
Leathea Poe 12/11/1845
Leila May Poe 11/4/1886
Sarah Catherine Poe 7/5/1847
Sarah Ella Poe 11/1/1879
Adelpha Poe 5/14/1849
Joseph W. Poe 4/8/1874
John Daniel Poe 5/15/1951
James O. Poe 8/23/1875

(James Daniel Poe Bible continued...)

Thomas Jefferson Poe 6/6/1853
Susan Poe 5/20/1855
Thomas Jefferson Poe d. 9/11/1854 Leathea Bridges d. 6/6/1881

Marriages

James Daniel Poe to Sarah Gardner 12/28/1538
Nancy E. Poe to James Russell Underwood 11/29/1860
Lucinda Poe to William H. Underwood 12/23/1860

SHERWOOD WHITE PARKER BIBLE
Owner: Carolyn S. Price, Montgomery, Alabama

Marriages

Daniel Parker to Mary Booth 7/20/182--
Thomas Parker to Mary Ann Atkins 11/8/1827
Sherwood Parker to Candis Kemp 10/14/1838

Births

Daniel P. P. Meadows 10/30/1818
Susan M. Parker 9/18/1804
Nancy Meadows 5/25/1823
Lucy Walker 5/9/1803
Miles R. Meadows 5/9/1800

Deaths

Daniel Parker, Sr. 8/14/1844

(Sherwood White Parker Bible, Deaths continued...)

Thomas Parker 3/19/1845
Lucy Parker 11/14/1845
George W. Parker, son, Sherwood Parker, 10/20/1841
Lucy Parker 8/31/1868, aged 65 yrs, 3 mos., 22 days

Marriages

Miles R. Meadows to Susan M. Parker 8/17/1823

Births

Lucy Ann White Meadows 11/11/1824
James Meadows 1/9/1827
Miless Philmon Meadows 2/14/1829
Rutha Meadows 3/7/1831
Benjamin Franklin Meadows 5/31/1833
Isom Medders 4/4/1810
Lucv Medders 12/15/1806
Alletha Medders 10/27/1812
Susannah Parker 9/1/1807
Polly Medders 9/20/1814

Births

Susannah Medders 1/5/1821
Daniel M. Parker 10/7/1839
Thomas Parker 2/14/1803
Madison Columbus Parker 3/25/1840
America Ann Medders 10/19/1825
Lucy Ann M. Parker 1/23/1829

298

George Washington Parker 9/19/1841
Anderson W. Parker 7/15/1843
Nancy Ann Parker 9/1/1833
James Madison Parker 11/27/1835
Sarah Martha Parker 8/8/1339
James Knox Parker 12/22/1844
Thomas Jefferson Parker 1/6/1844
Richard Thomas Parker 12/19/1845
Mary Elizabeth Parker 10/7/1849

Deaths

Madison Columbus Parker 6/16/1868, aged 27 yrs., 8 mos., 21 days
Candace Parker 3/8/1869
Sherwood White Parker 5/24/1870?
James S. Parker 8/14/1874, aged 29 yrs., 3 mos., 22 days

Loose Note in Bible:

Mollie E. Shepherd 3/25/1887, aged 38 yrs., 8 mos., 18 days

JAMES BRYANT PALMER BIBLE
Owner: Otis Worley Pruett, Ormond Beach, Florida

Births

James Bryant Palmer 10/24/1846
Mollie Elizabeth Cox 12/24/1851-2/16/1924
Otis Otto Worley 1/11/1871
Carrie Elizabeth Palmer 1/17/1874

(James Bryant Palmer Bible...)

Benjamin Franklin Palmer 10/12/1871
William Daniel Palmer 11/8/1883
Ruby V. Worley 4/30/1892
Otis May Worley 3/30/1895
Lizzie Ruth Worley 9/22/1097
Ruby Lucille Pruett 1/25/1949, Williams Hospital, Camilla, Ga., dau. of Mr. and Mrs. Samuel Thomas Pruett, Jr.

Births of Children of Otis V. and Virginia F. Pruett

Otis Worley Pruett, Jr. 3/13/1945, John Hodges Drake Inf., Auburn, Alabama
David Foster Pruett 10/22/---, John Hodges Drake Inf., Auburn, Alabama
Mary Leda Pruett 3/27/1952, Lee Co. Hospital, Opelika, Alabama Lee Nicholas Pruett 10/27/1963, Halifax Hospital, Daytona Beach, Florida

Marriages

James C. Palmer to Mollie E. Cox 11/12/1871
Cnrrie L. Palmer to Otis O. Worley 7/5/1831
William D. Palmer to Jillia May Spencer 11/3/1904
Ruby V. Worley to Samuel Thomas Pruett 10/22/1913
Otis Worley Pruett to Virginia Lee Foster 3/6/1863, Methodist Church, Auburn, Alabama
Louise Mattison 9/6/1914, Abbevllle Co., S. C.-d. 1964 Detroit, Michigan m. 5/1/1943, Baptist Church, Phenix City, Alabama
Samuel Thomas Pruett, Jr. b. 3/1914

Deaths

James Benjamin Palmer 3/22/1908, 62 yrs., 2 mos., 6 days
Otis Otto Worley 5/1/1945, Camilla, Ga.

Carrie Elizabeth Worley 4/7/1948, Camilla, Ga.
Samuel Thomas Pruett, Sr. 9/8/1958, Tuscaloosa, Alabama
Ruby Worley Pruett 6/1S/1963, Daytona Beach, Florida
William 0. Palmer 1/25/1969, Camilla, Ga.
Julia May Spencer 5/30/1943, Camilla, Ga,

Births

Samuel Thomas Pruett, Jr. 9/1J1914
Otis Worley Pruett 9/3/1317
Virginia Lee Foster, wife of Otis W. Pruett 3/6/1943

THOMAS JEFFERSON CHRISTIAN BIBLE
Owner: Mrs. Mable C. Ross
Rt. 4, Box 3083, Opelika, Ala. 36801

Thomas Jefferson Christian, son of William Pain Christian and wife, Sarah Maxwell m.
6/10/1829 Mary Jane, dau. of Rufus Christian and wife, Mary Oglesby.

Births of Children of Thomas Jefferson and Mary Jane Christian

Martha Ann Christian 7/29/1830
William Rufus Christian 9/5/1832
Cornelius Jeptha Christian 3/18/1834
Louisa Antionette Christian 4/27/1936
Thomas Maxwell Christian 4/1/1835
Meriwether Garret Christian 2/11/1840
Lucinda Jane Christian 3/11/1842
Asa Chandler Christian 2/11/1844
Mary Elizabeth Christian 7/24/1846

(Thomas Jefferson Christian Bible continued....)

Luther Martin Christian 11/16/1848
Sarah Emily Christian 3/28/1851
      Deaths

Martha Ann Christian 9/28/1839, aged 9 yrs.
Lucinda Jane Christian 7/2/1857, aged 15 yrs.
Thomas Maxwell Christian 12/31/1851, Lynchburg, Va. hospital, effects of wound on battlefield
at Manassas, aged 23 yrs. Meriwether Garret Christian 3/13/1862 in prison, as Confederate
Soldier at Elmira, New York, aged 22 yrs.
Luther Martin Christian, went with Confederate army when only 16 yrs. old, we do not know
What became of him.
Mary Jane Christian, wife of T. J., 3/28/1887, aged 76.
T. J. Christian 10/23/1891, aged 84, near Lafayette, Chambers Co., Alabama

ASA CHANDLER CHRISTIAN BIBLE
Owner: Mrs. Mable C. Ross
Rt. 4, Box 303, Opelika, Ala. 36801

Asa Chandler Christian of Jackson Co., Ga. m. Sophiah E. Shields of Jackson Co., Ga.
1/14/1879 at her   father's house by William Seay. Wits: Robert Shields, Stewart McElhannon.

Births

Asa Chandler Christian 2/11/1844
Sophiah E. Shields 1/23/1859-6/22/1301 Logansville, Ga.

    Births of Their Children

Lizzie May Christian 2/2/1880
William Shields Christian 8/27/1881

Thomas Jefferson Christian 12/13/1882
Robert Asa Christian 11/16/1884
Joseph Charley Christian 3/23/1888
Omer Chandler Christian 9/26/1890
Lee Christian 4/3/1892
Sallie Lonn Christian 10/3/1894
Susie Jane Christian 2/20/1897
Nettle L. Christian 2/4/1900

Deaths

Robert Asa Christian 1/3/1856
Nettie Lou Christian 1/17/1902
Asa Chandler Christian at home of Sue Christian Champion in Lafayette, Ala. 3/4/1928, bur. in Winder, Ga.

GEORGE NICHOLAS CHERRY BIBLE
Owner: Leda Cherry Foster, Auburn, Alabama

Florida May Foster m. George N. Cherry at Auburn, Ala. 12/22/1887

Father - George N. Cherry 6/22/1859 Opelika, Ala.-6/3/1934 m. 1887
Mother - Florida M. Cherry 5/26/1869 Auburn, Ala.-3/5/1941 m. 1887

Children

Foster Lamar Cherry 4/3/1889 Opelika, Ala.- 8/19/1933 m. 11/1/1911
Mattie Lee Cherry 10/6/1890 Opelika, Ala. m. 2/11/1907
Lewis Allen Cherry 2/9/1893 Opelika, Ala. m. 2/13/1921

(George Nicholas Cherry Bible continued...)

Mary Elizabeth Cherry 9/10/1898 Opelika, Ala.-2/21/1902
Leda Mae Cherry 5/8/1902 Auburn, Ala. m. 12/31/1921

Grandchildren

William Leroy Flanagan 5/15/1908 Auburn, Ala. m. 5/1933
George Douglas Flanagan 2/22/1912 Auburn, Ala. m. 9/12/1938 (above are children of Mattie Lee Cherry and james W. Flanagan)

Thomas Cecil Cherry 9/13/1912, Ridge Grove, Ala.

Frances Elizabeth Flanagan 4/1/1916 Auburn, Ala. m. 9/23/1935
Elsie Louise Cherry 5/20/1816
Ridge Grove, Ala. m. 3/30/1934

James Adam Flanagan 8/15/1921 Auburn, Ala. m. 9/13/1949
Virginia Lee Foster 7/30/1923 Auburn, Ala. m. 3/6/1943
Foster Lamar Cherry, Jr. 3/28/1925
Montgomery, Ala.
Mary Frances Cherry 11/16/1935, Opelika, Ala.
Marianne Stickle 10/1935 Washington, D. C.
John Tom Gaillard III 12/1/1936, Wetumpka, Ala.
James Douglas Flanagan 4/24/1939, Opelika, Ala.
Roy William Flanagan d. 5/4/1939, Jersey City, N. J.

Marriages

Foster Lamar Cherry to Annie Belle Thomas
Mattie Lee Cherry to James W. Flanagan

(George Nicholas Cherry Bible continued...)

Lewis Allen Cherry to Lillie Mae Golden
Leda Mac Cherry to David S. Foster
William Leroy Flanagan to Emily Rowe
George Douglas Flanagan to Cornelia Stevens
Thomas Cecil Cherry to Vena Nolan
Frances Elizabeth Flanagan to John Tom Gailliard
Elsie Louise Cherry to Charles W. Stickle
James Adam Flanagan to La Vern Taylor
Virginia Lee Foster to Otis Worley Pruett
Mary Frances Cherry to Rev. James Taylor

CLARK FOSTER BIBLE
Owner: Leda Cherry Foster, Auburn, Alabama

Births

Clark Foster, Sr. 9/28/1790
Elizabeth (Wheeden) Foster 10/19/1793
Miranda Foster 2/13/1811
Stephen D. Foster 10/24/1816
L. A. Foster 4/27/1812
Sylvia Foster 12/28/1818
David S. Foster 10/14/1814
Clark Foster, Jr. 11/24/1820
Martha Long 1790
Seth Foster 12/7/1822
Dorinda D. Long 7/30/1817
Catherine Foster 4/2/1825
P. H. Long 12/17/1818

(Clark Foster Bible continued...)

Sarah and Asa Foster 1/9/1827
S. H. Long 12/17/---

Marriages

Lewis A. Foster to Dorinda D. Long 12/15/1835
David S. Foster to Margaret Johnson 7/3/1839 (or Johnston)

Births

Clark W. Foster, son of David and Margaret Johnson, 10/13/1829, Talbotton, Ga.
Elizabeth and Janie (twins) 1841 James Douglas Foster 9/19/1844
Ella Naomi Foster 5/8/1858

Deaths

Asa Foster 12/2/1828
Martha Long 10/2/1861
Clark Foster, Jr. 4/21/1046
Miranda Foster Sargant 10/1/1882
Elizabeth Foster 8/15/1847
Sylvia Foster 2/11/1832
Sarah E. Foster 2/16/1360
L. A. Foster 9/7/1894
Clark Foster, Sr. 7/6/1868
Dorinda D. Foster 4/23/1897

HENRY FRANKLIN PLESS BIBLE
Owner: Mrs. Gervis Mullican, Dadevllle, Alabama 36853

Marriages

Henry Franklin Pless of Tallapoosa Co., Ala. to Mary Permelia Smith of Tallapoosa Co., Ala. 12/28/1879 at A. A. Smith's, by Henry Mosley, D. D.
James Monroe Pless to Lucinda J. Doon 12/25/1853 by Joseph Johnson, J. P.

Births of Their Children

James Rufas Pless 8/6/----l0/13/1861 m. Belle Machen
Minnie Lee Pless 11/23/1864-5/18/1860 m. Samuel Eugene Banks
L. B. (Elby) Pless 2/15/1887 m. Sarah Loduska Knight
Arrie Dale Pless 8/23/1890-3/28/1920 m. John Warner Slaughter
David Clifton Pless 9/19/1893-5/28/1972 m. Tyra Gunn
Eva Bell Pless 12/15/1996-12/19/1972 m. Andrew J. Easterwood
Mary Ophelia Pless 12/8/1900 m. Grady Abernathy

Births

Eva Bell Pless 12/15/1896 Tallapoosa Co., Ala.
Mary Pless 12/9/1900 Tallapoosa Co., Ala..
James Monroe Pless 5/25/1830 Heard Co., Ga.
Lucinda J. Pless 2/11/1838 Chambers Co., Fla.
Mary F. Pless 11/22/1854 Tallapoosa Co., Ala.
Amy Elizabeth Pless 1/17/1857 Tallapoosa Co., Ala.
Henry Franklin Pless 3/10/1859 Tallapoosa Co., Ala.
Esper Ann Pless 2/5/1861 Tallapoosa Co., Ala. Texas
Olia Pless 3/28/1563 Tallapoosa Co., Ala.
Mary M. Pless 4/5/1859 Tallapoosa Co., Ala.

307

James R. Pless 8/4/1882 Tallapoosa Co., Ala.
Minnie Lee Pless 11/23/1984 Tallapoosa Co., Ala.
J. N. Pless 2/15/1857 Tallapoosa Co., Ala.
Arrie Dale Pless a/23/1890 Tallapoosa Co., Ala.
David Clifton Pless 9/19/1893 Tallapoosa Co., Ala.

Deaths

Henry F. Pless 5/29/1927
Mary Permelia Pless 2/9/1937
Mary E. Pless 1/8/1908
E. A. Henderson 12/24/1905
A. E. Henderson 4/8/1903
Mother 8/24/1913
Arrie Dail Slaughter Destroid (killed in tornado) 3/28/1920
H. F. Pless 4/30/1927
Mary Permelia Pless 2/9/1937

JAMES MONROE PLESS BIBLE
Of Tallapoosa County
Owner: Mrs. Gervis Mullican, Dadeville, Alabama 36852

James Monroe Pless b. 5/25/1830 Heard Co., Ga. m. 12/25/1853
Lucinda J. Boone, d. Camp Douglas, Chicago, Ill. 11/3/1863
Lucinda J. Boone Pless b. 2/11/1838 Chambers Co., Alabama

Births of Their Children (all b. Tallapoosa Co.. Ala.)

Amy Elizabeth Pless 1/17/1857-4/19/1909
Henry Franklin Pless 3/10/1859-4/30/1927

(James Monroe Pless Bible continued...)

Esper Ann Pless 2/5/1861-12/24/1908 Texas
Ola Fless 3/28/1863-1/24/1943
Mary F. Pless (sister of James Monroe) 11/22/1854-1/8/1808

WILLIAM McKISSACK BIBLE
Owner: Mrs. Gervis Mullican, Dadeville, Alabama 36853

Marriages

William McKissack to Jennie Nolen 1/9/1870
----- McKissack 12/3/1891
Herman Cary Mulican to Kate Ozelia McKissack 12/6/1908
Jack McKissack to Ruth Lowry McCarty 11/30/1911
Edd Mulican to Clessie McKissack 12/23/1906

Births

William McKissick 6/5/1846
Thomas McKissack 5/10/1881
Jennie McKissack 1/22/1854
Jack McKissack 5/20/1883
Cage McKissack 4/4/1868
Kate McKissack 5/20/1883
Simmie McKissack 10/2/1874
Cleseye McKissack 8/21/1888
Jean McKissack 5/15/1876
Dorsie McKissack 11/30/1890
Josie McKissack 5/15/1877
Nolen McKissack 6/4/1834
Ida McKissack 4/12/1879

309

(William McKissack Bible continued...)

Deaths

Grandfather, Thomas Jefferson McKissack, 4/16/1888
Grandmother, Emelah McKissack 5/14/1900
Thomas Jefferson McKissack 8/1888
Jennie Lee McKissick 4/1923

HERMAN CARY MULLICAN BIBLE
Owner: Mrs. Gervis Mullican, Dadeville, Alabama 36853

Herman Cary Mullican m. Kate Ozelia McKissack 12/6/1908 at T. J. Clayton's, by Rev. Stevenson, Dadeville, Alabama

Births

Herman Cary Mullican 6/29/1888
Kate Ozelia McKissack Mullican 3/17/1856-1/30/1931
Mary Lucile Mullican 3/4/1910
Joe Cary Mullican 5/28/1911
Thella May Mullican 12/2/1912
Lisa Vaughan Mullican 4/1/1915
Andrew Jackson Mulican 6/30/1916
William Mack Mullican 5/17/1921
Mary Lucile Mullican 3/4/1910 Dadeville, Ala. m. 12/24/1931
Joe Cary Mullican 5/28/1911 Dadeville, Ala. m. 12/22/1935
Bob Mullican 6/30/1916 Dadeville, Ala. m. 12/18/1936
Candy Mullican 12/2/1912 Dadeville, Ala. m. 17/23/1939
Mac Mullican 5/17/1921 Dadeville, Ala.-l2/23/1914 n. 1/15/1941
W. F. McKissack 6/5/1846-9/26/1910
Clessie McKissack Mullican 1/1935

(Herman Cary Millican Bible continued...)

Thomas Jefferson McKissack 5/10/1881-5/17/1893
Kate Ozelia McKissack Mullican 1/30/1931
Cage McKissack d. 7/1937
William Mac Mullican d. 12/23/1944

Note: sp. Mulican, Mullicnn

JESSE LAWRENCE AND MARY FRANCES ELIZABETH DOLLAR EASTWOOD BIBLE
Owner: Mrs. GervIs Mullican
Dadeville, Alabama

Marriages

L. C. Easterwood 3/4/1906
Mary Elizabeth Ensterwood 1/lH/1903
R. H. Easteruood 12/27/1908
A. J. Easterwood 9/27/1916
Lena Easterwood 3/21/1915
Lois Easterwood 7/20/1918
Bessie Easterwood 5/1'!1921
L. C. Easterwood to Dannie Callaway 2/2/1930 (2nd marr.)
Lucious Easterwood
Susie Easterwood 5/16/1925

Births

Jessie Lawrence Easterwood 6/15/1859
Mary Frances Elizabeth Dollar 4/1/1861
Mary Elizabeth Easterwood 4/7/18A
Larkin Cleveland Easterwood 9/18/1884

311

Rich Henry Eastwood 6/10/1886
Susa Leona Easterwood 4/12/1888
Lucious Eligia Easterwood 4/6/1890
Martha Maglener Easterwooi: 5/22/1893
Andrew Jackson Easterwood 4/21/1894
Bessie Easterwood 4/21/1897
Lowyest Easterwood 7/26/1839
Flora Lodesta Easterwood h:2/1802

Jesse Lawrence Easterwood 6/15/1859-1/13/1931 m. 3/23/1882
Mary Frances Elsabeth Dollar
Mary Frances Elizabeth Dollar 4/1/1861-6/6/1931 m. 3/23/1852
Jesse Lawrence Easterwood
Mary Elizabeth Easterwood 4/7/i1883-3/3/1973 m. 1/18/1903
Charles H. Allen
Larkin Cleveland Easterwood 9/28/1884-2/15/1971 m. 1st, 3/0/1906
Lena Scogin, 2nd, 2/2/1930 Dannie Callaway
Richard Henry Easterwood 6/10/1886-5/17/1964 m. 12/27/1908
Dixie Maybell Fuller
Susie Leona Easterwood 4/12/1889-4/1963 m. 5/16/1925
Joe Thomas Banks
Lucious Eligia Easterwood 4/6/1890-3/3/1925 m. 5/5/1917
Holland Patterson
Martha Magdalene Easterwood 5/22/1892 m. 3/21/1915 George W. Davis
Andrew Jackson Easterwood b. 4/21/1894 m. 9/27/1914 Eva Bell Pless
Bessie Easterwood b. 4/21/1897 m. 5/15/1921 Calvin Howard
Lois Easterwood b. 7/26/1899 m. 7/20/1918 Coley Lee Gilbert

JOHN RANDOLPH PAGE BIBLE
Owner: Arthur E. Page, Jr.
2821 Martin Lane, Montgomery, Ala.

Births

William Byrd Page 4/25/1833 Chambers Co., Ala.
Henry Williamson Pace 10/14/1834 Chambers Co., Ala.
John Randolph Page 12/12/1836 Chambers Co., Ala.
Asa Thomas Page 7/26/1838 Chambers Co., Ala.
Robert Seldon Page 3/11/1840 Chambers Co., Ala.
Jesse Boring Page 4/19/1842 Russell Co., Ala.
Mary Ann Page 6/6/1844 Russell Co., Ala.
Lucy Edmonia Page 12/18/1843 Russell Co., Ala.
Walter Alexander Page 10/11/1851 Russell Co., Ala.
Maria Virginia Page 2/4/1853 Russell Co., Ala.
Frances Jane Byrd Page 10/8/1854 Russell Co., Ala.
Wiley McClendon Page 12/8/1887 Oak Dowery, Chambers Co., Ala.
Lucy Bird Page 4/29/1890 Oak Dowery, Chambers Co., Ala.
Walter Alexander Page 10/12/1891 Oak Dowery, Chambers Co., Ala.

Deaths

Maria Page 3/15/1848 Russell Co., Ala., aged 34
Robert Seldon Page 3/11/1862 Russell Co., Ala. aged 22
Henry Williamson Page 5/8/1872 Lee Co., Ala., aged 38
John R. Page 8/4/1804-10/26/1864 Russell Co., Ala., aged 60 yrs, 2
mos., 22 days
Walter Alexander Page 10/29/1838 Oak Dowery, Chambers Co., Ala.,
aged 47 yrs.

313

(John Randolph Page Bible continued...)

Lucy Cryer Page 4/1812-2/10/1890 Oak Bowery, Chambers Co., Ala., aged 78 yrs.

Marriages

John Randolph Page to Maria Williamsbn 6/26/1832, Harris Co., Ga.
John Randolph Page to Lucy Crier 3/20/1849 Auburn, Macon, Co., Ala.

WILLIAM F. AND MAGGIE CUMMINGS' BIBLE
Owner: Mrs. Clarence Cummings
P. O. Box 181, Phenix City, Alabama

Marriages

William Flynn Cummings to Maggie S. Godwin -/1/1889
Chester F. Bonnet to Sally Fannie Cummings -/15/1809
Jim J. Jones to Cerlera S. Cummings 6/21/1918
Ben Godwin Cummings to Cleo Mathew 5/22/--
Bryan Cummings to Thelma Warren Cubbage 5/22/1920
William Clarence Cummings to Minnie L. Maye 10/14/1924
John P. Vastine Cunmings to Essie Marie HeySack 6/18/1930

Births

William Flynn Cummings 11/8/1861 Maggie S. Cummings 6/28/1870
Sally Fannie Cummings 9/8/1890 Sally Fannie Cummings 9/8/1830
Ben Godwin Cummings 1/31/1892, twin James Gordon Cummings 1/31/1892, twin
Cerlera S. Cummings 6/17/1893 William Clarence Cummings 12/7/1894
Bryan Cummings 1/2/1897
John P. Vastine Cummings 10/20/1901

314

(John Randolph Page Bible continued...)

Mattie Grace Cummings 10/14/1906
Mary E. Cummings 6/18/1910

Deaths

W. F. Cummings 3/18/1941, funeral by Rev. Fred Davis
Mrs. W. F. Cummings 5/18/1945, funeral by Rev. Walton
Mrs. Willie Bonner Sanders 10/26/1945, funeral by Rev. Stanley
Mrs. Frances Cummings.Lunsford 12/17/1956
Mary E. Cummings 2/22/1859, funeral by Rev. Thomas Curtis Bryan Cummings 12/2/1967
Godwin Cummings 1/8/1981 Gordon Cummings 5/2/1981 Vastine Cummings 5/14/1982

ANDREW TAYLOR JACKSON
Owner: Don L. Clark
P. O. Box 353, Lafayette, Alabama 36862

Andrew Jackson Taylor b. 12/16/1846 Chambers Co., Ala., son of William Rufus and Martha Foster Jackson m. 12/24/1878
Lucy Ida Cryer b. 9/4/1860 Chambers Co., Ala.-d. 10/2/1933, dau. of George W. Cryer (1/1/1800-5/30/1877) and Elizabeth Mitchell (2/17/1823-

Births of Children of Andrew and Lucy Jackson

Erine Pauline Jackson 3/14/1881-11/3/1937
Herbert Bernard Jackson 11/23/1882-12/26/1959
Bertha Jackson 2/9/1885-1/12/1935
Florine Jackson 5/20/1888-1/30/1962
Charles William Jackson 2/2/1894-8/7/1954

315

HAVIS-REEVES BIBLE
Owner: T. J. Peddy, Columbus, Georgia

Wilton Wendell Webb m. Eloise Burkhead Harrell at Opelika, Ala.
Wendell Burkhead Webb, their child, b. 1933 at Hospital in
Montgomery, Ala.
Thomas Joseph Peddy m. Patricia Lambert 2/2/1938 in Spartanburg, S. C.
Thomas Larry Peddy, son of Thomas Joseph and Patricia Lambert Peddy, b. 10/4/1940 South
Highlands Hospital, Birmingham, Ala.

Neil Williams Webb, wife of Grady Webb, Sr. d. West Point, Ga. 1/20/1842
Martha Elizabeth Webb m. John King 7/3/1941, West Point, Ga.

John Minor Havis 5/26/1839 Chambers Co., Ala.-10/23/1879 m. 8/14/1866 Annie Elizabeth
Reeves 5/5/1845 Auburn, Ala.-11/30/1930 m. 8/14/1866
George William Havis b. 12/1/1867 Loachapoka, Ala. Jesse Minor Havis b. 3/14/1877 Newnan,
Ga.
Roy Calhoun Havis b. 12/30/1900 Atlanta, Ga.

THOMAS BROUGHTON BIBLE
Of Lawrence County
From: Rev. War Pension #W897

Thomas Broughton b. 4/19/1760, St. John's Parish on Cooper River in South Carolina, m. 1783
Edgefield District, S. c., Mary Wallace

Births of Children of Thomas and Mary Broughton

Robert Wallace Broughton 12/31/1784-6/29/1855
Ann Singleton Broughton 6/29/1786
Sarah Broughton 9/12/1789-10/23/1789

(Thomas Broughton Bible continued...)

Thomas Broughton 9/8/1791
Mary Broughton 5/9/1794
Isabel Stewart Broughton 3/15/1799
Ruth Broughton 5/14/1802 m. Josiah Penn

Note: Thomas Broughton lived in S. C. after war until 1818 when he removed to Rutherford Co., N. C. In 1819 he moved to Lawrence Co., Ala. where he d. 2/14/1836. Widow, Mary Broughton, applied for pension 6/9/1841, Gibson Co., Tenn., aged 78 yrs. She d. 4/22/1842.

ISAM SHEPHERD BIBLE
Owner: Louie Shepherd
Alexander City, Alabama

Marriages

Isam Shepherd to Rebecca Y. Godfrey 6/18/1851
Florence Isabella Shepherd to J. J. Nickerson 2/28/1878
Thomas H. Shepherd to Nancy Isabella McKelvey 10/10/1853
Louie Shepherd to Thelma Sproggins 11/20/1937

Deaths

Isam Shepherd 5/13/1871, aged 46 yrs., 1 mo., 24 days
Florence Isabella Shepherd Nickerson 4/21/1579, aged 19 yrs., 4 mos., 18 days
Howard Belle Shepherd 5/22/1892
Thomas H. Shepherd 4/2/1933
BDernard G. Shepherd 3/5/1948
Nannie McKelvey Shepherd 3/23/1957

317

(Isam Shepherd Bible)

Births

Isam Shepherd 3/29/1825
Rcbecca Y. Godfrey 3/21/1834
Hassle Shepherd, dau. of Warren O'Neal, 12/6/1906
John Tilleton Shepherd 4/17/1852
Buddy Shepherd 1/18/1854-8/7/1854
Warren O'Neal Shepherd 7/5/1855
Florence Isabella Shepherd 12/31/1859
Adolpha Shepherd 1/13/1862
Thomas H. Shepherd 5/20/1864
Nancy Isabella McKelvey 4/1/1870

W. A. HEARN BIBLE
Owner: Mrs. Lewis C. Hanna, Columbus, Georgia

Births (all in Alabama)

W. A. Hearn 12/31/1871
Georgia Hearn 8/20/1902
Mrs. Mittie Hearn 2/6/1874
Clarence Hearn 8/8/1907
Johny Hearn 12/7/1891
Lydia Hearn 7/17/1909
Willie Hearn 3/14/1893
Leroy Hearn 11/12/1912
Lelia Hearn 9/3/1895
Ruth Hearn 2/19/1925
Bryant Hearn 2/14/1900
Lillian Hearn 4/9/1926

Harrel Hearn 11/27/1920 Co.
Mack Hearn 12/13/1916 Ga.
William Taylor Burks 7/31/1899 Miss.

W. A. Hearn 12/31/1871 m. 12/25/1890
Permittie A. Hearn 2/6/1874-5/8/1893
Johnie Hearn 12/7/1891
Billie Hearn 3/1893
Willie May Hearn 9/3/1895
Bryant Hearn 2/14/1900
Clarence Hearn 8/8/1906
Leila Hearn 7/17/1905-3/1906
Roy Hearn 11/12/1913
Georgia Hearn d. 7/11/1906
A. M. Allen d. 9/26/1929

J. D. Hearn m. Annie Brantley 8/6/1821

Memorandum
Billie Hearn b. 11/7/1871
Lila Hearn b. 7/17/1909
Mittie Hearn b. 2/6/1874
Roy Hern 11/12/1912
Johnie Hearn b. 12/7/1892
Emma Hearn 7/18/1897
Willie Hearn b. 3/14/1895
Jack Hearn 12/13/1916
Leila Hearn b. 9/3/1897
Harrel Hearn 11/27/1920
Bryant Hearn b. 2/14/1900

(W. A. Hearn Bible, contd....)

Ruth Hearn 2/19/1925
Georgia Hearn b. 8/20/1902
Lillian Hearn 4/9/1926
· Clarence Hearn b. 8/8/1906
Annie Hearn 4/26/1902

William Taylor Burks 7/31/1899

Record of Births of Billie Hearn and wife's Family

Billie Hearn 12130/1872
Georgia 8/20/1904

Mrs. Mittie Beam 2/6/1874
Clarence 8/20/1907
Jonnie (boy) 12/7/1892
Lila Willie 7/14/1895
Roy 11/12/1912
Lelia 9/2/1897
Ruth 2/19/1925
Bryant 2/14/1900

Deaths

Jimmie Hearn 2/20/1870-7/11/1926, bur. 7/12/1926, aged 56
M. Allen 9/30/1856-9/26/1329, bur. 9/27th, aged 79
Mrs. Corrie Bankston, 70 yr., 1904-6/21/1874
Mrs. A. M. Allen b. 8/1857
Mrs. Mittie Hearn b. 2/6/1874, d. 61 yrs.

(W. A. Hearn Bible, contd....)

From Loose Paper:

Harry Carpenter 11/1/18-4
Juanita Carpenter 7/1/l947
W. A. Hearn 12/31/1871- -:5/1949
Mary Lee Hearn 3/15/- - 9/30/1956
A. M. Allen b. 9/30/1850
George Allen b. 8/1857
A. M. Allen 1850-9/26/1929, bur. 9/27th, aged 79
Willam Taylor Burks and Lila Hearn m. 9/5/1332 Separated 6/3/1934
Mrs. Mittie Hearn d. 4/12/1935, aged 61 yrs., bur. 4/14th

Obituaries in Bible:

"Mrs. Mittie Hearn. Funeral services for Mrs. Mittie Hearn, wife of W. A. Hearn who dlr.d...at
her home on Crawford Road four miles west of Phenix City....interment in Girard cemetery....She is
survived by one daughter, Mrs. Lila Burch of Phenix City, three sons, W. A., Jr, J. B. and L. R. Hearn of
Phenix City, three brothers, J. W., B. T. and W. R. Allen of Phenix City, three sisters, Mrs. C. Farmer,
Mrs. J. E. Lloyd ; and Mrs. C. F. Hearn of Columbus and several nieces, nephews and grandchildren...

"William Andrew Hearn, Rt. 2, Phenix City, died Monday at Phenix M Memorial Hospital....
A native of Marris Co., Ga., he was b. 12/31/1871....Survivors are a daughter, Mrs. H. R.
Favors. Phenix City, three sons, Willie Hearn, Phenix City, *and Bryant and Roy Hearn , Miami,*
Fla., a brother, George Hearn, Columbus , four grandchildren, six great-grandchildren and
several nieces and nephews.

"Opelika, June 22, Funeral services of Mrs. Arthur Bankston, 30, who d. Tuesday....She was b.
at Brantley, Ala. and moved from Columbus, Ga. to Opelika where she m. Arthur Bankston
2!14/1820....She is survived by her husband, Arthur Bankston, one son, Arthur Bankston, Jr., two
sisters, Mrs. Annie Pearl Reese of Phentx City and Mrs. John Griggs of Girard, one brother,
Albert Hearn, of Columbus."

321

WILEY THOMAS WILLIAMS' BIBLE
Owner: Mrs. Willie M. Speakman
2012 Second St., N. W.
Birmingham, Alabama 35215

Marriages

W. T. Williams of Chambers Co. Ala. to Susan Frances Dorman of Tallapoosa Co. 3/6/1892 at W. C. Dormans. Wits: W. C. Dorman. /s/C. W. Biddell, Minister Gospel

Births

W. T. Williams 3/16/1866
Susan Frances Dorman 3/15/1873

Lula C. Williams 1/4/1893
Stella J. Williams 9/13/1902
Daniel Cullen Williams 1/4/1995
Thomas Walter Williams 2/26/1905
Lewis Williams 3/1897
James Velpean Williams 7/26/1339
Frances W. Williams 8/23/1900
Emma Frances Williams 5/15/1928

Deaths

Infant son 1/10/1908
infant son 1/28/1912, aged 5 days
Stella Dillard 8/1/1920, aged 17
L. F. Dorman 1/1/1921, aged 78

Thomas Walter WIlliams 2/2/1973

(Wiley Thomas Williams Bible, Deaths, contd....)

Lula Kate McAuley 3/2/1874
Frances Willard Hawkins 12/1/1974
James Velpean Williams 8/8/1975

Daniel Williams m. Catherine B. Williams 9/3/1846, William C. Davis, J. P.

Births

Daniel Williams 5/10/1822
Catharine B. Slaughter 3/24/1824
Martha Elizabeth Williams 11/3/1847
Henrietta Williams 5/10/1849
Susan Victoria Williams 10/18/1850
Missouri Catharine Williams 2/3/1853
Terrisa Dalsoria Williams 2/21/1855
Nancy Eugenia Williams 3/1/1857
William Franklin Williams 1/10/1859
Jefferson Daniel Williams 6/1/1861
Carrie D. Williams 8/8/1863
Wiley Thomas Williams 3/10/1866

Loose Papers in Bible:

Births

Lucendy Frances Poe 8/9/1842
Lela Dorman 4/3/1881
J. B. Underwood 1/22/1862
M. L. Dorman 10/12/1876
W. Dorman 2/9/1864
Le E. Dorman 7/18/1878

(Wiley Thomas Williams Bible contd....)

T. J. Dorman 10/25/1870
W. L. Dorman 9/13/1884
S. F. Dorman 3/15/1873
W. C. Dorman 2/1/1844

Deaths

Stella Williams 8/1/1920
Ruth Brown 10/22/1914
Dollie Miler 10/3/1918
C. W. Dorman 4/4/1318

Marriages

Susie Dorman to W. T. Williams 3/4/1892
C. W. Dorman to O. E. Milner 11/5/1893
J. B. Underwood to Olo Barrow 12/28/1886
T. J. Dorman to M. F. Slaughter 10/1/1898
Ella Dorman to James Milner 1/2/1898
Lizzie Dorman to T. J. Brown 4/1899
Ada Dorman to L. B. Wright 1/26/1902
Leila Dorman to G. H. Nelson 12/20/1908

Newspaper Clipping in Bible:

"To the memory of Roy Akin. In loving remembrance of Roy Akin, who passed away Feb. 21, 1912. He was the son of Mr. and Mrs. C. L. Akin. He was 16 years 2 months and 1 day old....

SAMUEL JONES' BIBLE
Owner: Mrs. Herbert Walton
Rt. 4, Opelika, Alabama 36801

Births

Samuel Jones II, 8/27/1798 S. C.
Sarah Truesdel Jones 4/20/1802 S. C
William Jones 12/1/1819 S. C.
Elizabeth Jones 8/28/1821 S. C
John Jones 11/30/1823 S. C
Rebecca Jones 9/10/1825 S. C.
Samuel Jones III 8/16/1827 S. C.
Erasmus Jones 5/4/1829 S. C.
James Jones 4/30/1831 S. C.
Calvin Jones I 3/21/1833 S. C.
Decalb Jones 1/21/1835 S. C.
Columbus Jones 1/11/1837 Ala
Hilton Jones 8/10/1839 Ala
Louisa Jones 11/27/1841 Ala
Vandoozen Jones 8/29/1844 Ala.
Sherrad Jones 9/22/1847 Ala.
Frances Moore, 2nd wife of Samuel Jones -
Thomas Jones 8/25/1856 Ala

Franklin Jones 8/5/1561 Ala. Jasper Jones 11/11/1863 Ala. Sally Jones 4/2/1865 Ala. Jane Jones 1/29/1868 Ala. Mollie Jones 4/15/1871 Ala.

Births of Children of Richard H. Barnett and Rebecca Jones

Samuel Barnett 10/20/1849 Ala.

(Samuel Jones' Bible contd....)

Martha Jane Barnett 11/20/1851 Ala.
Sarah Barnett 3/7/1854 Ala.

Births of Children of R. H. Barnett and Louisa Jones

John Calvin Barnett 8/24/1856 Ala.
Nancy Jones 7/1/1859 Ala. Elizabeth Jones 9/30/1861 Ala.

Births

Thavey? Truesdel 8/5/1799 S. C.
Mary Holinsworth Truesdel 3/6/1803 S. C.
Milly Truesdel 3/8/1805 S. C.
John Truesdel 10/26/1807 S. C.
Henry Truesdel 11/23/1809 S. C.
Elvia Truesdel 3/8/1812 S. 6.
Jane Rebecca Truesdel 6/29/1814 S. C.
James Simmon Truesdel 8/11/1816 S. C.
Decalf (Jeff) Jones m. 7/7/1853

Deaths

Erasmus Jones 8/16/1831
Sarah Truesdel Jones 12/28/1854
Rebecca Jones Barnett 7/7/1854
Columbus Jones 8/7/1862
Elizabeth Jones 8/16/1854
Sherrad Jones 3/8/1865

326

GARRET MORRIS BIBLE
Owner: Mrs. Ralph Lane, Monroe, Louisiana

Births

William Morris 10/30/1755
Sarah Terry Morris 7/22/1757
Elizabeth Morris 3/26/1779 m. George Wilson
--- Morris 3/8/1781
John Morris 5/15/1783 m. Nancy Hubbard
Thomas Morris 7/8/ 1785
William Morris 7/9/1787 m. Hannah Gillespie
Driscilla Morris 4/13/1789 m. Ist David Richardson, 2nd, Daniel Hartley
Sarah Catherine Morris 12/24/1790 m. Robert Niers
Garret Morris 3/31/1792 m. ist Mary Jones, 2nd, Nancy Jones, 3rd, Mary Key, 4th, Mrs. Lavonia Earp Bowie
Benjamin Morris 1/21/1795 m. Polly Seals
Caty Morris 5/28/1797 m. 12/2/1814
James H. Hubbard, Abbeville Dist., S. C., d. 1/16/1892, Coosa Co., Alabama
Rhody Morris 9/23/1799 m. Joseph Ward Cook
Garret Morris 3/31/1792-6/7/1875

JOHN R. HARRIS BIBLE
Owner: Mrs. Lee Templeton, Dadeville, Alabama

Marriages

John R. Harris to Margaret J. Burnett 10/10/1965
Henry David Harris to Jessie Spraggins 6/15/1923
Lee Templeton to Jonnie Sue Harris 12/19/1953

(John R. Harris Bible continued...)

Barry Lee Templeton to Brenda Leigh Colbin 12/2/1977
Audrey Suzette Templeton to Clyde Alison 11/17/1979
John R. Harris b. 10/26/1038 Margaret J. Harris b. 11/23/1840

Births of Children of John R. and Margaret J. Harris

Charles M. Harris 9/25/1866
Anna Emeline Harris 3/14/1874
John Taylor Harris 2/14/1869
Henry David Harris 8/27/1877
William Pink Harris 1/6/1872
Lee Templeton 3/4/1929
Jonnie Sue Harris 4/29/1932
Barry Lee Templeton 1/13/1955
Thomas Zacary Templeton 8/20/1956
Audrey Suzette Templeton 8/9/1957
Renwick Dirk Templeton 12/27/1958
Forrest Tyler Templeton 4/29/1961
John Wyatt Templeton 11/18/1962
Christopher Lynn Templeton 7/24/1978

Deaths

John Taler Harris 7/1/1927
Anna Emeline Harris 4/8/1351
Charles M. Harris 12/8/1886
Wm. Pink Harris 4/5/1951
Margaret J. Harris 12/10/1910
Henry David Harris 11/27/1964
John R. Harris 2/10/1916
Jessie Spraggins Harris 1/19/1964

328

CHARLES B. HARRELSON BIBLE
Owner: Mrs. Lovie Harrelson
Second Ave., Phenix City, Ala.

Husband: Charlie B. Harrelson b. 9/26/1900 Tallassee, Ala., son of M. C. Harrelson and Fannie Harrelson
Wife: Lovie N. Harrelson b. 5/31/1905 Brown Spring G. A.

Births

Jack L. Harrelson 3/13/1923
Charlie D. Harrelson 9/26/1900
Juanita Marrelson 11/10/1925
Lovie N. Harrelson 5/31/1905
Charles Ashby Harrelson 5/5/1928

Marriages

Charles B. Harrelson to Lovie N. Favors 12/24/1921
Jack L. Harrelson to Joan Barfield 11/2/1946
Juanita Harrelson to Raymond Erickson 4/16/1946
Ashby Harrelson to Shirley Mims 8/31/1961

Deaths

Charlie D. Harrelson 4/21/1967

329

GUSTAVUS A. GROSS BIBLE
Owner: Mrs. Curtis Hicks
504 W. Pryer St., Athens, Ala. 35611

Gustavus A. Gross m. Martha A. Newell 12/12/1867

Births

Baby girl 11/13/1868
C. M. Gross 12/30/1880
J. R. Gross 8/11/1870
A. J. Gross 10/16/1883
J. T. Gross 2/8/1873
C. O. Gross 6/14/1856
S. C. Gross 10/5/1875
baby girl 5/21/1891
G. A. Gross 3/9/1878

Marriages and Deaths

John Robert Gross 8/11/1870-12/6/1966 m. 8/12/1597 Molly Tomlinson b. 3/28/1880
James Thomas Gross 2/8/1873-3/22/1948
Solomon Cornelius Gross 10/8/1875-11/8/1969 m. Cora Chaffin
Gustavus Adolphus Gross 3/9/1878-2/13/1910 m. Ida Taylor 1/9/18784/4/1954
Charles Monroe Gross 12/31/1880-7/8/1960 m. Georgia Traylor
Andrew Jackson Gross 10/16/1883-3/22/1965 m. 6/15/1916
Ruth Harrell. She d. 12/25/1954
Cornelius O'Neal Gross 6/14/1886-12/2/1959 m. Effie Cannady 1/22/1859-7/8/1921

Marriages

Edmond Hammack 3/18/1844-1/3/1932 m. 6/22/1866
Margret Velvet Boland 11/13/1850-7/11/1911

Births

George Lewis Hammack 3/25/1867
Frankling Hammack 2/13/1879
Sarah Ann E. Hammack 3/1/1869
Janie Hammack 1/5/1651-3/18/1892
Henry L. Hammack 3/20/1871
Emma Hammack 12/3/1592
Alice Hammack 1/11/1873
Annie Hammack 9/9/1885-1947
Elle Hammack 4/8/1875
Ara Hammack 7/22/1889
Mary Hammack 4/19/1877-7/15/1972

Deaths

Sarah Ann E. Hammack 9/7/1869
Janie Hammack 3/1892
Franklin Hammack 8/13/1933

JOHN AND SUE DENNIS BIBLE
Owner: Mrs. Jack Caldwell, Dadeville, Alabama

Births of Children of John and Sue Dennis

Mary Alice Dennis 8/22/1871
Wade Dennis 11/3/1880
Almond Dennis 2/26/1873
Banks Dennis 6/21/1882
Jady (Carrie) Dennis 3/31/1875
Homer Dennis 12/14/1885
Ola Dennis 7/4/1877

Deaths

Mrs. Sue Dennis 6/9/1925
John Dennis 6/2/1327

Births of Children of John Henry and Jackie Dennis Williams

Mattie Williams 2/17/1893
Roby Williams 8/22/1902
Carrie Williams 11/25/1895
Eunice Williams 10/28/1912

THOMAS J. SPRAGGINS' BIBLE

Marriages

H. D. Harris to Miss Jessie Spraggins 6/18/1923
Tommie Junior Spraggins to Miss Dora Ray 10/14/1928
William (Jackson) Spraggins to Margaret Martin 10/28/1928
Arthur Vernon Milam to Mary Lou Spraggins 2/21/1931
Hillard (Benjamin) Spraggins to Lois Virginia Sharpe 10/19/1935
James Marvin Griggs to Sally Spraggins 8/25/1936

Births

Jonnie Pinell Spraggins 11/26/1895
Thomas Wesley Spraggins 11/29/1896
Lessie Spraggins 1/30/1898
Jessie Spraggins 4/22/1899 or 1900
Tommie Junior Spraggins 2/6/1902
Harry Spraggins 6/4/1904
William Jackson Spraggins 12/6/1905
Hillard Benjamin Spraggins 4/14/1908
Mary Lois Spraggins 4/24/1910
Carl Henry Spraggins 5/18/1912
Marion Olander Spraggins 7/26/1914
Sally Estelle Spraggins 10/20/1916
James Edward Milam 11/4/1931
Billy Gordon Milam 7/24/1933
Sarah Lee Milam 4/16/1935
Boby Lou Milam 6/28/1937

(Thomas J. Spraggins Bible continued....)

Deaths

Jonnie Pinell Spraggins 2/26/1896
Thomas Wesley Spraggins 9/11/1898
Marion Olandar Spraggins 11/30/1915
Mrs. Emma Spraggins (Sweetie) 1/18/1918
Thomas Jefferson Spraggins 12/20/1926
James Edward Milam 1/14/1938
Tommie Junior Spraggins 5/11/1961
Jessie Spraggins Harris 1/19/1964
Hillard Benjamin Spraggins 3/1964
Carl Henry Spraggins 5/18/1970
Lessie Nancy Spraggins 9/17/1978

JAMES L. FLOWERS' BIBLE
Owner: Brady Wilson, Columbus, Georgia

Marriages

John Flowers to Nancy Williamson of Pike Co., Ala. 11/22/1825
William Willis Flowers to Mary Conway Wilson
Silas Wright Flowers to Mary Conway Wilson 1865
James L. Flowers to Sophie Lee (b. 11/1/1863) 2/24/1877, Pike Co., Ala.

Births of Children of John and Nancy Flowers

Kiziah Flowers 9/1/1826
William Willis Flowers 2/29/1538
Alexander Formi.Flowers 6/27/1828
Heland Elizabeth Flowers

334

(Bible of James L. Flowers' continued...)

John Calvin Flowers 7/30/1830 7/21/1841
Morilda Ann Flowers 10/11/1832
Luke Isham Flowers 9/20/1843
Lucretia Flowers 11/2/1834
Silas Wright Flowers 2/24/1846
Ignatious Flowers 12/6/1836
Mary Jane Flowers 3/1/1849
James Lorenzo Flowers b. 8/11/1866, son of Silas Wright and Mary
Conway Wilson Flowers

Births of Children of James L. and Sophie Lee Flowers

Lilla Lee Flowers 12/21/1889
James Marcus Flowers
Silas Calvin and Sophia Cairo Flowers, twins, 4/1/1893
Roy Lawson and Ralph Atlas Flowers, twins, 10/5/1895
Elsie Flowers 6/27/1898

James L. Flowers m. 2nd wife, Emma Frances Vaughan (b. 5/31/1871) 12/26/1839.

Births of Children of James L. and Emma Frances Flowers

Cephus Morgan Flowers 1/29/1901
Charlotte Dora Flowers 3/12/1902
Oscar Culver Flowers 9/4/1903

Joseph Gilman Flowers 10/31/1905
Travis Curtis Flowers 1/27/1909
Clem Gibson Flowers 12/11/1911

Mary Conway Wilson Flowers, mother of James L. Flowers, b. 5/14/1843, dau. of Reuben and Mary Ray Wilson, Pike Co., Ala., from N. C.

335

(Bible of James L. Flowers' continued...)

Deaths

Silas Wright Flowers 7/14/1872, father of James L. Flowers
James Marcus Flowers 1/21/1891 son of James L. Flowers Elsie Flowers 11/5/1900, dau. of
James L. Flowers
Sophia Lee Flowers 3/7/1899, 1st wife of James L. Flowers
Mary Conway Wilson Flowers 6/23/1920, mother of James L. Flowers
James L. Flowers 7/29/1947
Emma Frances Vaughan Flowers 2/27/1950

Marriages

Silas Wright Flowers to Mary Conway Wilson 1865
James L. Flowers to Sophia Lee 2/24/1857
James L. Flowers to Emma Frances Vaughan 12/26/1899
Otis Addington to Lilla Lee Flowers 8/20/1906

REUBIN AND MARY WILSON BIBLE
of Pike County
Owner: Brady Wilson, Columbus, Ga.

Reubin Wilson b. 3/23/1793, son of James and Lydia Wilson, N. C. Mary Ray b. 5/13/1801 N. C.
m. 5/21/1826

Births of Children

James Wilson 5/19/1828
Mary Conway Wilson 5/14/1849
Allis Wilson 11/15/1830
Daniel Wilson 7/23/1846
Samuel Wilson 7/2/1832

(Reuben and Mary Wilson Bible continued...)

Jane Wilson 1/1/1848
Nancy Ann Wilson 1/25/1833
Jeremia Wilson 4/14/1849
Reubin Anderson Wilson 7/9/1838
Henry Wilson 3/30/1850
John Duncan Wilson 1/5/1841
Mariola Wilson 12/16/1851

Deaths

Reubin Wilson 1/6/1876
Mary Ray Wilson 5/1/1880

JAMES AND MINERVA WILSON BIBLE
Owner: Brady Wilson, Columbus, Georgia

James Wilson b. 5/19/1825, son of Reubin and Mary Ray Wilson m. Minerva A. Clawson b. 12/3/1835, dau. of James and Cinderella, Macon, Bibb Co, Ga. at Troy, Pike Co., Ala. on 12/1/1853

Births of Children

Victor Oscar Wilson 10/10/1854 -
Lenora Wilson 6/24/1865
Thomas Horace Wilson
Obed Wilson 3/21/1872
Reubin Guy Wilson 8/30/1858
Nevada Edward Wilson 11/25/1874
Anderson Lafayette Wilson 11/14/1861
John Duncan Wilson 5/26/1867
Mary Wilson 11/13/1876
Willis Wilson 8/22/1880

(James Wilson Bible continued...)

Deaths

James Wilson 7/18/1907
Minerva A. Clawson Wilson 4/7/1919
(Both bur. New Hope Cemetery in New Hope, Coffee Co., Alabama)

SAMUEL AND HANNAH WILSON BIBLE
Owner: Brady Wilson, Columbus, Ga.

Samuel Wilson b. 7/2/1832, son of Reubin and Mary Ray Wilson m. Hannah Flowers b. 7/13/1840, dau. of Richard and Lucinda Graves Flowers at Brundidge, Pike Co., Ala. on 1/13/1859

Births of Children Richard Reubin Wilson:

Susan Frances Wilson 5/14/1862 Joseph William Ferry Wilson 5/28/1564
Mary Lucinda Wilson 10/16/1569 Willie Linda Wilson 11/30/1871
Nancy Jahasy Wilson 12/31/1873 Shadic Wilson 6/18/.1876
Emma Jane Wilson 3/28/1878
Melissa Wilson 1/21/1880 Veloxie Wilson 4/28/1884
Zenobva Wilson 9/25/1886

Deaths

Samuel Wilson 8/31/1909, Brundidge, Pike Co., Alabama Hannah Wilson 11/22/1921, Brundige, Pike Co., Alabama

MICHAEL LEONARD SHOCKLY BIBLE
Owner: Mrs. R. Earl Wilson
Rt. 6, Box 10, Arrowhead Rd., Alexander City, Alabama 35010

Michael L. Shockly b: 1/11/1784 (Worcester Co., Md.) m. Frances O'Rear in Greene Co., Ga. in 1808.

Births of Children

Friend O. Shockly 11/19/1809
John Shockly 11/5/1811
Elizabeth Shockly 2/23/1814
Susan Shockly 1/23/1516
Benjamin S. Shockly 2/18/1818
Mary Ann Shockly 9/11/1820

Francis Shockly 1/17/1823
James M. Shockly 9/26/1826
Harriet Shockly 2/4/1830
Andrew J. Shockly 1/20/1832
Jonathan N. Shockly 8/2/1835

JAMES D. PHILLIPS BIBLE
Owner: Mrs. J. H. Strother

James D. Phillips b. 12/31/1813 m. Sarah Ann McNeill b. 3/12/1818 on --/19/1838.

Marriages of Their Children:

Leora Ashton Phillips to Charles D. Condon 10/30/1860
Frances Henrietta Phillips to William O. Massey 4/11/1867
Mary Alice Phillips to Jackson Baggett 9/3/1869
Virginia Adelaide Phillips to John C. Chambliss 3/18/1863
Virginia Adelia Chambliss to James Q. Baker 11/9/1871
J. S. Phillips to Gertrude Nichols 5/21/1893, Gertrude the only child of George Robert Nichols
Of Mt. Pelier, Vt. and Sara Louise Cadwell.

(James D. Phillip Bible continued...)

Births

Leora Ashton Phillips 8/5/1839
Mary Alice Phillips 1/2/1841
Frances Henrietta Phillips 2/15/1842
Virginia Adelaide Phillips 3/20/1844
Lachlin Eli McNeill Phillips 4/28/1845
Josephine Otelia Phillips 11/6/1846
William John Phillips 5/8/1845

James Charles   Phillips 10/2/1849
Celestina Ann   Phillips 8/18/1855
Thaxton Yelventon Phillips 8/18/1857

Josiah Samuel   Phillips 11/14/1852
Lucius Conner   Phillips 3/17/1856
Clem Austin Phillips 5/7/1861

Jane E. McNeill, wife of Lachlin McNeill, dau. of Horacia and Sarah Wades, b. 1739
Lachlin McNeill, son of John and Hancy McNeill, b. 5/27/1769

Deaths

James D. Phillips 9/2/1866 in Dadeville Alabama
Sarah Ann (Hampton) Phillips 5/13/1906, Dadeville, Alabama

Deaths of Children Lachlin Eli McNeill Phillips 5/2711845

Lucius Conner Phillips 10/4/1856

On Loose Paper:

(James D. Phillip Bible continued...)

Births

Mannie Mac Phillips, dau. of Thaxton and Annie Phillips, 8/19/1884 in Oxford, Alabama
William Thaxton Phillips 5/15/1887 in Atlanta, Ga.
John Lachlin Phillips 5/24/1830 in Atlanta, Ga.
Pay Belie Phillips 7/21/1892 in Atlanta, Ga.
Charley McNeill Phillips 9/7/1894 in Atlanta, Ga.

Deaths
John Lachlin Phillips 8/ 3 1/ 18 90 in Atlan ta , Ga. Fay Belle Phillips 5/27/1895 in Atlanta, Ga.

J. D. PHILLIPS BIBLE

"Presented to Mrs. S. A. Phillips by her daughter, Otie, 12/25/1903"

Parents Names:

Husband - J. D. Phillips
Wife - S. 8. Phillips b. 3/12/1818

Deaths

James Dowd Phillips 9/2/1866 Sarah Ann Phillips 5/14/1906
Thack Phillips, son of above named, 5/10/1911 Charlie Phillips, son of above named, 6/11/1913

Newspaper clipping in Bible:

"*Mrs. S. A. Phillips was born March 12, 1818 at Fayetteville, N. C. When a young lady she
came with her people to Socopatoy, Coosa County, Alabama. June 19, 1838, she was
married to J. D. Phillips, who came from Fayetteville, N. C. to Blabama....In 1866 he was
sheriff of Tallapoosa county....He died Sept. 2/1866 and his remains rested In the old*
341

cemetery behind the M. E. Church until Tuesday when they were exhumed and laid by the side of his wife from whom he has been separated 40 years, Mr. and Mrs. Phillips had 14 children, eleven of whom he left to the care of Mrs. Phillips....Mrs. Phillips was 89 years old."

"J. L. Condon, 75-year old independent oil operator, died at University Hospital. Mr. Condon, who was a resident of 3411 Kings Highway, was admitted to the hospital last Monday. A native of Troy, Alabama, he moved to Jackson in 1932...Mr. Condon is survived by two sisters, Mrs. Maude Wynn and Mrs. Mary C. Baker, both of Jackson, a stepdaughter, Mrs. Jennie D. Smith and a stepgrandson, jack P. Smith, both of Silver Springs, Maryland....His body will be taken to Birmingham, Ala. where graveside service will be held at 11 a.m. Friday in the Elmwood Cemetery."

"Died at her residence in Clay County, Ala., August 4, 1885...Mrs. Mary J. McGehee. Mrs. McGehee was born in North Carolina on Sept. 17, 1820, but when very young her father Major McNeil moved to this State, where she was married, June ;, 1540 to Mr. Samuel McGehee

MANNING LANGLEY BIBLE
Owner: A. W. Washburn, Lafayette, Alabama

Marriages

Manning Langley to Tappenus Harrelson 1/19/1826
Martha Bnn Langley to James D. l;and 10/26/1848
David A. Langley to Sarah Ann Mainor, widow, formerly Frasier

Births

Manning Langley 5/25/1805
Tappenus Langley 10/20/1805

(Manning Langley Bible continued...)

Their Children:

Martha Ann Langley 5/30/1827
George W. Langley 9/5/1837
David A. Langley 8/9/1829
James M. Langley 5/31/1840
Alexander Langley 1/5/1832
Mary Ann Sophronia Langley 10/13/1842
Manning J. Langley 2/15/1844
Elijah Langley 8/15/1833
Edmund B. Langley 6/10/1834
William T. Langley 9/5/1847
Jasper Langley 4/15/1836
Thomas J. Langley 7/15/1851

Deaths

David Langley, father of Manning Langley. 4/10/1822
Jasper Langley, son of Manning and Tappenus, 6/1/1836, age 6 wks.
Alexander Langley, son of Manning and Tappenus Langley, 4/29/1852, aged 20 yrs, 3 mos., 24 days
Manning Langley, husband of Tappenus Langley, 6/26/1864, aged 59 yrs., 1 mo., 1 day
Mary Ann Sophronia Langley, dau. of Manning and Tappenus Langley, 7/10/1864, aged 21 yrs., 8 mos., 27 days
Tappenus Langley, consort of Manning Langley, 5/24/1896
Sister Martha Land, dau. of Manning Langley, 1/8/1914, bur. near Algoods at Sardis Church
J. M. Langley, son of Manning and Tappenus Langley, 2/22/1919,aged 79 yrs., 9 mos., 21 days
E. B. Langley, son of Manning and Tappenus Langley, 7/2/1920, aged 86 yrs., 22 days
William T. Langley, son of Manning and Tappenus Langley, 4/3/1931
Thomas J. Langley, son of Manning and Tappenus Langley, 4/4/1932

(Manning Langley Bible continued...)

Manning J. Langley, son of Manning and Tappenus Langley, 10/25/1932

THOMAS ARNOLD BIBLE
From: Rev. War Pension #W5640

Births of Children of Thomas and Mary Arnold

Temperance Arnold 11/25/1759
William B. Arnold 7/1/1791
John Arnold 4/4/1793
Thomas K. Arnold 4/27/1799
Ann H. Arnold 6/22/1802

Temperance Arnold m. 8/15/1804 Peter Ross Ann H. Arnold m. 3/11/1824 Hance H. Dunklln

Births of Children of Peter and Temperance Ross

Thomas A. Ross 7/4/1805
Lucinda Ross 8/14/1812
Mary Ross 9/6/1807
Andrew J. Ross 11/25/1814
Susan Ross 4/20/1810
Note: Thomas Arnold applied for pension 4/16/1833, Autauga Co., Ala. He was b. 10/4/1763 in Buckingham Co., Va. Mrs. Mary Arnold was living with her grandson, William A. Dunklin in Selma, Ala in 1854. William A. Dunklin m. Drucilla Hartsfield.

INDEX

350

351

Joe, 155
Joe H., 155
John A., 154
Katy R., 155
Mary E., 122
Mary E. R., 154
Oma, 154, 155
Philip, 122
Terrsa, 122
Tyre, 122
Butt, Nicholason Forsyth,
 204(2)
Butts, Barnard, 182
 Bernard Lee, 182(2)
 Charlie, 181(2)
 Clara, 182
 Cora, 180
 Cummy, 182
 Ethel, 182
 Horace, 181, 182
 Kathryn, 182
 Wade, 182

-C-

Callaway, Dannie, 311(3)
 Eunice, 231
Cambell, Charley J. T.,
 49
Cameron, Barnabas C., 193
 Louise L., 193
 Martha A., 193
 Thomas P., 192

 Campbell, Albert A.
  Suttles, 113
 Albert Archibald
  Suttle, 112
 Andrew, 114
 Davis, 113
 Davis J., 113
 Davis Jasper, 114
 H., 113
 Harris, 112, 113
 Ida Geneva, 114(2)
 Jane, 112
 Julia Margret, 114

Martha Jane, 114
Martha Paralee, 112
Mary Beneter, 114
Mary Jane, 112
Morea Smily, 112
Morris, 112
Phadre Isadora, 112
Ruth, 114
S. M., 113
Saphra Catharine, 112
Sarah An, 114
Sarah Martha, 114
Sophran Sarah, 112
Susan Eloise, 112
Sylvester Myconiu, 112
T. J., 114
Thomas Henry, 114
Walter H. D., 113
Walter H. Sawson, 112
Washington Davis, 114
William, 113, 114
Willson, 113
Wilson, 114
Cannaday, Effie, 330
Cannon, Allay C., 188
 C. B., 71
 C. M., 71
 C. O., 72
 Caleb B., 70
 E. O., 72
 Ella Ossa, 71
 L. S. L., 72
 M., 72
 M. I., 71
 Margret Ida, 70
 N. J., 72
 Nannie Jane, 70
 R. Y., 72
 T. L. M., 71
 Thomas Linton
  McWhorter, 70

 W. D., 71
 Willie D., 70
Capps, Ella O., 275
 Emma Lou, 275
 James Wesley, Rev.,

355

356

357

364

365

366

372

373

374

375

376

384

385

387

389

391

392

393

394

398

399

402

403

405

406

416

Other Heritage Books by Jeannette Holland Austin:

1860 Paulding County, Georgia Census

Alabama Bible Records

DeKalb County, Georgia Probate Records

Fayette County, Georgia Probate Records: Volume II
Annual Returns, Inventories, Sales, Bonds, 1845-1897

Georgia Bible Records, Supplement, 1772-1940

Georgia Obituaries, 1740-1935

Georgia Obituaries, 1905-1910

Jackson County, Georgia Tombstones
Jeannette Holland Austin and Dorothy Holland Herring

Masters of the Low Country: A History of the Georgia Colony

North Carolina–South Carolina Bible Records

The Georgians Database: Genealogical Notes

Virginia Bible Records

www.ingramcontent.com/pod-product-compliance
Lightning Source LLC
Chambersburg PA
CBHW050558270326
41926CB00012B/2103